'We Pulled Together ...and Won!'

Hard work and sacrifice
saw America through
World War II. These are
the memories of strong people
who united for victory—and
prevailed—when a world at
war demanded their best.

A CELEBRATING THRONG poured out of downtown Seattle's office buildings, as sirens announced the end of WWII. Gay Sorensen, who now lives in Lacey, Washington, was in the crowd that day...the excited 18-year-old appears in detail at right. See her story on page 155.

Publisher: Roy J. Reiman
Editor: Deb Mulvey
Contributing Editor: Clancy Strock
Assistant Editors: Mike Beno, Michael Martin, Kristine Krueger, Henry de Fiebre
Art Director: Gail Engeldahl
Art Associates: Sue Myers, Jim Sibilski, Janet Thalken
Photo Coordination: Trudi Bellin
Editorial Assistants: Blanche Comiskey, Joe Kertzman

Production Assistants: Ellen Lloyd, Julie Wagner
©1993 Reiman Publications, L.P.
5400 S. 60th St., Greendale WI 53129

Reminisce Books
International Standard Book Number: 0-89821-112-3
Library of Congress Catalog Number: 93-84612
All rights reserved. Printed in U.S.A.
Cover photo by Seattle Post Intelligencer
Collection/Museum of History & Industry

For additional copies of this book or information on other books, write: Reminisce Books, P.O. Box 990, Greendale WI 53129. **Credit card orders call toll-free 1-800/558-1013.**

Contents

This book is dedicated not only to the fighting men of World War II, but to strong
women everywhere. They were the glue that held America together, joining
the armed services with bravery, mastering industrial jobs with aplomb and
keeping the home fires burning until their men came home.

Prologue

By Clancy Strock, Contributing Editor, Reminisce Magazine

*A*mericans were feeling pretty good about things in 1941, but the picture looked bleak for our friends in Europe. Great Britain was in mortal peril and there was a raging debate about how much we should help out, if at all.

The view wasn't much better across the Pacific, as the Japanese Empire planted its flag on the Asian mainland.

But those problems seemed awfully far away to most Americans, and we felt secure behind our two-ocean moat. Best of all, the grinding days of the Great Depression were behind us, and Americans were hopeful and smiling again.

The Depression had seemed like a stalking animal that slowly but surely nibbled away at us all. But not World War II.

It arrived on a Sunday afternoon. Bam! *The United States had been attacked!* One moment we were enjoying peace and a fledgling prosperity, the next, we were at war.

Sure, Americans had been involved in wars before. We'd buried husbands and sons on foreign soil as we helped our friends overseas. We'd lost tens of thousands in our own Civil War. We'd charged up San Juan Hill in the trumped-up Spanish-American War.

But for the first time in more than a century, a foreign power had attacked us. The unthinkable had happened.

In It Together

In an instant, the entire nation dropped its differences. Republican or Democrat, Easterner or Westerner, man or woman, Jew, Catholic or Protestant, rich or poor, a city mouse or a country mouse—we were in it together because *we had been attacked!*

World War II was *our* war, uniting us as a nation like nothing before or since.

There have been millions of words written about World War II. As this book is being compiled, it has been 50 years since we were embroiled in that conflict. Historians and scholars are able to take the long view and put things into better perspective.

Some of their statistics are astonishing. More than 10 million men and women served in some branch of the military, including 300,000

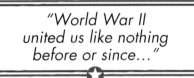

"World War II united us like nothing before or since..."

women who volunteered to be WACs, WAVEs, WASPs, SPARs and Women Marines.

Some 3.5 million women reported to armament plants, helping produce 300,000 aircraft, 71,000 naval ships, 5,500 cargo ships and 2.5 million trucks in 4 years. Nearly 1.5 million citizens volunteered to be air raid spotters—and then never spotted a single hostile aircraft.

Just 11 months after Pearl Harbor, the U.S. put troops ashore in North Africa—an amazing accomplishment considering the U.S. Army was virtually nonexistent and unequipped prior to December 7, 1941.

When it all was over, we had lost more than 300,000 of our fittest and brightest young men. But that's just a number. Its full impact doesn't really hit you until you see one of the many cemeteries on foreign soil, with row after row of white markers in perfect alignment, almost as though the dead were standing one last inspection on a grassy parade ground.

So how do you tell the story of a

momentous event that, in one way or another, touched the lives of all Americans who lived through it?

War, like all of life, is lived one person at a time. The only war you know is your own.

An infantryman's war is quite unlike an airman's war. A nurse's war is not the same as one fought by a submariner. Our war in Africa and Europe was nothing like our war in the Pacific, where even Guadalcanal was quite unlike Iwo Jima and Okinawa.

Then there was the war experienced by the welders who turned out Victory cargo ships in just 17 days. (Can you imagine it—building an ocean-going vessel in a little over *2 weeks*?) There was the war lived by long rows of farmers' wives and widows and young mothers and retired men, loading explosives into an endless procession of bullets and bombs.

And these wars weren't at all like the one endured by the mother with five sons in the service. Especially when she soon had two gold stars hanging in the front window.

The Red Cross volunteer who helped those in her hometown saw a different war from that lived by the USO volunteer in Rome, and neither saw the war that the medical corpsman saw in the Philippine Islands.

Each Experience Unique

This book is about World War II, as seen and remembered by those who experienced it. It won't be like anything else you have ever read about that war, because it has been written by hundreds of *individuals.* Each one remembers "their" war. Some shared priceless photos from their own family albums to help explain the feelings they felt during that historic, terrible and heady time.

World War II forever changed those who were in it. For example, I had rarely set foot outside of Whiteside County, Illinois. My universe extended from Chicago on the east to Ames, Iowa on the west, and as far south as Springfield, Illinois.

I enlisted 6 weeks after Pearl Harbor and was discharged 4 years later, having seen most of the United States plus chunks of Hawaii, Eniwetok, Leyte and Luzon. (And, so you don't misunderstand, I never heard a shot fired in anger that whole time. I was one of the lucky ones.)

I ate my first Mexican food (in San Antonio), my first seafood (in Galveston), saw my first oil wells and cotton fields (also in Texas) and shared a tent with a black man (in Oklahoma) for several months.

I learned a little Spanish and Tagalog (in the Philippines), lived with men from Philadelphia and Charleston and Pittsburgh and Denver plus small towns in Kansas and Nebraska and Louisiana. I listened to each of these men passionately explain why *his* hometown was the garden spot of the earth.

Old Army Habits Remain

To this day, I still roll up my socks Army-style before putting them into my sock drawer. I fold my underwear and stack it neatly, and hang all my shirts and jackets facing the same way in the closet. Some habits, hard-learned, just won't go away.

Multiply that experience by 10 million and you see why Americans could never be the same again. A lot of walls came tumbling down and a good many horizons were stretched all the way to the ends of the earth.

"We Pulled Together...and Won!" is a patchwork quilt pieced together with scraps of memories, all about that single event called World War II. It is an attempt to capture and record some of the myriad of memories that common folks recall about the most uncommon of times.

Those memories make this quilt so warm and colorful that we think you'll agree it is truly one of a kind. For our part, it's been an honor to assemble it...and we hope you'll feel the same way as you feel the warmth in the pages that follow.✪

ONE SHARP SOLDIER! The smart-looking serviceman in the photo above had good reason to smile with pride. This 1945 picture was taken when Lieutenant Clancy Strock graduated from Officer's Candidate School in field artillery.

Clancy took a troop ship to the Philippines later that year, and was part of the Allied force that was staging to invade Japan. The atomic bomb and Japan's surrender ended those plans.

"I never saw action, and today I make no bones about telling people that," Clancy says. "I feel very lucky."

Though he never saw combat, Clancy served his country for 4 long years during World War II. As contributing editor of this book, he uses that experience to provide deep insight into a time that united all Americans like never before or since.

TODAY, Clancy is Contributing Editor of *Reminisce* magazine. He recently retired as vice-chair of the advertising department in the College of Journalism at the University of Nebraska.

CHAPTER ONE

Remember Pearl Harbor

Remember Pearl Harbor

THE NEWS of December 7, 1941 hit Americans with all the violent force of a hurricane. Pearl Harbor had been attacked, and within hours the United States would be at war. It was a shattering moment that touched all Americans. After December 7, their lives would never again be the same.

CASUALTY OF WAR. The USS California, hit by two torpedoes and a bomb, was one of 18 warships crippled or sunk at Pearl Harbor. The crew abandoned ship when burning oil from other ships engulfed the stern.

*T*he way it's being told today, you'd think most everyone knew that we were on the brink of war with the Japanese.

Nothing could be further from the truth. Things were starting to feel "normal" again to most Americans in this post-Depression year of 1941. People were able to move back into homes of their own, buy cars, enjoy a decent diet, wear new clothes and make plans for the future.

Then it happened. Pearl Harbor. The "day that will live in infamy".

If you were alive on December 7, 1941, you can never forget exactly where you were, what you were doing and who you were with at the moment you heard the news.

I was studying in my room at college. The radio was on. It was a quiet, tranquil Sunday afternoon.

Heard Special Announcement

And then the announcer broke in: "The Japanese have attacked Pearl Harbor." (I still get a chill when I hear a rebroadcast of that announcement.)

First question: Is this another Orson Welles *War of the Worlds* hoax?

Second question: Where in the dickens is Pearl Harbor?

Word spread throughout the house where I lived with several other students. Soon a dozen bewildered young men were clustered around the radio, pondering what it all meant. There had been talk for months about whether or not the U.S. should become more involved in the war in Europe, and arguments ran strongly on both sides. With our attention focused on Europe, somehow the thought of an attack *on us* had never occurred. And certainly not an attack by Japan.

For those in Hawaii, the reality of war was painfully clear. Their pleasant Sunday morning was shattered by the worst single military pounding in U.S. history.

But for most other Americans, the real truth didn't dawn until December 8, when President Roosevelt spelled it out. *We were at war!*

People across the land clustered around their radios. When the President ended his brief speech, all I can remember is the total silence as we each tried to sort out what the news meant to our own lives.

It Would Be Up to Us

One thing was clear enough. As young men in our late teens and early 20s, this for sure was going to be *our* war. What we knew about war was what we had heard from our dads and others their age who had served in World War I. We'd heard the stories of Verdun and the Meuse-Argonne. Poison gas. Life in filthy, muddy trenches. Daring pilots dogfighting in the clear, blue French air.

But that was history, the stuff of fiction and legends. It had nothing to do with our lives.

Now we were faced with making some history of our own. There were big decisions ahead. Wait to be drafted or enlist? Become a sailor? (I couldn't swim.) Join the Army? (Dad's experiences didn't sound like anything I wanted to repeat.) Be an airman? (I'd never been higher than the haymow, but it sounded exciting.)

So we stood together, each overwhelmed with new thoughts. Brave thoughts. Scared thoughts. In just 24 hours our lives had been thrown into turmoil.

Yes, this one was going to be our war.

There was a lot to think about.

—*Clancy Strock*

Even 'Good Soldiers' Shed Tears

By Sandra Lloyd
Lancaster, California

MOST IMAGES stored in our memories fade with the passing years. But for me, when the date recalled happens to be December 7, 1941, those mental pictures remain vivid, even though they were seen through the eyes of a 6-year-old.

That beautiful Sunday morning in Hawaii began in typical fashion. Dad, a warrant officer in the Army Air Corps at Wheeler Field in central Oahu, was reading the newspaper with Mother, who had one leg in a cast. She also was pregnant.

A few minutes before 8 a.m., I slipped out of bed and walked sleepily to their room. Just as Dad handed me the comics, we heard the roar of planes low over our house. Dad glanced out the window. He knew instantly the planes weren't from the local squadrons.

"Those must be the new ones from the States," he said, kneeling for a better look. I started toward the window, too, only to recoil as the panes shattered. Wood and plaster jumped off the walls. *Rat-a-tat-tat! Rat-a-tat-tat!*

"Duck!" Dad screamed over the roar of the diving planes. "We're being attacked!" He shoved me to the floor and covered me with his body. Mother had already dived to the floor.

BA-ROOOM! Our house shook with such force that the ceiling plaster turned to dust. Japanese planes were bombing us! Another burst of machine-gun fire rippled through the walls. Dad cradled us in his arms until a siren blast told us the danger had passed. He jumped up, checked Mom and me, told us to get dressed, then grabbed his uniform.

Made "Bomb Shelter"

Dad pulled the mattress off the bed and lugged it to my bedroom. Then he grabbed every pillow, cushion and blanket he could find and converted my room into a makeshift bunker.

"I've got to go now," he said. "Just keep down. I'll see you. Keep safe. I love you both." With a hug and a kiss, Dad was gone.

Mom sobbed quietly, but I was determined not to cry. Dad always told me, "Good soldiers don't cry". I wanted to be a "good soldier" for him. Then the air-raid sirens wailed and Mom

BRAVE SOLDIERS rushed women and children to shelter when Pearl Harbor was attacked, and stood guard until their charges could safely return home.

prayed as we huddled together.

It seemed like ages before the "all-clear" sirens sounded again, followed by frantic pounding on the front door. A soldier burst in and quickly helped us gather a few belongings.

He took us to a stone house against the side of a mountain, where several other women and children were already seeking refuge.

"Sarge", as I called him, calmed us down, then showed us how to put on a gas mask. I was small, even for a 6-year-old, and Sarge kept me close to him, "just in case".

I left his side to get a dipperful of water from a jar in the kitchen when the sirens blew again. Sarge screamed, "Down!" I was standing next to an old-fashioned refrigerator with 12-in. legs, and nothing could've seemed safer. I dove underneath it.

After the all clear, Sarge counted noses and came up one short—me. He finally saw my feet sticking out from under the refrigerator. Apparently I'd slid under so fast that my head banged into the stone wall, knocking me out cold.

Sarge gently cradled me in his arms, carried me to the couch and began to weep quietly. That's when I remember looking up and seeing his face. Mom said later that my first words to him were, "Good soldiers don't cry".

"Only if they're sad," Sarge replied softly. For the rest of the time he guarded us, he never let me out of his sight.

Did He Fire First Shot?

By Bob Munroe
Sunland, California

Editor's Note: The USS Tangier was the first ship in Pearl Harbor to open fire on attacking Japanese planes. Bob Munroe, a 19-year-old seaman second class, was aboard the Tangier that day. Bob is believed to be the man who fired the first shots in defense of Pearl Harbor on December 7, 1941. The evening after the attack, he wrote this account. Recently he shared those historic words so they might be published here.

SUNDAY MORNING at 7:50, I was reading when I heard a long, powerful dive from the air. I didn't think much of it, because nearly every day we heard our own Navy planes taking practice dives. When the first dive was followed by two more, I took notice.

Suddenly I heard a tremendous explosion. I ran to the captain's cabin and yelled, "Captain, it's an air raid!"

"Man your gun!" he yelled back, on the run.

I scrambled out the starboard hatchway to a terrible sight: Two torpedo bombers dropped what looked like long silver fish, and those torpedos ran smack into the side of the battleship *USS Utah*, moored right behind us.

I ran to my .50-caliber machine gun and yanked off the cover. I looked up to see the *Utah* on her side, sinking fast, with men sliding over the side and swimming to shore.

The first raid had come and gone and I hadn't even had time to put on my helmet or life jacket. I put them on, cleaned and oiled my gun, and got ready for the next attack. It was only a matter of minutes.

At about 8:19, out of the clouds and smoke came a bunch of planes straight down, and they were *moving*. I couldn't count them all because I was too busy shooting. The planes all laid straight for the battlewagons, and the *USS Arizona* was blown sky high. It burned all day and is still burning as I'm writing this.

Plenty of planes dove straight for the *Tangier*. I know I hit several of them,

---
"'Man your gun!' the captain yelled..."
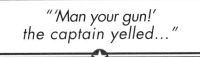

---

but not enough to bring them all down.

Soon, six or seven more dove at us. When they got within 1,500 ft. they peeled off, some going for the aft part of the ship, some forward and one or two straight at me, amidships.

Gunner Selby was screaming his lungs out to open fire. I waited for the planes to get a little closer, then I opened up. I followed my tracers straight into the nose of the plane, and my heart was in my mouth for fear he would open up on me before I could get him. His engine started to smoke,

JAPANESE BOMBERS were bearing down on the *USS Tangier* (top) when Seaman Second Class Bob Munroe (above) began to return fire.

then burst into flames. I realized I had gotten my first plane.

At 9:35, we heard 30 or 40 planes high overhead, but because of the smoke from the burning *Arizona*, we couldn't tell whether they were ours or not. They weren't. Two dive-bombers broke out of the smoke, out of range.

The next second, two bombs hit the water next to the ship. The aircraft had only a split second to aim, and had it not been for the smoke from the *Arizona*, I wouldn't be here to write all this down.

That was the last direct run on our ship, and with all the destruction around us, it was really a miracle that the *Tangier* survived.

We had never had the opportunity to operate the ship's guns before today, except in test firing. Afterward, the captain sent up word to all hands: "You are good enough for my money!"✪

Days, Nights in Honolulu Were Filled with Fear

By Marjorie Willcox
Hendersonville, North Carolina

ABOUT 7:55 a.m., right after breakfast, we heard a distant rumble that sounded like thunder—very unusual for Honolulu. Then it grew louder and the rumble was continuous. We thought it was target practice.

Then the radio announced, "The island of Oahu is being attacked by the enemy. All policemen and firemen, report for duty at once."

After a bit of music, we heard: "All civilians keep off the streets. Do not use your car." From then on, the program was interrupted frequently to repeat orders and add new ones.

Finally, we heard this announcement: "The enemy has been identified as the Japanese."

The sound of guns and bombs was ominous. I heard a bomb whistle by, then saw a plane with the Rising Sun on it drop a bomb near St. Andrew's Priory, where I was a teacher. One man was killed there. A car was flattened, and plate-glass windows were shattered.

That night, a total blackout was ordered. No one was prepared for that, and darkness fell early. Another teacher and I put mattresses on the floor

BARBED WIRE lined Waikiki Beach (top), and residents like Marjorie Willcox were issued gas masks.

Attack Took Toll on Civilians, Too

THE ATTACK on Pearl Harbor was horrible for civilians as well as military personnel. My husband worked for the government there. The morning of December 7, we watched gray planes with red orbs on each wing fly low over our house on their way to wreck Hickam Field and bomb the harbor.

Blackouts started that night. Gas rationing began the next day. Our children, ages 7 and 9, found spent bullets near our house. On December 9, we lined up with many others to send telegrams to relatives in the States.

Months later, the children and I were evacuated in a large convoy to California. Before we sailed, we were required to sign a form agreeing not to divulge any knowledge we had of the war.

It took us 8 days to reach San Francisco. Each morning, an hour before daylight, we heard the order "general quarters"—which, for civilians, meant rushing to our lifeboat stations. Even now, when I hear that phrase on a TV program about the Navy, it sends a chill down my spine. —*Mrs. L.M. Graves*
San Jacinto, California

BOMBING AFTERMATH. When the smoke cleared, Hickam Field was littered with rubble. The home of Air Force bombers was a primary target.

and settled in for a long night.

Everything that happened after dark seemed frightening: the crack of gunfire; a voice calling "halt"; the sound of planes; even the shrill voice of a neighbor calling her poodle, "*Jiggsy, Jiggsy, come back here!*"

A Night Long Remembered

In the days that followed, rumors ran rampant. Was the damage as bad as reported, or worse? Were the Japanese returning? When?

We lived under martial law; guards were everywhere. Our boarding students were sent home as soon as possible. We began sewing for the destitute refugees from Pearl Harbor. Air-raid drills became common; shelters were dug just outside the priory. Gas masks were issued, and rolls of barbed wire lined the beach at Waikiki.

The war altered our lives, but we were grateful the enemy did not return.

In June 1942, I was given 24 hours' notice that, if I wished, I could sail home to the mainland on a troop ship. I did!

BILLOWING SMOKE filled the sky in Battleship Row as Japanese bombs and torpedoes found their targets. To keep the enemy guessing about the extent of the damage, many U.S. newspapers didn't publish photos until months later.

His Photos Documented 'Day of Infamy'

DECEMBER 7, 1941 was a sailor's nightmare...I know, because I was a Navy photographer at Pearl Harbor.

The first half hour of the attack was a mixed bag of surprise, shock, anger, confusion and just trying to survive, combined with screamed commands, exploding bombs and ships, droning planes and cries for help.

I was taking pictures of the damage and my film supply ran out quickly. I was heading back to the photo lab when I heard a dive-bomber start his run, and I hit the ground. The bomb exploded just a few hundred feet from me—about a thousand feet short of the first vessel in Battleship Row.

The bomb left a crater in the street that was 28 ft. wide and 18 ft. deep. I still have a bomb fragment that fell close enough for me to grab.

During a lull between raids, I was told to go to the Navy Yard and take pictures. On my way, I felt a rifle in my back. There was a Marine at the other end. His commanding officer let me go after I explained I was an official Navy photographer. If I got stopped

By Harold Fawcett
Bridgeport, West Virginia

again (and I did), I was to say, "St. Peter said it was okay." Thirty years later, I learned that wasn't a code, but the commanding officer's name!

I wasn't too familiar with the Navy Yard, so I stopped at the commander's headquarters for instructions or orders. The first person I saw was another Navy

> *"I couldn't take pictures of shipmates in distress..."*
>
>

photographer, who told me in no uncertain terms to get out of there. He was essentially under house arrest and had been forbidden to take photos.

"Do not let anyone confiscate your film," he told me. "You know who you can trust." From then on, I was very careful.

I helped with rescue and aid efforts, but was able to keep shooting. One pic-

ture, which appeared in Walter Lord's book *Day of Infamy*, shows a destroyer lying on its side, its flag hanging in the oily waters of the dry dock. Whenever I see the U.S. flag, I see that scene in my mind, along with the picture I couldn't bring myself to take. The crew was on the dock, their uniforms covered with oil and blood, while an officer tried to hold muster to see who was missing, wounded or dead. I couldn't take a picture of shipmates in distress.

Another picture of three destroyed ships ran a full page in the San Francisco papers—but not until a year later. The delay was to keep the Japanese from learning the terrific damage they'd inflicted.

In the months that followed, we were called upon to take many more pictures, from an unexploded torpedo in the bowels of a battleship to salvage photos vital to the recovery of the destroyed Pacific fleet. Many of those pictures have never been seen by the public, but I'm proud to have taken them. They were very important to shortening the war and saving lives.✪

'Our Lives Would Never Be the Same'

THAT SUNDAY started as routinely as any other. Little did we realize our lives would never be the same.

As I browsed through the newspaper, my husband, Chet, busied himself at his basement workbench. Our radio churned out an old favorite, *Ramona*. Suddenly the music stopped and a somber voice interrupted to announce, "Pearl Harbor has just been heavily bombed by a surprise Japanese aerial attack."

I hurried to the basement door and called down, "What or where is Pearl Harbor? I've never heard of it."

"What about it?" Chet replied.

"They just cut into the music to announce it's been badly bombed—that's all I know. Is it something serious for us?"

Chet's tools clattered to the bench and he bounded up the stairs three at a time. For the rest of the day, he was practically glued to the radio. There was no more music, and all programs were either canceled or interrupted frequently. By now I'd learned that Pearl Harbor was in Hawaii, and yes, it was indeed important to the United States!

I couldn't grasp the whole event; it seemed so far away from Detroit. How could it affect us in our busy lives? Chet was too engrossed in the news reports to tell me much about the implications.

At work the next morning, all we talked about were the reports, the angles, the possibilities. We clustered around the only radio to listen as President Roosevelt asked Congress to declare war.

Before the battle in the Pacific was

TUNING IN. Radio programs were interrupted with frequent bulletins about events in the Pacific.

over, six of the men in our immediate family were taken, one after another. All personal plans were laid aside; we knew what "for the duration" really meant. "V for victory" became our slogan.

As the sons of our family left to serve their country, the women saved anything the government said needed saving for the war effort. We grew victory gardens. And we worked and prayed as never before. By no stretch of the imagination was life to be the same as before. —*Ruth Corbett*
Sun City, California

Neighbors Gathered To Hear Radio Reports

MY PARENTS owned a small neighborhood tavern in 1941, and I helped out however I could. Mom and I were washing glasses there one morning when we heard on the radio that the

Japanese had bombed Pearl Harbor.

I froze, my arms deep in the water, and looked at Mom. Her eyes were filling with tears, and I knew this had to be something bad. We told Father the news, as well as my Uncle Frank, who lived with us then. He said, "I will have to go."

We usually didn't have any business on Sundays, but before long, people began pouring in to listen to our radio, one of the few in the neighborhood. Everyone was quiet and somber, and some of the older men began to cry. Our family had emigrated from Italy, and our neighbors were European emigrants, too; they knew what war meant.

I was only 11 years old at the time, but that scene has never left my mind. It never will. —*Eleanor Santucci Flower*
Ottawa, Illinois

Youth Didn't Know He Was Listening in on History

WE HAD company that afternoon, but as a boy age 12, I was much more interested in listening to a professional football game on the radio. Leaving the grown-ups, I went to our basement and tuned in.

I vividly recall being annoyed by all the news bulletins interrupting the game. Finally, in a juvenile tantrum, I ran upstairs and asked the grown-ups, "Where in the world is Pearl Harbor?"

"I think it's in Massachusetts," one guest said. "Well," I replied, "the Japanese are bombing it." Little did I know that I was announcing an event that would change the history of the world.
—*Robert Greene*
Pleasant Hill, California

'The Shadow' Never Showed

THE RADIO was the main source of entertainment when I was a child. The whole family enjoyed listening to The Great Gildersleeve, Edgar Bergen and Charlie McCarthy, and Fibber McGee and Molly.

On December 7, my brother Kenneth and I settled in to listen to our favorite show, *The Shadow*. We got comfortable on the floor as we waited for the Shadow's scary voice…*Who knows what evil lurks in the hearts of men?*

We never heard that familiar line. Instead, an announcer told us that, at 7:55 a.m., the Japanese had attacked Pearl Harbor. There were many casualties, and many ships had been lost.

My brother ran to get Mother and Daddy, and I rounded up the rest of our siblings. For the next hour, the whole family sat listening to the news. Tears streamed down Mother's face. Daddy was restless—he'd sit for a while, then pace the floor, muttering.

The teacher brought a radio to school the next day, and we listened to President Roosevelt's "day of infamy" speech, in which he asked Congress to declare war. That night, on my knees, I prayed for my country and the soldiers who would be fighting. —*Leona Hall*
Nashville, Tennessee

GRIM NEWS affected children, too. Leona Hall was 12 when the bombing occurred.

SERVICEMEN like Ralph Herbison, photographed in his Navy garb in 1943, appreciated the warm send-offs they received from civilians.

Crowd Gave Soldiers Unforgettable Send-Off

I REMEMBER December 7, 1941 as though it were yesterday.

I heard the news while attending a hockey game with friends at Madison Square Garden in New York City. We were all devastated, thinking of the lives already lost and the loved ones who might be sent overseas.

Suddenly a booming voice came over the loudspeaker, asking all servicemen to report to their bases. At first there was dead silence. Then, as the boys started to rise and file out, the crowd gave them a standing ovation and thunderous applause. I haven't seen or heard anything as moving since.

—*Paula Mealy, Ridgewood, New York*

War Shattered Tranquility Of Quiet Rural Community

OUR LITTLE rural community of Pleasant Grove, Florida was safe and peaceful. Most of the problems of the world didn't seem to touch us.

My family had a battery-operated radio and people came by often to learn what was happening. December 7, 1941 was no different. I was only 6 then, but I still remember the sound of President Roosevelt's voice, and the worried faces of people who had been happy only moments before.

I heard strange words—"war", "bombs", "Pearl Harbor", "Japan"— and talk of young men we knew who might have to give their lives. My grandmother walked the floor with tears in her eyes; her oldest and youngest sons were in the Army, and she was afraid they wouldn't come home again.

I walked into the kitchen and asked my mother, "What is war?" She explained as best she could to a 6-year-old, but her troubled look told me more than her words. I asked her why Grandpa didn't stop the war (I thought Grandpa could do anything).

She replied, "Honey, there are some things Grandpa just can't fix."

I went to the room where my 7-month-old brother slept and pulled him close, wondering if he'd have to go to war when he grew up.

It was a traumatic time for a child, and perhaps, it was the time I began to grow up. Never again did I feel completely secure in my own little spot in the world.   —*Dorothy Kinkey De Funiak Springs, Florida*

'We All Sang the National Anthem Through Our Tears'

I REMEMBER exactly the announcement of the attack on Pearl Harbor.

My husband, Norman, and I had gone to a movie that afternoon. Suddenly, the picture screen went dark, the house lights came up, and a booming voice came from nowhere. "The Japanese have bombed Pearl Harbor. Some of our ships have been damaged. The attack came early this morning."

There was dead silence, then a wave of moans as everyone stood, feeling the crushing blow that would affect us all. Then the American flag appeared on the movie screen. As the strains of the National Anthem filled the theater, we sang, our eyes filled with tears.

In my heart, I knew my Norman would be going to war. I remember it all exactly. We must never forget!

—*Marilyn Russell Belleair Bluffs, Florida*

GI Had Speedy Trip Back to Fort Dix

DO I remember Pearl Harbor Day? You bet I do!

I was hitchhiking back to Army camp at Fort Dix, New Jersey after a weekend pass, and was amazed at how easily I was getting rides.

The instant one car dropped me off, another immediately picked me up. Getting rides was usually not difficult for a man in uniform, but this was ridiculously quick.

Finally, one driver opened his door and said, "Have you heard the news, buddy? The Japanese have bombed Pearl Harbor and all service personnel are ordered to return to their posts immediately," he said.

I never got back to camp quicker than I did that day! In fact, I arrived a little sooner than I would've liked, because as soon as I got back, I was issued a rifle and sent to guard the bakery! That night on guard duty was one of the coldest I can remember.

—*Owen Carpenter Tucson, Arizona*

STAYING CLOSE. Many Americans stayed close to their radios throughout the war, anxious for information on how their troops were faring.

SHOCKING STORY. Radio announcers were first to break the news to the public about the Pearl Harbor attack. From big-city stations like this one in New York, to the small-town station manned by Warren Deem whose story appears here, the unnerving news swept the country.

Teletype Bells Signaled Alarming News

By Warren Deem
San Marcos, California

I WAS the only person on duty at a small Iowa radio station that Sunday, serving as technician, announcer and newscaster.

Suddenly, I heard a persistent DING-DING-DING-DING-DING coming from the news Teletype down the corridor. The bell rang when reports were transmitted; the more bells, the more serious the news. As I approached the Teletype, the bells rang incessantly. Was there something wrong with the machine?

Then I picked up the sheet of paper winding out of the Teletype and read:

White House says Japanese attack Pearl Harbor.

I felt as though I'd been doused with a bucket of cold water. I dashed back to the microphone and interrupted the program to read the report twice, adding, "Further details when they become available."

The news was unnerving; my palms and brow were damp. But there was little time to think. The bells were ringing again. I raced down the hall, tore off the latest bulletin and rushed back to read it on the air. This one said:

Washington—The White House says the Japanese have attacked the American Naval Base at Pearl Harbor, Hawaii.

That bulletin was followed by two more:

Honolulu—A naval engagement is in progress off the coast of Hawaii. At least one black enemy aircraft carrier has been sighted in action against the Pearl Harbor defenses.

Washington—President Roosevelt has ordered the Army and Navy to carry out undisclosed orders prepared

---
"The news was unnerving; my palms were damp..."
✪
---

for the defense of the United States.

A short time later, there was a War Department bulletin:

Washington—The War Department has ordered all military personnel in the United States into uniform.

Then another flash set off a new frenzy of bells:

Japanese Imperial Headquarters announces state of war with United States...

The first regular news story to move on the war was a brief one:

Washington—The Far Eastern situation has exploded with a Japanese attack on Hawaii.

President Roosevelt has just announced that Japanese warplanes have attacked the big American Naval Base at Honolulu. This followed days of unprecedented tension between Japan and the United States and Britain over Japan's ambition in the Orient.

Attacks also were made on what were summed up as all naval and military activities on the principal island of Oahu. Presidential Secretary Stephen Early read the White House statement to newsmen. No further details were given immediately.

Later, as more detailed reports were transmitted, the unfolding story was broadcast to unbelieving listeners across the country.

Those strips of Teletype paper are yellowed and fragile now, but I still have them. Many of us have witnessed history in the making, but few events are so momentous that we can remember precisely where we were and what we were doing at the time. December 7, 1941 is one of them. ✪

Wife Held Back Tears—for 45 Years

By Ruth Bishop
McMinnville, Oregon

IT WAS a clear, quiet Sunday morning. Dad was in the living room, reading the paper and listening to the radio. Mother and I were in the kitchen, bathing my 2-month-old daughter, Janice.

I was trying to decide whether to mail my husband's Christmas presents; he was due for discharge from the Navy, but had to wait until his ship, the *USS West Virginia*, returned from Hawaii.

Dad came to the kitchen and said he hoped we wouldn't be disappointed about missing our favorite radio programs, but a tube had burned out and he couldn't replace it until tomorrow. Then he asked Mother to come read an article in the paper. That wasn't unusual, so I paid no attention.

A few minutes later, a neighbor stopped by on her way to church and asked Mother about Janice. Then the phone began to ring. Each time, Mother or Dad answered but didn't talk long. My friend Theresa came by; her eyes were watering, especially when she looked at Janice or helped me wrap Earl's presents.

It was a busy day—so much company and so much to do. An uneasy feeling had come over me, but I was so tired that I managed to sleep.

I woke early the next morning, and the unease was even stronger. I went outside to get the paper. It wasn't there. Could it have not been delivered? For the first time in *years*? I didn't think so.

I ran to the garage, hunted through Dad's car and found the paper tucked under the front seat. The headline read: "JAPANESE ATTACK PEARL HARBOR. USS WEST VIRGINIA SUNK WITH ONLY TWO SURVIVORS."

I began to yell, using words and phrases I ordinarily would never have used. I was *mad*. My parents came out and helped me into the house. They sat me down and told me headlines are often wrong, especially after a disaster.

No Tears Now

My anger began to fade. If there were only two survivors on that ship, Earl was one of them. I had to be strong, not only for myself, but for Janice. A deep coldness settled over my emotions. I didn't cry.

Dad plugged in the radio for more news. He had disconnected it the day before, hoping good news would come before I learned about the attack. But the news was confusing; there was little information.

The mail brought two letters from Earl, both dated before December 7, saying he was sure he'd be home for

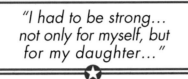

> "I had to be strong...
> not only for myself, but
> for my daughter..."

Christmas. But now the newscasters were saying the *West Virginia* was at the bottom of Pearl Harbor. The number of survivors either wasn't known or wasn't released.

The following Friday, Theresa and I were drinking tea with Mother and a friend when we heard the unmistakable rattle and clatter of the telegram deliveryman's Model T. It stopped in front of our house. We all knew why

he was there. I answered the door, but couldn't take the message, even though the deliveryman insisted it was good news.

Mother took it and read: "EVERYTHING OK, WESTER WOOD." Nobody knew who Wester Wood was, but at the moment, he was my best friend!

A few days later, a postcard came from Earl. It contained no news, but was dated after December 7, so I knew he was all right. (He later told me he was able to leap from the *West Virginia* to another ship and walk ashore.)

Earl came home February 8 and was later reassigned to the *USS San Juan*. By July, he was in combat in the South Pacific.

In 1986, Earl and I flew to Hawaii. As the plane approached the airport in Honolulu, the pilot announced that we would fly over Pearl Harbor. I looked out the window, listening as Earl described what had happened there so many years before.

It was then that all the tears I had not cried back in 1941 began to flow.✪

CRIPPLED SHIPS. The **USS West Virginia** and the **USS Tennessee** were pounded by Japanese bombs and torpedoes. Seven torpedoes hit the **West Virginia** alone.

'I Want to Go There To Remember...to Cry'

I WAS roller-skating at a park when suddenly the music stopped and a voice on the loudspeaker said, "May we have your attention, please...all military personnel are ordered to return to their bases immediately. The rink is closing, and we ask everyone to please leave and return to your homes as soon as possible." My bewildered friends and I did just that, but we couldn't imagine what was wrong.

When I walked into our house, Mother was on her knees, praying. That night, we went to a special service at our church. I was amazed by the size of the crowd and the frightened looks on all those faces. I can still see them!

As the months passed, my two oldest brothers entered the service. It was so hard on Mom. The whole time they were gone, she'd do her housework very fast. "I feel the faster I do it, the faster the boys will come home," she'd say. Luckily, both returned safely, but many of our friends didn't.

All my life I've had one dream—that someday I'll visit Pearl Harbor, to remember, to see it, to cry. I know I'll probably never get there, but I'll never, ever forget. Nothing has affected my life more than that Sunday afternoon in 1941. —*Elaine Hoskison Paradise, California*

'We Couldn't Believe It...'

ON THE FARM where I grew up, we only had one radio, a crystal set, which

ANSWERED PRAYERS. Elaine Hoskison's mom's prayers were answered when sons Leo and Russ, shown with Leo's children, returned from the war.

we powered with a car battery. To conserve power we only listened to that radio once a week, on Saturday nights, to hear *The Grand Ole Opry*.

My brother heard about the Pearl Harbor attack at a friend's house on a Sunday. What a shock it was when he came home and told us! We couldn't believe it until we hooked up our crystal set and heard Walter Winchell describe the attack. For better or worse, that fateful day united Americans like never before. —*Daniel Hanes Huffman, Texas*

Eric Sevareid Heard News from Neighbor

I WAS sitting in my home in Chevy Chase, Maryland when I heard the news that Pearl Harbor had been bombed. I looked out my window and saw our neighbor Eric Sevareid, then a radio reporter, playing with his twin boys in the snow.

I ran over to Eric's home and told him the news. He took his sons inside and raced off to his radio station in Washington, D.C.

It was a sad day for everyone, and a very busy one for our neighbor Eric. —*Mrs. Francis Vincent Cambridge, Maryland*

Show Was Short-Lived For GI's at Theater

I'D JUST been drafted 3 months before and was attending a show in a theater in California. In the middle of the program, a military policeman stepped onstage and said all service personnel were to report outside and board waiting trucks immediately.

None of us knew what was happening, but we obeyed. It wasn't 'til we got back to the base that we learned Pearl Harbor had been bombed. —*John Heimann, Madison, Wisconsin*

Youth Decided to Enlist

MY COUSIN and I were playing cards with our girlfriends when we heard about the bombing. I got up and said, "Well, that's it—I'm going to enlist tomorrow." And I did. I served in the war as a radio operator in the 9th Air Force Fighter Squadron. —*Harold Ludeker, Milan, Indiana*

Attack Turned Draftee Into Gung-Ho Soldier

I WAS DRAFTED into the peacetime Army almost a year before Pearl Harbor. Gosh, how I *hated* it—the pay, the rations, the antiquated weapons. Being sent to Texas, 2,000 miles from home, didn't help, either. (That was a long way, back in 1941!) I did my job and was proud of it, but I could hardly wait for my year of duty to expire.

It wasn't to be. After the sneak attack on Pearl Harbor, many unhappy "1-year draftees", including me, had a complete change in attitude. We be-

Archive Photos

RECRUITING STATIONS did brisk business after Pearl Harbor was bombed. Eager to do their patriotic duty, many young men rushed out to enlist the next day.

came gung-ho soldiers, appreciative of the training we'd received and ready to do battle.

All told, I put in 5 years of military service and advanced in rank, becoming a commissioned infantry officer. I'm proud of my military service, and while I wouldn't want to go through it again, I certainly would if my country needed me! —*William Barnes Temple Hills, Maryland*

Patriotic Memento Had Unusual Twist

ON DECEMBER 7, 1941, our local fire company had a celebration to raise a new flag donated by Spanish-American War veterans.

As the flag was raised, a white dove flew out from among its folds, and dozens of smaller flags that were tucked inside fluttered down over the crowd. My husband was president of the fire company, so I picked up one of those small flags as a memento.

After the ceremony, the crowd went into the firehouse for a program of entertainment. My husband came to me and said, "Go home and turn on the radio. They say we're at war with Japan."

My small flag was forgotten until I got ready for bed that night. I picked it up to look at it, and it was then that I saw the ironic words printed on the stick: "Made in Japan".

I still have that flag, and it always reminds me of the feelings I felt on Pearl Harbor day. —*Frances Webber Reading, Pennsylvania*

News of Attack Spurred Teen to Join Marines

THE MORNING of the "day of infamy", three of my buddies and I set out from my hometown of Buffalo, New York in my 1935 Ford for Rochester, about 70 miles away.

On the way back, we stopped to have the car serviced and I heard a ra-

dio blaring in the station. Suddenly an attendant ran out and asked if we'd heard the news that Japan had attacked Pearl Harbor.

We hadn't, but we all agreed then and there that we were going to do something. As we roared homeward, all we could talk about was joining the Marines.

I told my parents I wanted to sign up, but I was only 17 and they refused to grant their permission. There was nothing I could do but wait to turn 18, when I promptly enlisted. The Japanese put three slugs in me on Saipan and two more on Iwo Jima, but I have no regrets for doing my tour of duty. Some of my buddies, however, paid the supreme sacrifice. —*Jack Claven Glendora, California*

Split-Second Decisions Changed Lives Forever

ALTHOUGH I was just a little girl, I remember well the events of December 7, 1941. We were at my grandparents' house, visiting with my aunt and her sweetheart, who was serving in the Army Air Corps.

Suddenly the radio announcer broke in with a bulletin about the attack on Pearl Harbor. All servicemen were or-

dered to return to their bases.

Americans everywhere were forced to make split-second, life-changing decisions that day. My aunt and her soldier decided to get married immediately. Granny had reservations; she didn't think they'd known each other long enough.

But she was wrong. My aunt's marriage was a lifelong love affair that lasted until her husband died in 1989, and his exciting military career took them all over the world. —*Nancy Smith, Midville, Georgia*

Family Gave Servicemen Rides to Military Bases

OUR FAMILY was driving home to Chicago after visiting relatives in Indiana, and we heard the news on our car radio. I was too young to understand the significance of the announcement, but I noticed my parents became very quiet.

We stopped several times to pick up hitchhiking servicemen trying to get back to their bases. The situation was urgent, so we didn't stop for meals, but the GIs shared their candy with me whenever I got hungry. It was an exciting trip for me, but a sad one for my parents. —*Mary Lee Robertson Green Bay, Wisconsin*

BUDDIES ENLISTED. Larry Sullivan of Milwaukee, Wisconsin (at right and second from left above) and pals were pinsetters in a bowling alley when a patron took their picture December 7. All eventually enlisted.

SHIPS WRECKED. Bombs destroyed the dry-docked *USS Cassin* (left) and *USS Downes*. One sailor likened their eruption to a huge, horrible fireworks display.

L.A. Blackout Brought The War Home

RUMORS that the Japanese might attack the California coast had been going around for months, but they were only rumors. Besides, there were all those P-40s at Hamilton Field to protect northern California, and twin-tailed P-38s to defend the Los Angeles area.

My husband was working in the booming aircraft industry in Los Angeles. The plants were busy, but not yet working 7 days a week, so that Sunday we visited friends. We were fixing a picnic lunch when we heard the news of Pearl Harbor on the radio. The news was startling, but we felt safe enough—Honolulu was half an ocean away.

We took our lunch to Mt. Wilson, where we could gaze down at Los Angeles and the suburbs and neighboring cities that stretched for miles along the Pacific Coast and inland valleys. It was a rare clear day, and the view was dazzling. We stayed until twilight fell.

Glittering below, brighter and thicker than the stars, were the lights of all the cities and towns. The men pointed out and named each community, and could even identify some of the thoroughfares. It was a spectacular scene of thousands of gleaming lights.

Then lights started winking out randomly here and there—streetlights, advertising lights, house lights. More and more of them were extinguished, faster and faster. Moving headlights decreased and then disappeared. The vast metropolitan expanse below us became as dark as a stretch of uninhabited desert!

The news of Pearl Harbor had spread. Fear of an attack on California had taken over. This was a blackout—and not in faraway London!

The war had come to us.

—*Isabelle Van Nice Winship*
Warden, Washington

Stunned Students Listened as FDR Addressed Congress

THE STUDENTS in my high school seemed numb from shock the day after Pearl Harbor was bombed. The mood was solemn, and there was little laughter.

Just before noon, I asked our principal if we could listen to President Roosevelt's address to a joint session of Congress, scheduled for 1 o'clock our time. After checking with the superintendent, he told us we could listen to the speech in our homerooms. The school borrowed radios from several homes to provide enough for each room.

Come 1 p.m., every student was waiting to hear the President's message. The applause that greeted him in the House chamber was prolonged by shouts, cheers and rebel yells. When the crowd finally quieted down, the President spoke slowly, solemnly and distinctly.

"Yesterday, December 7, 1941—a date which will live in infamy—the United States of America was suddenly and deliberately attacked by naval and air forces of the empire of Japan," he began.

When he asked Congress to declare war, the chamber erupted in clapping, cheering and shouting that lasted a full 6 minutes. Then the cry rose: "Vote! Vote!" The Senate and House quickly passed the resolution, and the President signed it, officially declaring the United States at war. —*Bob Witkovsky*
Bay City, Michigan

EXTRA! EXTRA! Newspapers published "extra" editions to report the unprovoked attack on Pearl Harbor.

EXTRA

RACE RESULTS

Los Angeles Times

NIGHT Pictorial

VOL. LXI   Three Parts—38 Pages   ***   MONDAY MORNING, DECEMBER 8, 1941.   Page A   DAILY, FIVE CENTS

IT'S WAR!

Hostilities Declared by Japanese; 350 Reported Killed in Hawaii Raid

U.S. Battleships Hit; 7 Die in Honolulu

NEW YORK, Dec. 7. (A.P.)—Three hundred and fifty men were killed by a direct bomb hit on Hickam Field, an N.B.C. observer reported tonight from Honolulu.

In addition to these casualties from an air raid by planes which the observer identified as Japanese, said three United S...

LATE WAR BULLETINS

SHANGHAI, Dec. 8 (Monday). (A.P.)—The Japanese have sunk the British gunboat Petrel as it lay off the International Settlement waterfront.

HONOLULU, Dec. 7. (U.P.)—Parachute troops were sighted off Pearl Harbor today.

Air Bombs Rained on Pacific Bases

WASHINGTON, Dec. 7. (A.P.)—The White House announced early tonight that the Navy had advised the President that Japan has attacked the...

CHAPTER TWO

Off To War

Off To War

Jefferson Barracks, Missouri
March 8, 1942

Dear Mom and Dad:

You asked what it's like here in basic training. Here's a sample of a typical day: Friday we loitered around in bed until 5 a.m. Then a hoarse-voiced corporal came down our row of huts, banging on the wooden sides to wake us up. We got dressed, made our bunks and reported for roll call at 5:20. Still pitch-dark outside. After a mile-and-a-half walk we reached the mess hall, where we leisurely ate our breakfast in 10 minutes and then sauntered back to our huts at 120 steps to the minute.

By 6:45 we had cleaned the ashes from the stove, swept and mopped the floor, refilled the fire basket, hung our clothes up, with everything buttoned and on separate hangers, and shined three pairs of shoes, whether they needed it or not.

Then we were called out to stand in the cold until 7:30, when we marched to the parade ground. We drilled under a screaming sergeant until 10:30, then stripped off our overcoats and did calisthenics for 25 minutes.

Finally we went to the noon mess. Normally there would have been more drills, but this afternoon we got our shots. A few fainted and others got sick...

Instant Fighting Men

There's no such thing as an easy transition from civilian life to the military, as my letter above attests. Perhaps it was worse than usual in World War II, as the country was faced with the need to create a vast force of sailors, soldiers, airmen, medics and Marines nearly overnight.

We left our homes full of excitement. We arrived scared and bewildered. Equally bewildered were the people charged with turning us into soldiers. There were no mattresses for the beds, no uniforms, no training equipment, not enough doctors—not enough of anything. No one in the military had any experience trying to create an instant fighting force.

Those of us who went to Jefferson Barracks were told to arrive with only the clothes on our backs, because we'd receive uniforms when we got there. Alas, there were no uniforms for more than a week. Our civilian shoes went to pieces in a hurry in the snow and mud that February, and our civilian clothes were no match even for a St. Louis winter.

We stood for hours in endless lines. Lines for food. Lines for clothing. Lines to fill out forms and lines to take tests. As part of the physical conditioning, we ran wherever we went. "Hurry up and wait" was the wry joke in every branch of the service.

There were lots of rumors and exaggeration but very few facts. We'll be here 3 months...no, we'll ship out Thursday. We're all headed for the infantry...no, they're going to make us into paratroopers. Forty-two men died of pneumonia yesterday because there's no medicine...

Meanwhile, members of the regular Army valiantly tried to turn us into soldiers. We learned how to salute and what to salute. We watched propaganda and personal hygiene movies. And mostly, we were yelled at from reveille until taps.

It was no easy job, turning a bunch of high-spirited, independent, rambunctious young men into a fighting force. Basic training was just the start.

The real stuff was still ahead.

—*Clancy Strock*

ONE DAY after the bombing of Pearl Harbor, America found herself at war. Young men across the nation swarmed to recruiting stations and eventually train stations, fighting back fears about the future. All they knew was that their country needed them. And that was enough.

A SOLDIER'S FAREWELL. A new recruit kissed his sweetheart one last time before shipping out on a troop train. Along their routes, many trains were met by townsfolk who offered the soldiers food and moral support.

CAR

Harold M. Lambert

Sarge Made His Point with Raw Recruits

By Ed Knapp
Three Rivers, Michigan

"COME ON, let's go, let's go! Move it, double-time, let's go!" The rumble of the first sergeant's gravelly voice filled the air above Camp Crowder, Missouri. His rantings seemed merciless to the trembling recruits in basic training.

"Fall out, you miserable excuses for soldiers!" he'd yell at us. "I never saw such a sad bunch of men in my long Army career."

While we stood at attention, Sarge laid out the ground rules, making it perfectly clear that anyone who disobeyed them faced court-martial or death, whichever came first. Hands on hips, he'd stare us down and bellow, "If you don't believe me, just try me out." Nobody ever did.

Most of us had only recently been coddled teenage civilians, and we felt abused. But we were helpless to object. We learned to suffer in silence.

He Was *Tough*

Facing Sarge was a daily trial. His rough-hewn, unsmiling face always seemed to be glowering. Dark circles outlined his cold blue eyes. Whenever I was summoned to his office, I felt like a man about to face a firing squad.

When Sarge needed to flush out low-ranking men for "extra detail", he'd barge into the barracks without warning and announce, "I need some volunteers for a detail."

I tried to keep a low profile, acting as though I hadn't heard him and avoiding eye contact. It usually didn't work. When no one volunteered and Sarge snapped, "You, you and you", I knew that one of those "yous" was me.

I seemed to be his favorite target at Saturday-morning barracks inspections, too. My shoes weren't shined enough, my hair wasn't short enough, my footlocker wasn't properly arranged. I got so much KP I developed dishpan hands.

Some 37 years later, my old outfit had a reunion and I had a chance to see Sarge again. He was shorter than I recalled, the eyes had warmed, his manner was thoughtful, and the thunder was gone from his voice. I hardly knew him. This was a regular guy, someone I even liked.

Out of curiosity, I asked him why I'd been on KP so much. The answer was quick and decisive. "Kid," he said, "you did such a good job on KP, we just kept calling you back."

To this day, one of Sarge's commands stays with me. Whenever the battalion was parading for the military brass, Sarge was right there to make sure we didn't goof up.

He'd march alongside us, muttering under his breath, "Keep in step. You're bouncing too much. Dig in your heels. *Dig 'em in*." Today, whenever I walk for any distance, I still find myself digging in my heels. I guess Sarge will be with me forever. ✪

Train Crew Paid Daily Tribute

MY COUSIN John Geesaman of Cedar Rapids, Iowa was just 18 when Pearl Harbor was bombed. He enlisted in the Navy the next day, and eventually was sent to the South Pacific.

John had lived next to the Milwaukee Road railroad tracks, and like many youths, he was fascinated by the big steam engines and streamliners. There was a whistle-stop near his home, and he went down there every day to wave at the trains. The only time he missed a day was when he was sick.

Suddenly one train crew realized the young man who used to wave to them wasn't there anymore. The engineer decided he had to know what had happened. He stopped the train, walked up to John's house and knocked on the door. My aunt answered and explained that John was serving in the Pacific.

Then and there, the engineer told her that until John returned, the trains would make a couple of extra "toots" each time they passed. And they did—until John came home.

—Bev Johnson
Cedar Rapids, Iowa

GONE BUT NOT FORGOTTEN. When a young GI shipped out, local railroad workers kept him in their thoughts.

Harold M. Lambert

Familiar Phrase Kept Soldiers' Spirits Up

By Dale Gooch
Granite Falls, Washington

CAMP WOLTERS, west of Fort Worth, Texas, was not only a basic training camp for infantry recruits but an Army "reception center". It was there, on a bus with about 20 other draftees, that I got my first glimpse of military life.

As we pulled through the gate, a few recruits in fatigues were trying to look busy, picking up cigarette butts, gum wrappers and other trash. When they saw our bus, they broke into grins and shouted at us in perfect unison, "You'll be sorrr-eee!"

Later, as we were marched to the post barbershop in our civilian clothes, we heard the same taunt echoing from every direction. I couldn't wait to get into an Army uniform, just to cover up the

---

*"If the Army
didn't have jobs,
it invented them..."*

✪

---

indignity of being a raw recruit. Little did I know that a uniform wouldn't help.

The next morning, our metamorphosis from civilian to soldier continued. We stood in line all day—for clothes, for shots, for another physical, for IQ tests. And in each line, we heard, "You'll be sorrr-eee!"

It became clear that no matter how long we were in uniform, there'd always be someone who'd been at it a little longer.

After about a week, we'd taken all our tests, received all our shots and filled out all our paperwork. We were ready to be shipped out to other posts for basic training. It was a time of waiting; where we went depended on our test results and the needs of training camps around the country.

But it wasn't a time of leisure. If the Army didn't have jobs that needed to be done, it invented them. One morning after chores were doled out, we were loaded into a truck for a cleanup detail. As we rode past the barbershop, we noticed a line of new arrivals waiting to be sheared. We couldn't resist the temptation. "You'll be sorrr-eee!" we chorused. It felt great!

Voice in the Night

I eventually was assigned to Camp Callan in California, arriving on a troop train in the middle of the night. As we lined up for roll call, a voice from the darkness broke the stillness of the night: "You'll be sorrr-eee!" Would we *ever* escape the stigma of being just a little greener than everyone else?

After further training, I was shipped out for Europe. As I walked the gangplank to board the troop ship, I heard the familiar cry again. By then, I would have felt let down if I hadn't.

Our ship arrived in Naples, Italy several days later. The destruction all around us made it clear we were in a war zone. Somber drivers loaded us onto trucks. As our convoy moved through the countryside, we saw more and more destruction. We thought of those who'd arrived before us, and the

many who had paid with their lives. Soon we might serve our country in battle and make the same sacrifice.

It was a serious moment. But the wit and humor of the American soldier has a way of turning up in even the gravest situations.

As we rode along, I noticed a farmhouse just off the road. Its roof was gone, and one corner had been blasted away. Clearly visible on the white plaster walls, in crude English letters, appeared the immortal reminder: "YOU'LL BE SORRY!" It made my day.✪

Snow Foolin': Rookie Drill Sergeant Forgot Commands

MY BOOT TRAINING was at Fort Snelling, Minnesota during the big winter of 1941. The snow was knee-deep the day one of the sergeants gave a rookie the chance to drill us.

He started marching us in close formation, and things were going along pretty well until we reached a high bank of snow. The farther we marched, the deeper into the snow we got.

But the flustered rookie couldn't remember the command "To the rear, march!"

Instead, he sputtered a few choice words and finally yelled, "Stop, you crazy fools!"

—*J. Fershee, Monroe, Ohio*

SHEAR PLEASURE it wasn't, as this group of U.S. Navy "boots" received their regulation haircuts at the regimental barbershop. The trimming occurred at the U.S. Navy Training Station in Farragut, Idaho in 1944. This picture postcard was saved and shard by Leo Selz of Tomah, Wisconsin.

Recruit Quickly Learned Hazards of Volunteering

ON OUR FIRST day of Coast Guard training, we were marched to the base barbershop for haircuts. As we sat on the lawn, waiting our turn, an officer came up and asked if anyone could drive a truck. Several eager hands shot up.

The officer chose one man, took him into the base barbershop, handed him a broom and told him to sweep all of the hair off the floor. I learned right then and there never to volunteer for anything.

Later, we took commando training with submachine guns on an island off the California coast. Whenever the leader yelled "Down!", everyone was to hit the dirt in firing position. One day when the order came, we hit the dirt...and popped right back up. We'd hit the ground in an area where a large flock of sea gulls roosted at night! We got the rest of the afternoon off to wash our clothes.

—*Melvin Dunsworth, Quincy, Illinois*

Boot Camp Lessons Lasted a Lifetime

By David Oglesby
Clovis, California

NOBODY COULD teach me to swim. Many had tried and failed. I was deathly afraid of water, and ashamed of my tall, skinny frame, so I resisted all efforts to teach me to swim. When everyone gave up on me, I was secretly relieved.

Then came World War II. In June 1944 I gave up my deferment and asked to be inducted in the Navy. I was accepted, said good-bye to my wife and daughter and set out for boot camp.

We were immediately divided into groups of swimmers and non-swimmers, and my agony began anew. Of course, I'd have to learn how to swim!

The classes were traumatic. The instructors were hard-nosed and the water

was ice-cold. The weeks dragged by, and one by one the other swimmers passed the test—swimming the length of the pool and back, then jumping feet first off a 10-ft. diving board and swimming to the edge of the pool. Only five of us were left, and none of us had even dog-paddled as much as 5 yds.

One night, our grizzled old drill instructor took us aside. "Fellas," he said, "in 2 more weeks it'll be time to break boot, and you'll go home for a few days. But if you don't pass your swimming test, I can't certify you as having completed boot training. You won't go home, and I'll have to hold you over for another 12 weeks."

I didn't sleep much that night, but when I reported to class the next day, I'd made up my mind. Nothing was going to stop me from seeing my wife and

daughter! I bowed my head, prayed silently, jumped in—and swam the length of the pool and back. Then I climbed the 100-ft. diving tower (well, it *looked* that tall) and jumped in. Fighting panic, I shoved off the bottom and swam out. Never in my life had I experienced a greater personal victory!

We later learned that the DI was using a little applied psychology on us about holding us over—but we didn't know that then.

That experience taught me two valuable lessons. One was that I could do anything if I wanted it badly enough—a big help later in life, when I was struggling through college and the seminary while supporting a family. The other lesson was to never say "no" to a challenge. Even when I fail, I'm always enriched by giving my best.✪

Parachuting Left Pilot On Horns of a Dilemma

DURING 1945, we were training people to fly the new B-32 bomber in Fort Worth, Texas. Maynard was an instructor taking up new pilots for a practice run.

Summers in Forth Worth are terribly hot, and in those days, our planes weren't air-conditioned. On the hottest days, fliers often would strip down to nothing but a parachute harness, undershorts, shoes and socks before takeoff.

Maynard and his crew were practicing maneuvers when an engine caught fire. Attempts to extinguish the blaze failed, and Maynard told the crew to bail out. After setting a course that would crash the flaming ship in a remote area, he bailed out, too.

Maynard came floating down quietly and serenely beneath his parachute, looking for a place to land. He spotted an open field and steered for it. His landing was uneventful, but as he began gathering up his chute, Maynard heard the sound of pounding hooves behind him.

He glanced over his shoulder and saw a Brahma bull bearing down on him! Apparently the bull had taken Maynard's intrusion into the pasture as a direct challenge.

Maynard sped off, desperately trying to beat the bull to the pasture fence. He had to make several quick turns, feints and dodges, but finally made it to the fence line—just in time for the bull to give him "a little help" over it.

So Maynard escaped the bull —but now he was stranded in the Texas countryside wearing nothing but his undershorts, shoes and socks! How would he ever explain that? He was carrying no identification and hadn't worn his dog tags. Fortunately, the military found him before he had to make any explanations.

—Roger Bowlus
Reynoldsburg, Ohio

Cadet 'Bailed Out' the Hard Way

By Joseph Brabenec, Reed City, Michigan

AS PART OF the Navy's V-5 Aviation Program, we were learning how to fly in two-seat, open-cockpit biplanes at a small airfield near Athens, Georgia.

Each small group of cadets was assigned to a civilian instructor, flying with him each day. Our instructor, Thomas Shoemate, was a competent pilot and a jolly fellow, but a little heavy-handed.

On our second training flight, we were to make 180-degree turns back

"What did you do... lose one?"

and forth over some railroad tracks while maintaining an altitude of *exactly* 500 ft. We were watching Mr. Shoemate's plane return from a flight with Cadet Ketchum, when we realized the rear cockpit was empty! *Where was Ketchum?*

When Mr. Shoemate landed and climbed down, our commanding officer, a pilot himself, ran up to Instructor Shoemate and exclaimed, "What in

the world did you do, *lose one?*"

We later learned that Ketchum had been doing very well with his 180-degree turns, but in concentrating so hard on turning he had trouble maintaining altitude. Mr. Shoemate kept barking that the plane was too high, and on Ketchum's fifth attempt, the instructor took a more forceful approach.

Without comment, Mr. Shoemate slammed the control stick forward, throwing the plane into a violent dive. Ketchum's seat belt wasn't fastened, and he suddenly found himself "sitting on air", watching the plane fly down and away from him! He immediately pulled the rip cord on his parachute, and had just enough altitude for it to open and return him to earth unharmed.

These planes had no radios, so when Mr. Shoemate realized he'd lost his student, all he could do was circle to see that he'd landed safely. Later, a vehicle was sent to pick up Ketchum and return him to the airport.

As it turned out, Cadet Ketchum ended up being one of the very few students in our class to earn his wings and commission!✪

WILD FLIGHT with Instructor Thomas Shoemate (center) left a cadet "sitting on air". Joseph Brabenec (second from right) saw that two-seater plane come back with the instructor, but no cadet.

Older Recruit Proved He Was No Soldier

MOST RECRUITS gave their drill instructors little trouble, but one wore out quite a number of DIs in his attempt to prove he wasn't Army material.

By Floyd Hedge
Mountain Home, Arkansas

ONE FELLOW in our platoon at Fort Bragg was named Frank. He was in his 40s, and I don't know how he ended up in the same outfit with a bunch of us young bucks. But the Army was determined to make a soldier out of him no matter what his age, whether he liked it or not.

Frank did not. In fact, he was just as determined not to become a soldier as the Army was to make him one. He made every mistake in the book, and came up with several new ones. When it came to fouling up, he was in a class by himself…and he was more fun to watch than a three-ring circus.

When marching in close-order drill, he could stay out of step all day long, which takes some doing. About half the time he'd turn and go the wrong direction. Sometimes he'd stumble and pretend to fall. And often he'd manage to drop his rifle—an unpardonable sin in basic training.

He'd stand at attention while being chewed out and suddenly begin swaying from side to side until it seemed he'd topple over. He could keep this up for hours, wearing out one drill instructor after another while staying perky as a pup himself. And he did it all without so much as cracking a smile.

The drill instructors took turns at him, drilling him alone for hours on end. Once our own drill instructor actually had us fall out for a break so we could watch Frank in action. I laughed so hard my stomach hurt. We all knew what he was up to, especially when we saw him look our way and wink.

After a few weeks of this, the Army finally gave up on Frank and sent him home to St. Louis. He became a photographer, traveling around the countryside with his camera and tripod. I know this because one day he showed up at my mother's house!

When he asked if she had any little ones that he could photograph, Mom said, "No, my little one is in the Army." Frank spotted my picture on the mantel and said, "Wait a minute! I know that boy. I was in the Army with him at Fort Bragg."

Mom began to cry, and they had a long discussion about me. Later, she wrote to me about it. I could hardly wait to tell the rest of the men in the platoon! They were glad to know Frank had made it home safely, though we all missed the fun of having him around. ✪

An Unflappable WAC

OUR infantry regiment was at Camp Swift, Texas, preparing for assignments in Europe. I was a member of the medical detachment, performing physicals and giving shots.

All the men, wearing only shoes and socks, were making their way from room to room for shots and examinations. At least 20 naked men were standing in the front room of the dispensary, waiting for their final paperwork.

Suddenly the dispensary's front door flew open, and in walked a WAC with a stack of hospital reports. She was about two steps into the room when she realized what was going on. Her face reddened and she started to leave, then she thought better of it. With military bearing, she walked briskly across the room, laid the reports on a desk and left.

While she was there, you could have heard a pin drop. But once she left, you should have heard all the laughter. I've often wondered what she told her unit when she got back! —*Cletus Wunderlin, Platteville, Wisconsin*

THE NAKED TRUTH. Inductees who disrobed for shots and physicals never expected a WAC to walk into the room!

"OUR HOUSE IS YOUR HOUSE." Many families lived that philosophy during the war, inviting soldiers into their homes for meals and conversation.

Ranch Was 'Home Away from Home'

By Julie Larsen
Oakhurst, California

MY FAMILY moved to a California ranch in 1942. When the military established a rifle range nearby, soldiers poured into the area for training before they were shipped overseas. The men started coming to our house to buy eggs, milk and produce, and my parents quickly became well-acquainted with the troops and commanders.

Before long, we had soldiers at the ranch every day. I was 4 years old then, and those soldiers showered me and my brother with attention. We were thrilled when they took us for rides, letting us honk the horns as we drove over the country roads. I remember the strong arms that held me, and the gentleness of all those men. But I had my favorites— Sarge, Slim and McDonald.

As the weeks went by, those soldiers spent more and more time with us. Mother made fresh lemonade for them every afternoon. We shared whatever we had, and the soldiers were always welcome. Many were from big cities, and they'd never seen peaches, plums or apricots growing on trees. They'd never seen a cow being milked, either.

One summer night we had a slide show for them under the sycamore tree on our large front lawn. The soldiers began arriving just after sundown and sat on folding chairs we'd borrowed from the local school. Daddy showed slides of the family, trips we'd taken and places we'd lived. The men seemed touched and grateful to be part of a family again. Most of their own families were very far away.

I don't remember when the soldiers

"We shared whatever we had...the soldiers were always welcome..."

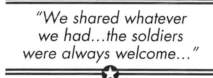

---

stopped coming. I don't remember saying good-bye. One day they disappeared from my life as quickly as they had come. I was overcome with sadness.

I do remember the end of the war. Grandma and I were listening to the radio when an announcer said the war was over. She threw her hands in the air and cried, "The war's over! Thank God. Now Donny and Jack can come home!" She grabbed me and hugged me hard, and I knew something important had happened to my family and my country.

Thankfully, my cousins Donny and Jack did come home. I've prayed, many times, that Sarge, Slim and McDonald made it home, too.✪

Family Gave Servicemen A Place to Call Home

MY FATHER was a security guard at Pier 32 in San Francisco, California. When the war started, he went to work on the ships that came in, and befriended many servicemen who were on leave while waiting to ship out. Most of them were young boys who had never been away from home before.

Many of these men had nowhere to stay, so Dad brought them home. It was nothing to get up in the morning, stumble into our living room and see one serviceman asleep on the sofa, another in each armchair, and two or three on the floor. Army, Navy and Air Force hats lined the back of the couch, and shirts and ties hung from the floor lamp.

My mother would be in the kitchen, cooking a big breakfast of pancakes and two or three pots of coffee. We had only one bathroom, and the boys would all line up outside it, talking and drinking coffee while waiting their turn.

After breakfast, the boys would sit and talk about their hometowns, families and sweethearts. They all had pictures to show each other.

FAST FRIENDSHIPS were made during boot camp, and later in the field. This snapshot of military buddies was shared by Warren Engeldahl of Houston, Texas.

When they left, each one went up to my parents to thank them. One young boy gave Mother a big hug and said, with tears in his eyes, "Ma'am, no matter where I am, I will always remember you."
—*Carolyn Schiro*
San Jose, California

Family 'Adopted' Soldiers Before They Shipped Out

MY FATHER worked at one of the military bases in Louisiana. As a World War I veteran, he knew the servicemen would enjoy home cooking, and regularly invited them to share Sunday dinner with us.

Soon the men were coming more often, for coffee with lemon pie or chocolate cake in the afternoon, or to share a picnic with our family. They sure seemed to appreciate everything we did to return some degree of normalcy to their lives.

Sometimes there were soldiers sitting around the wood stove in the kitchen while my mother and I prepared a meal or an afternoon snack. They seemed at home with us, and we were very comfortable having them there. They lis-

tened as we talked and sometimes laughed at our slow drawl and odd pronunciations. We in turn learned to speak more clearly—and to laugh at ourselves.

When our friends left to go overseas, it was hard to say good-bye to them. We made our partings as quick and painless as possible, and prayed for their safe return.
—*Dorothy Longfoot*
Pineville, Louisiana

Rented Rooms Kept Kin Close to Soldiers' Camp

WHILE YOUNG MEN were being transformed into infantrymen at Camp Barkley in Abilene, Texas, their family members wanted to stay as close to them as possible. Many residents, including my family, rented out rooms to these relatives so they could be with their loved ones up until they were shipped overseas.

I was moved to the dining room and my parents rented out my bedroom for $6 a week. People from as far away as Wisconsin and Washington stayed in that room, and they all became like family. I remember Mother hurriedly summoning the preacher and borrowing flowers from a neighbor so one couple could be married in our living room.

Mother kept a map of Europe on the kitchen wall, and marked it with pins to show where the boys were fighting. Whenever a family let us know their loved one had fallen in service, it was as though we'd lost one of our own.

Many of the young men at Camp Barkley worshipped at our church. It became a custom for them to stand in the front of the church after services so the ladies could invite them home for Sunday dinner.

Mother always brought a couple of them back for a home-cooked meal such as pot roast, mashed potatoes, fresh tomatoes, green beans and chocolate mocha cake. Afterward, the soldiers read the newspaper, listened to the radio or played games until evening, when Dad took them to their shuttle bus back to camp.

I remember one very cold Christmas Eve when Mother let me open my gifts early, while the soldiers were there. I got a Monopoly game, and we all played until the last possible moment before the bus left. Those homesick soldiers left with big tears in their eyes.
—*Mary Ann Brame, Dallas, Texas*

OFF TO WAR went GIs on the Pennsylvania Railroad. This patriotic ad, which appeared in *The Saturday Evening Post* April 8, 1944, reminded readers to buy war bonds.

Son Helped Mom Deliver Goodies to Troop Trains

By Maxine Setzer
Hutchinson, Kansas

OUR WOMEN'S LODGE met the troop trains that came through Hutchinson, Kansas and provided the men with items like magazines, pencils, playing cards and homemade cookies.

The engineers signaled us with two whistle blasts whenever a troop train was making a stop. We displayed our goodies on "trays" made from cardboard box lids, and everyone got to select something.

We always spent some time chatting with the soldiers. Some gave us their addresses and asked us to write to them.

Most days, my 3-year-old son, Mike, would come to the train with me. He was very outgoing and the soldiers adored him. He always seemed to remind them of a son, brother or neighbor they'd left behind.

When the troops couldn't get off the train, we'd lift Mike through the window so the soldiers could chat with him. One soldier gave him his Army pin, which I still have—attached to a picture of Mike in his own Army uniform years later.

MOTHER'S HELPER. Little Mike Setzer (with his mom, Maxine) lifted spirits of soldiers on troop trains.

Postcards Kept Relatives in Touch

By Naomi Crowley
Parker, Colorado

OUR HOUSE in McPherson, Kansas was right across the street from the railroad tracks, and it wasn't unusual to see troop trains stopped there. The windows were always open in good weather, and sometimes even in bad weather, so the men could chat with the local folks on the platform. The men often asked where they were and which direction their train was headed.

Sometimes they threw out empty chocolate boxes with their names and their families' names written inside, asking that someone write their folks to let them know where they'd been. Other times they gave their APO address, asking that someone write to them.

After the trains left, I would walk through the ditch and pick up every box I could. Mother never let me write to soldiers, but if there was a family address, we'd send them a postcard to let them know when their loved one had passed through. Mother had three sons in the war and knew how it felt to worry about a son's whereabouts.

We also saw many flatcars loaded with military equipment. Tanks, large guns and crates were secured with chains. Other cargo was covered with canvas. When these trains stopped, an MP was usually stationed at each corner of the flatcar. They took their duties seriously, and didn't chat with us.

Taking pictures of the trains was prohibited. One neighbor took a few snapshots one morning, only to have a government man confiscate the film by evening. He returned all the photos except those of the train. As time went on, we all became very security conscious. "Loose lips sink ships!" ✪

SENDING THEM OFF. Civilians eased soldiers' journeys by meeting troop trains with food, drinks, magazines and personal items. Some sent postcards to soldiers' families, who rarely knew where their loved ones were headed.

He Kept Dad's $5 Gift 50 Years!

By James Albrecht
Wauwatosa, Wisconsin

ON OCTOBER 20, 1942, my dad drove me to the armory in New Ulm, Minnesota to join other draftees for a bus ride to Fort Snelling. A friend used Dad's old Kodak box camera to capture our parting handshake.

At that moment, Dad handed me a $5 bill. At first I declined it, but Dad insisted. He said if I didn't need it, I should carry it through the war.

Can you believe it? That $5 bill has been in my billfold for over 50 years! I carried it through army camps in the United States, and with the 11th Armored Division in England, France, Belgium, Luxembourg, Germany and Austria.

It came home with me in 1946, and its sentimental value has increased every year since. It's also quite a conversation piece, especially every October 20.✪

SO LONG, SON! When James Albrecht's dad saw him off at the Greyhound depot, a friend snapped this picture. James' dad slipped his son a $5 bill then, and this keepsake has stayed in his wallet ever since!

He Raced from Chicago to Colorado on 72-Hour Pass

By Robert Lohr, Hereford, Texas

I FINISHED high school in Colorado in 1943 and enlisted that fall. After attending boot camp in Idaho, I was assigned to service school in Chicago.

One beautiful spring day I got a 72-hour pass. I went straight to the train depot and boarded the Denver Zephyr, which luckily had room for one more sailor. I was heading home.

The picture of my father and me was taken during that leave in front of our house in Loveland, Colorado. My dad, Charlie, was a National Guard veteran who worked at the local sugar factory, helping to manufacture food for the armed forces and the nation.

After an all too brief visit, it was time to head back to Chicago. Getting back on time was half the fun. I boarded the Zephyr without a reservation, but it was standing room only for many miles.

In Chicago, several of us hired a cab for the final dash to the main gate. Once inside, we raced to our various destinations on base. Whew! I made it with about 5-1/2 seconds to spare!✪

BRIEF REUNION. Sailor Robert Lohr (left) raced home to Colorado from Chicago on a 72-hour pass. He posed for this happy photo with his dad, Charlie, a National Guard veteran.

Small-Town Fib Led To Big Embarrassment

WHEN I was serving with the WAVES during World War II, it seemed nobody wanted to admit being from a small town.

One afternoon I boarded a train in Dallas, Texas on the way to Utah and sat beside a handsome sailor. He asked the question all service personnel asked each other: "Where are you from?" I thought he'd never know if I fibbed, so I said, "I'm from Dallas. Where are you from?"

"Houston," he said.

Minutes later a Shore Patrol man came through the train, checking leave papers. He looked at mine and read aloud, "Turkey, Texas!" Then he looked at the sailor's and announced, "Goose Creek, Texas!" He was chuckling as he walked away.

The strange-sounding names gave him a good laugh, but that sailor and I were so embarrassed we wanted to crawl under our seats!

—*Lee Nelson*
Waco, Texas

Harold M. Lambert

CROWDED TRAINS pulled into tiny towns, giving servicemen a break from the monotony of travel.

Moberly, Missouri Was an Oasis to Parched Soldiers

By James Mund
Bedford, Texas

WE WERE FRESH out of basic training and being shipped to Army Air Corps technical school on a "troop sleeper", the Army's Spartan version of a Pullman car. The interior was jammed with rows of bunks stacked three high, with an undersized rest room at one end.

The cars were crowded and hot, and there was no air-conditioning—not in 1943! We kept the windows open, despite the soot and smoke that blew in.

The food provided us no solace—it wasn't even as good as what we'd had in the mess hall during basic training, and that had hardly been gourmet fare.

Our destination was classified. We meandered generally north and west of Miami, Florida, but we could only guess the rest. Whenever we approached a city or town, we craned our necks to look for an identifying sign.

As the train slowed to a stop for coal or water, someone called out, "Hey! We're coming in to Moberly. Anybody know where Moberly is?"

"Yeah, Missouri."

"Looks like a nice, clean little town."

We came to a dead stop near the small passenger station. Along the loading platform, the townspeople had set up rows of folding tables laden with paper cups and plates, pitchers of juice, ice water and soft drinks, and stacks and stacks of homemade cookies.

The ladies of the town apparently waited in the station for the troop trains to come by, then came out and walked alongside the cars, serving refreshments through the windows or open doors. It was their "extra-mile" contribution to the war effort, and it was wonderful.

I particularly remember one slim, pretty redhead. She was about my age, and I wished I could somehow get her name and address. But she quickly moved on to the next car and was gone.

"Well, maybe I never heard of Moberly, Missouri before," I told a fellow soldier as the train pulled out, "but I'll never forget it!" To us, Moberly was like an oasis in the middle of America on that hot, humid August afternoon.✪

'I Enlisted by Being Run Out of Town on a Rail!'

I WAS CLASSIFIED as 1-A in April 1943, and was to report to the Marine Corps recruiting depot for duty August 18. Between those dates, I saw a newspaper story in the *Chicago Tribune* that said fathers with two or more children would not be inducted for service. Since I had two kids, I figured that was the end of the matter, and forgot all about it.

That September, I was at work running a tractor and loader in suburban Chicago when I noticed two men standing on the sidewalk, watching me. I climbed off the idling machine and asked those fellows what I could do for them. They asked if I was Joseph Bird. I said I was. They asked where I was on August 18. I said I couldn't remember.

Then they pulled out FBI badges, informed me I was a draft dodger and started to lead me away! I explained to them about the news story, but they said that meant nothing, and that I was to come with them. They didn't even want to wait to let me shut off the tractor.

We walked 2 blocks to the train depot and boarded a train to downtown Chicago. From there, I was put on a westbound train for the Marine base in San Diego. I wasn't allowed to contact my wife, who had no idea what had happened, until we reached Omaha. She was indignant, to say the least!

When we arrived in San Diego, I was inducted, outfitted, had my hair chopped off, and was turned over to a drill sergeant who made the detectives look like sissies.

So that's how I entered the Marine Corps—by being run out of town on a rail! I eventually was cleared of the "draft dodger" status, earned an expert rifleman award, and was honorably discharged 2 years later.

—Joseph Bird Jr., Winfield, Illinois

War Separated Newlyweds Sooner Than Expected

MY FIANCE, Ralph, was a young sailor when he proposed to me on Christmas Eve 1943. When he returned the following November, we had a nice wedding—although we'd had only 10 days to prepare for it!

After the wedding, we enjoyed a brief respite from the war—Ralph was temporarily assigned to stateside duty. Unfortunately, the assignment that was supposed to last 6 months lasted only 6 weeks! We had only a few hours' notice that he was being reassigned to a mine-sweeper that was leaving for the Pacific.

I managed to find a ride to his ship, and Ralph and I said our good-byes in heavy fog at the end of the pier. Whenever I hear the song *Harbor Lights*, it still brings back that night and our sad parting.
—*Jean Pelletier*
Palm Springs, California

"WILL YOU MARRY ME?" Jean Pelletier with fiance Ralph after he proposed on Christmas Eve 1943. Ralph had stateside duty after the wedding, but soon was sent back overseas.

Poignant Moment Moved Departing GIs to Tears

IT WAS DUSK when our ship pulled away from the pier in Seattle. None of us had any idea where we were headed, although we suspected it was Hawaii.

As we stood on deck to watch the lights of the good old USA slowly recede, about eight black soldiers put their arms around each other and formed a circle. Slowly, softly, they began to sing *Harbor Lights*.

An eerie quiet fell over the deck as everyone stopped to listen. More than a few had to brush away their tears.
—*Joseph Petti, Bayonne, New Jersey*

This Shipload of Seasick Servicemen Longed for Dry Land

MY ANTIAIRCRAFT outfit boarded the *Queen Mary* in New York Harbor on December 23, 1943.

We got under way, and many of the men were seasick even before we hit rough water a few miles out. We soon learned that this ship's great size didn't keep her from rolling and pitching on the big waves.

By Christmas Day, many of us had real problems. And it didn't help that our holiday dinner was kidney stew, apricots and tea!

The *Queen Mary* was such a fast ship that she didn't travel as part of a convoy. We were out there all alone. We'd zig and zag, trying to evade the German subs. We heard later there had been a reward for any German officer who sank her.

It took us 6 days to get to Scotland. What a happy and thankful group of soldiers we were when we finally got our feet back on land!
—*Fred Ortwig, Exeland, Wisconsin*

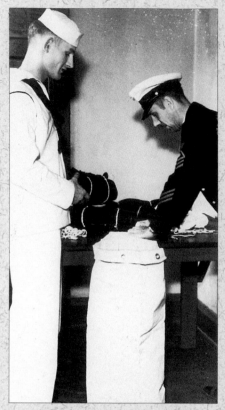

STOWING IT. Apprentice Seaman D.T. Rohde (left) gets a lesson in how to roll his clothing and stow it in a seabag. "If done correctly, the clothes were surprisingly unwrinkled when unrolled," says Rohde, who went on to become a Navy commander. Now retired, he lives in Los Osos, California.

SHIPPING OUT. When sailor Dean Nicholson had a brief leave before being shipped overseas, he visited his father at the Todd Shipyards in Seattle, Washington. Dean's dad helped build destroyers there. Dean now lives in Mount Vernon, Washington.

Archive Photos

Secret Journey Kept Soldiers on Edge

ONE DAY AT CAMP, we were told to write our last letters home and pack our bags. None of us knew where we were going, or when. We joked that maybe we'd just be sent somewhere else on the West Coast, or that we were being moved only to confuse the enemy. But many of us didn't sleep well that night.

After chow the next morning, we piled into a convoy of Army trucks. Two hours later, we saw the docks and big ships and realized this was not a dry run—in fact, it would be rather wet. As we jumped off the trucks, our packs seemed twice as heavy as before.

We descended into the bowels of our ship…down, down, down, until at last we reached our quarters—on F deck, right at the waterline. This was our new home? Heaven forbid! It was dark, hot and musty-smelling; the cots were three-high and cramped. My bunk was on top, and every time I moved, I bumped something—the ventilator, the guy next to me, the steel beam over my head.

My company drew KP duty, and I was chosen to pour coffee, which was a steaming-hot job in the torrid mess hall. I longed to be on deck.

The ship left at 1:30 the next afternoon, and loneliness set in quickly. For a few days, everyone just stood around (you can't sit on a transport—no room)

By Norm Whiton
Deerfield, Massachusetts

looking dismal and sad. Our only link to land were the sea gulls and albatross that followed in our wake.

Meanwhile, rumors flew thick and fast about where we were headed—Chile, Australia, Alaska, the Fiji Islands, New Caledonia. Some men honestly believed we were just trying to confound the enemy and would be back home the next morning. They were wrong. This was the real thing—a dangerous and secret mission.

Our fourth day out, the men started shooting craps. Betting was prohibited,

---

"Rumors flew thick about where we were heading…"

✪

---

so they played for matches, although the matches were occasionally exchanged for money in darkened corners. Others caught up on reading or chatted about the loved ones they'd left behind.

At 7 every night came the much-mimicked announcement: "Prepare to darken ship, prepare to darken ship. Show no lights about the ship. Close all doors and ports. Smoking is prohib-

ited on outer decks until sunrise."

We knew we were moving in a southerly direction, but still didn't know our destination. All we knew was that the weather was getting warmer.

One day the foghorn blew, indicating we'd crossed the equator. We'd left the spring of the northern hemisphere behind and were now coasting into autumn in the southern latitudes.

The crossing meant my KP stint was over, too. At last I was free to come up on deck and enjoy the fresh clean air of the tropics. At night, the ship's bow churned up a strange phosphorescence in the water. Overhead, the heavens and the Southern Cross appeared in the upper portion of the sky.

Star watching helped us appreciate just how far from home we were—the North Star had vanished.

Finally, after nearly 4 weeks at sea, we spotted the mountains of New Guinea, our new home. Although we had no idea what was in store, anything would be better than staying on the overcrowded ship.

We saw the coral reefs that challenged our navigator, then the beaches, coconut groves and dense jungles. We slept peacefully that night, our ship safely anchored and its lamps lit. Our trip was finally over.✪

These Little Boys Found 'Big Brothers'

Ewing Galloway

HEROES ASHORE! When four boys stumbled onto a Marine training exercise, they forged bonds of friendship they've never forgotten.

By Richard Mackie
Concord, California

WE WERE WALKING along the beach near Coronado, California when we saw two ships anchored about a half-mile offshore. We watched in amazement as eight or 10 small rectangular boats emerged from those ships and started heading straight for us. To four preteen boys, the scene was too entrancing for us to think about running!

Before we knew it, the first rectangular boat had reached shore, and its entire front end burst open. Out charged 30 to 40 armed Marines, whooping and shouting as they ran for the beach. When they reached the sand, they dove in on their bellies and began firing their rifles.

Everything happened so fast! Marines were running right by us as if we weren't even there. Others were setting up machine guns and firing with abandon at an unseen enemy. Within a minute, the rest of the rectangular boats reached their destinations, and the beach was crawling with hundreds of shouting men.

Within 5 minutes, the Marines had "secured" the beach and began to sit down in groups. Now I was really getting scared. I expected an officer to yell at us any minute for getting in the way of this training exercise. I was sure we'd all be put in jail, or worse! But no officer came.

Finally, we started walking tentatively toward a group of six Marines sitting in a circle, eating. The soldiers smiled and invited us to join them. When we sat down and opened our lunch bags, the bartering was immediate. In short order, we traded apples, oranges, sand-

---

"Out charged the Marines, shouting as they ran for the beach..."

★

---

wiches and cookies for C rations, K rations, several dimes and a knife.

This was like heaven! We were breaking bread with new friends far more exciting than Gene Autry, Tom Mix or any of our other current heroes. These were real Marines!

All too soon, the Marines had to return to their ships. We said our good-byes reluctantly, but promised to meet again the next day. We were comforted in knowing they'd be back to "take" the beach again tomorrow.

By 10:30 the next morning, we were sitting on the beach, eyes glued to the ocean. We'd brought plenty of food this time—a sack of oranges, a bag of cookies, extra sandwiches, several apples and three candy bars.

About 11, the two ships appeared on the horizon, and in another 20 minutes the landing crafts started for shore. Our friends were back!

We cheered them on as they "invaded", beat back the "enemy" and secured the beach.

This was better than any movie Hollywood could ever produce. We were right in the middle of all the action, and some of the "actors" were our personal friends! We could hardly wait for the Marines to settle down for lunch.

They'd Made Friends

By the end of the fourth day of training, we four boys had become fast friends with the six Marines. The chatter was much like what one would expect among family members. We were thrilled to have the biggest, strongest, smartest Marines in the world as friends. And the Marines seemed delighted to have "little brothers" to relieve some of their homesickness.

I think we also helped them forget for a few minutes their ultimate destination. They were, after all, being trained to invade some island in the Pacific—an island protected by Japanese soldiers trained to fight to the death.

On this fourth day, the Marines announced they wouldn't be coming back. They had completed their training and were ready to put it to the test. Our final parting was filled with sadness and lots of bravado. Large hands tousled the hair on small heads. Lips quivered as we struggled to hold back tears. The Marines knew what they were about to face. We sensed it, too.

We held the Marines' hands as we escorted them back to their landing crafts. The silence said far more than any words ever could. The bonds would last a lifetime.

We sat on the beach and watched the crafts take our friends back to the big ships for the last time. Then the ships slowly and silently moved away, until they disappeared over the horizon.

CHAPTER THREE

On the Home Front

On the Home Front

IT WASN'T enough to support the troops in spirit. Winning the war required sacrifices at home as well as abroad, so Americans everywhere rolled up their sleeves and got to work. The war wasn't fought on battlefields alone. Those on the home front helped win it.

POTS, PANS AND MOVIE FANS. Youngsters thronged to this "aluminum matinee" at the State Theater in Minneapolis, Minnesota in 1941. Each child with an aluminum item was admitted free. Pam Kroschel of Post Falls, Idaho shared this photo. Her mom, Marceline Foy, is behind the "U" on the banner, waving a pan lid.

There was scarcely an American who wasn't involved—in one way or another—in World War II.

Some served coffee and doughnuts to troops as they boarded ships for overseas duty. Others rolled bandages, collected scrap metal and went to work in factories that produced everything from bullets to bombers. Quite a number manned air raid lookout posts, or made home calls to help bewildered young mothers who suddenly were totally on their own.

They also had to cope with something new called rationing. First call on everything went to the military. What was left over was doled out to those left at home. There were food coupons and gas coupons and shoe coupons and tire coupons—coupons for just about everything you needed. Use up your monthly allotment early and you went without. And if someone in the family was lucky enough to be coming home on furlough, all the relatives hoarded their precious stamps so there could be steak on the table and a full tank of gas for visiting the girl who had been left behind.

You'll read dozens of those stories in this next chapter. And one aspect of life on the home front may glimmer through as you read—that's the millions of small everyday kindnesses bestowed upon servicemen.

Free Food and Fare

There were restaurant owners who wouldn't let anyone in uniform pay for their meal. And cab drivers who "forgot" to drop the fare flag when the passenger was in the service.

There were the people who took soldiers and sailors into their homes for Christmas and Thanksgiving meals. I particularly remember being invited to the home of a woman, hobbled with arthritis and age, who in her younger days had performed in the Metropolitan Opera. She prepared lunch with her own hands, and we sat talking the entire afternoon.

She had never met an Illinois farm boy. I had never met an opera star. I'm not sure which of us enjoyed the chat more. Nor had I ever tasted her beverage of choice, a 50-50 blend of iced tea and ginger ale. (It's worse than it sounds, by the way.)

The local USO always had free tickets to movies, concerts and sporting events—all donated by people who wanted to do something for their troops. One bizarre entertainment sticks in my mind to this day—the Houston Symphony playing the accompaniment for several large men who mud-wrestled on stage. Only in Texas…

Cautious parents gingerly permitted their daughters to be hostesses at service club dances. You had a chance to spend a few hours back in "the real world", and meet young ladies with strange and beguiling accents, to boot.

To a youngster far from home, these small kindnesses made you feel that all of America was your hometown, and all Americans were your family. Tired as they were from long days in defense work, they still had time and a smile for those of us in uniform.

The history books tell us about the celebrities who entertained troops, sometimes within sound of gunfire. They tell about the Stage Door Canteen, the USOs and the American Red Cross. Important, every single one of them.

But what put a lump in your throat were the unexpected small kindnesses from all those people who didn't want your thanks—because it was their way of thanking you.

—*Clancy Strock*

For Uncle Sam.....
ALUMINUM!
FOR NATIONAL DEFENSE
From Minneapolis Kiddies

LITTLE PATRIOTS. Students at Israel Putnum School in Meriden, Connecticut posed proudly with the paper they collected in a 1944 drive for the war effort. One pupil was Joyce Witkovic, now of Newport, New Hampshire, who shared photo.

Patriotic Fire Burned Bright in Boy's Heart

THE JAPANESE did a lot of damage when they bombed Pearl Harbor. Little did they know they had started a patriotic fire that burned in every American, young and old, from head to toe.

The word on everyone's lips, and behind every thought, action and effort, was "victory". Instead of waving to those we passed, we gave the "V for victory" sign. We didn't just have gardens, we had *victory* gardens, planted in the shape of a "V".

I was only 8 years old, but even our school days were planned around this great effort. We gathered tin cans, newspapers, iron, copper, even milkweed pods—anything that could be recycled or made into something useful.

We gathered cans after school, and when our gunnysacks were full, we hauled them to the schoolhouse. We walked the lanes and ditch banks, filling sack after sack with milkweed pods. These activities made us feel important, a part of the team. We were so proud!

We sang patriotic songs in school, too. My favorite went like this:

Buy Jeeps, buy Jeeps,
Send thousands of Jeeps o'er the sea,
  the sea.
Buy Jeeps, buy Jeeps,
And bring back my loved one to me.

One Jeep lost its driver in battle,
Kept on fighting enemy tanks.
It pushed them all down in a canyon,
Then gave three cheers for the Yanks.

By Jerald Oldroyd
Glenwood, Utah

One day a week, we could bring our dimes and quarters to school to buy savings stamps—10¢ for a red stamp, 25¢ for a green one. A stamp-filled book could be exchanged for a war bond.

Now, in those days a dime was big money, and hard to come by. A dime could buy two candy bars, two bottles of pop or 10 pieces of penny candy. So I had a choice—candy or stamps. It wasn't a hard choice to make. I wanted to help buy one of those Jeeps that pushed enemy tanks into a canyon.

One day, a classmate said his family had received a box from his soldier brother and invited us to come by after school to see what was in it. When school let out that day, we looked like a herd of cattle stampeding to his house!

What Would They Find?

His mother took a few personal things from the box first, then lifted out a captured German flag. I couldn't believe it! There was the black spider-like swastika, circled in white with a red border. The flag felt coarse, cold and threatening, and it didn't smell very good. Touching it made me feel awful. I wanted to wash my hands as soon as possible.

My friends and I often walked around town to see where the "star mothers" lived. Each star in a window represented a son at war. Then one day it happened: One mother had a *gold* star in the window. Her 19-year-old son

had been killed in action. A dark cloud of sorrow and anger settled over our little village.

I wanted so much to go to that young man's funeral, but 8-year-old boys didn't do that. So I decided to go to the cemetery and watch his burial, stationing myself on a small hill overlooking the cemetery.

I watched as six neatly dressed soldiers removed the casket, draped with the flag of my country, from the hearse. Then the order was given and seven rifles fired three shots each, giving the traditional 21-gun salute for a fallen soldier. From close by came the clear, beautiful sound of a bugler playing *Taps*. Like a faraway echo, the sound was repeated, floating up and across the cemetery.

Something happened to me in those moments. A chill ran down my back, and something caught in my throat. My heart hurt so much I thought it was going to explode. The feeling struck me so hard that tears began to form in my eyes.

The soldiers took the flag from the casket and folded it neatly. One soldier handed it to the mother, then stepped back to give her a military salute.

Right then, on that little hill, I began to weep. Tears streamed down my face, and at that moment I wouldn't have cared if the whole world saw me. In that moment, I promised that I would always respect, honor and stand by my wonderful country and flag forever—whatever the cost. And I have. ✪

'Soldiers Without Uniforms' Fought on Home Front

By Ruth Corbett
Sun City, California

DURING THE war, we civilians lived with daily admonitions. "Back up our boys." "Conserve your tires." "Buy U.S. defense stamps." "The car in your future is the car in your past—it's the car you have now, so you'd better make it last." "We've *got* to win the war!"

World War II has been studied by historians, novelists, journalists and military experts, but little has been said about the faceless army that fought just as hard back home. We worked in many capacities to supply material for the allies first, then our own soldiers.

We soldiers without uniforms fed the factory machines, grew victory gardens to supplement the food supply and patched everything with the hope it would last "for the duration"—a phrase heard often in those years.

We were sometimes called the "home guard", and our role in the war effort should not be underestimated. Everyone played his or her part, from the lonely air raid warden walking a beat on a moonless night to the woman riveting a fighter plane to those who cut fresh cardboard soles to line shoes that had worn through.

Those born two generations later have little idea what civilian life is like when one's country is engaged in all-out war. Such a war reaches into the most insignificant corners of everyday life, changing and twisting it until all its familiar patterns are gone. As we tried to adapt, we listened to the news daily, working and praying for peace, wishing we could do more.

We're often told not to dwell on the past. But we can get a better perspective on the present by learning and remembering all that was done by that army of soldiers without uniforms.✪

WOMEN AT WORK. Women joined the work force in unprecedented numbers during WWII, helping to build airplanes and other military equipment.

'I'll Always Treasure My Memories of Those Days'

IN 1942, I was in the first group of women to go to work at the newly activated Harding Field sub-depot. We were all "green as grass" and hardly knew what to expect.

Because of gas rationing, we rode the city bus to the airport, arriving just as the sun came up. I was assigned to the propeller shop and had a wonderful boss with the patience of Job. It wasn't long before I could manage a few chores.

On Saturday nights, all the single gals flocked to the community club for "military maids" dances. What a wonderful bunch of servicemen we met! Although we were chaperoned to and from the dances, there was no rule against inviting these young men to our homes. They were so easy to entertain, happy to share a home-cooked meal, listen to records and just socialize. I think many of them were just lonely, and maybe a little homesick.

Eventually, I met and married a wonderful man from Oregon who was the chief aircraft tower controller at the base. We had many wonderful years together until his death in 1976.

Even though times were difficult, I'll always treasure my memories of those days and the sacrifices made by so many. It was truly an all-out effort.

—*Virginia Darnielle, Baker, Louisiana*

PEDAL POWER! Faculty of Purdue University in West Lafayette, Indiana rode to work on balloon-tired bikes to conserve precious petroleum.

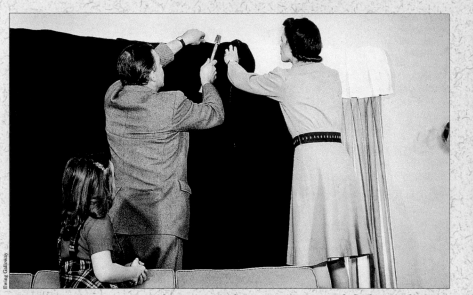

Ewing Galloway

BLACKOUT CURTAINS were hung in windows to ensure total darkness during air raid drills. Wardens made sure no lights were visible.

Blackouts Left Young Messenger in the Dark

FOUR DAYS before my 13th birthday, I signed on as a messenger for the Air Raid Warden Service in the District of Columbia. Messengers carried messages from one command center to another— a sort of courier service to carry on if communications were knocked out.

I knew my neighborhood very well, but during air raid drills the city was totally dark, and on moonless nights it was all but impossible to get my bearings. I never felt so small or alone in my life. No one but air raid wardens, messengers and police were on the streets, and then only in very small numbers.

Normally, the air was filled with the sights and sounds of a big city at night. During an air raid alert, there were no cars, no pedestrians, no sounds of people going from one place to another, no traffic or radios or even doors opening and closing—just total silence in near-total darkness.

I actually had to feel my way from one place to another, an experience few people ever have in the middle of a big city. To a 13-year-old, it was spooky, scary and *exciting*.
—*John Elvans Smith, Pueblo, Colorado*

'I'd Watch as Each Light Went Out Over the City...'

THE WAR LEFT a big impression on me. I had my own victory garden in the backyard, and Dad built a wooden fence around it to keep our dog out. I'd water the garden every day, and when my carrots were ready to pick, I'd run upstairs and give them to Mother. The carrots were only as big as my thumb, but Mother always praised me for a job well done.

My dad was an air raid warden and took that job very seriously. I can still see him jumping out of his chair when the siren went off, running for his helmet and flashlight so he could make sure all the neighborhood lights were off and the streets were clear.

I had a ritual, too. Our house was up on a hill, and from the sun porch that ran across the back we could see all of San Francisco below. I would run there as soon as the sirens began and watch as each light went out all over the city until all I could see was a sheet of blackness. When the "all clear" sounded, I'd run there again to watch the city come back to life.
—*Carolyn Costello Schiro*
San Jose, California

Son Saw Humor in Dad's Job As Air Raid Warden

MY FATHER became an air raid warden in suburban Boston in 1943. He was issued a white metal helmet complete with chin strap and a 3-ft.-tall "stirrup pump". This hand-operated fire extinguisher was a galvanized cylinder with a hose coming from the bottom and a pump handle on top.

Each evening, my father would set up his pump at the end of the driveway, to be used in the event of an incendiary attack anywhere on our street. If German air raids reduced the local fire department to chaos, he was ready.

Fortunately, Father never had to put out any fires. When filled, the pump was so heavy he never could have run up the street with it. Besides, vigorous pumping would generate only a thin stream of water for about 5 ft.

Dad's only job was making sure every house's blackout curtains were drawn at night. The slightest sliver of light would bring a knock at the door.

Some of these actions may seem silly now, but at the time there was a patriotic fervor that made my father very serious and proud about doing his duties.

Incidentally, Dad's metal helmet was later converted to a flowerpot, and the pump became a valuable garden tool in years to follow.   —*Robert Bruce*
Manchester, Connecticut

Harold M. Lambert

CHECKING IT OUT. A dutiful warden checks a driver's identity during a blackout. Citizens were asked to stay home during blackouts and air raids.

For Kids, Air Raid Drill Was a Thrill

By Marvin Kincaid
Columbus, Ohio

FOR THE kids in Trotwood, Ohio, the most excitement of the whole war was the night of the air raid drill. Our village of 600 was protected by the town marshal, Ed Bunger, who also picked up trash on Mondays. Ed was the chief air raid warden, and my dad assisted as the warden for our block.

One summer night in 1944, Dad got to perform his duty. An air raid drill was scheduled for 9 to 9:30 p.m. His job was to enforce the blackout and keep people off the streets.

Promptly at 9 p.m., the firehouse siren wailed. Dad rushed out of the house, calling over his shoulder, "Turn out all the lights and stay inside!" As Mother went from room to room, turning out lights, all three of us kids slipped out the back door.

Dad went to his post in the middle of the street under the darkened streetlight. My brother, sister and I stationed our-

---

> "Over a dozen of us
> kids were AWOL from
> our darkened houses..."

---

selves where he couldn't see us and waited for the emergency to begin. In a few minutes we were joined by a dozen or so equally curious friends, also AWOL from their darkened houses, plus one girl's dog.

As we huddled together, waiting for Dad's first emergency, we saw it. Mr. Seabold's lights were on! His house stood out like a full moon in a dark sky.

We watched silently as Dad climbed Mr. Seabold's porch. We couldn't hear Dad's end of the conversation, but Mr. Seabold was a bit deaf and spoke as if addressing the whole world. "What? Turn off my lights? You need my drill? I can't turn off my lights! I can't see to change the radio in the dark!" With that, he shut the door, leaving my bewildered father outside.

He Gave Warning

Suddenly, Dad blew a loud blast on his warden's whistle, sending our group scattering. That's when he spotted us. "All you kids, go on home!" he yelled.

ON THE LOOKOUT. Civil Defense wardens patrolled streets during blackout conditions and air raids. This warden also was a fire-watcher, responsible for spotting bombs or incendiary devices so fire crews could be summoned quickly.

"You're not supposed to be on the streets! This is an air raid drill!"

We scurried away, disappearing into the darkness. We had no intention of going home. Some of the girls crept under our cherry tree and began telling ghost stories.

The dog had been with us the whole time, but he was being quiet, too, as though he were part of the conspiracy. My brother Jimmy fixed that by tying a tomato can to the dog's tail and giving him a shove. The dog took off yelping, with the can clanging behind him—and ran right past Dad. At the same moment, one kid began shouting, and a girl under the cherry tree screamed.

Dad came at us again, really mad this time. "I told you kids to get off the street! Go home, all of you! This is a

serious drill!" To emphasize his point, he gave another loud blast on his whistle.

As we ran around to the back of our house, we heard the town dump truck pull up. Ed Bunger got out to have a word with Dad.

"What's going on in your block, Kincaid?" he asked. "I was over on Maple Street and heard your whistle and kids yelling and screaming, and a dog yelping. Can't you keep order here? And why doesn't Mr. Seabold have his lights out?"

Before Dad could answer, the "all clear" sounded and streetlights came on all over town. The air raid drill was over.

The next day, all the kids agreed the drill couldn't have been better. But Dad had his fill of air raid drills. He turned in his helmet and whistle, and someone else became warden for our block.✪

Teen Volunteers Scanned Skies for Enemy Planes

By Bill Hallstead
Sanibel, Florida

"ARMY FLASH, six nine six."

I still remember that important-sounding code I once used as a volunteer aircraft spotter in the early days of the war.

My brother, sister and I had collected every ounce of scrap metal we could lay our hands on, but I yearned for more active participation in the war effort. I was only 17, and too young to enlist.

I volunteered for observation duty with the Aircraft Warning Service (AWS), which used volunteers to watch for incoming enemy planes.

My post was a frame tower in a graveyard atop a hill in a suburb of Scranton, Pennsylvania, a 9-mile bike ride from home. The tower had a roofed deck about 6 ft. square with two chairs and a telephone—a direct line to the warning service's "plotting room".

That room was set up in the First National Bank building in Scranton. It featured an elaborate "board game" setup to help the AWS keep track of

aircraft. Sometimes the man working in that room was my own father, a World War I veteran who wanted to do his part in this battle, too.

Spotted as a Team

I shared the watch with a jovial fellow my age named David Westlake. We thought of ourselves as two adventurers

AIRCRAFT SPOTTERS scanned the skies, watching for enemy planes like this Japanese bomber squadron.

helping to guard the nation against the wily Hun. When we spotted a suspicious plane we were to call in our code, "Army flash, six nine six", followed by the type of plane, its direction and altitude.

David and I stared at the sky for many long, boring afternoons. One day we finally broke the monotony by reporting passing airline DC-3s. Small private planes from the municipal airport were to be disregarded, but nobody had told us that we were supposed to leave the airlines alone.

"Army flash, six nine six! One twin-engine type, heading north at about 6,000..." (we pictured a tiny wooden plane being moved across the board down at the bank). No sneaky Nazi who'd pilfered a DC-3 in Philadelphia, intent on dropping hand grenades on Syracuse, was going to get past *us* unreported!

That volunteer service was the most exciting period of my teen years—until I enlisted in the Army Air Force when I turned 18.✪

Many Fought in 'Battle of the Potomac'

By June Drebing
Minnetonka, Minnesota

IN WASHINGTON, D.C., military personnel and civilians alike fought the so-called "Battle of the Potomac". My

contribution was serving for 2 years as an antiaircraft volunteer.

We worked in crews of about 15, taking telephone reports of aircraft sightings from soldiers who scanned the skies continuously. Every plane's movement was plotted on a huge map of the District of Columbia, Maryland and Virginia so no enemy aircraft could arrive undetected.

The soldiers often got bored and liked to chat with the girls in our office, although this was a no-no. One soldier I talked with got around the restriction by reporting a P-47 "very, very low". When I asked for more information, especially concerning the altitude, he said, "They're dragging it behind a tractor!"

Volunteers worked 4 hours every third evening in addition to regular full-time jobs, many of them in defense. There was no such thing as having a regular bowling night or taking university classes—our free time belonged to the Army. But we didn't mind. Our jobs were important, and we felt we were an essential part of the Battle of the Potomac.✪

P-47 TALE gave one soldier an excuse to chat with a female anti-aircraft volunteer. Photo of P-47 (left) depicts one of those fighter planes the serviceman referred to.

PICTURE PERFECT. Juni Dunklin (far left) struck a happy pose with her photo studio staff during the war. Many of their clients were servicemen preparing to ship out.

Photographs Provided Precious Memories

By Juni Dunklin
Sandersville, Georgia

I OWNED a photography studio in an office building in Winston-Salem, North Carolina during World War II. Several boot camps were nearby, and thousands of soldiers were stationed only an hour's drive away at Fayetteville. Many of our subjects were men and women who wanted to be photographed one last time before being shipped overseas.

I said good-bye to hundreds of wonderful young people, some so young it broke my heart. They'd stand at the desk picking out poses for Mom and Dad, and if they shed as much as one tear, I'd join them in a good cry. I was always saddened by the thought that these young people might never return home.

One blond boy told me he had six brothers in the service. When I expressed amazement, he said, "That's nothing—Father had eight brothers in the service in World War I!" What fierce loyalty that family must have felt for its country!

On weekends, we invited as many service people as our house could hold for cookouts, dances and talent shows. We also held parties at the studio with a live "band", which amounted to a violin, guitar and piano. Anyone else in the office building was welcome to join us. In fact, the elevator attendants often deserted their posts to sing!

Many times soldiers came to us flat broke, but still wanting their photo taken. We never turned them away. Some sent us payment years later.

We kept our negatives on file, and

> *"Some servicemen were so young it broke my heart..."*

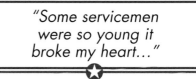

sometimes families would write us for duplicate photos of their sons who had died. In the last year of the fighting, we would ship out hundreds of portraits to the soldiers' families. Many thanked us, and some wrote to me for years.

It may not seem like much, and I know a portrait camera cannot be compared to a service gun, but we "shot" for a compelling cause—the families of the men and women who were sacrificing their lives. I still look back on those days as magnificent times of togetherness and love.❂

Departing Soldiers Treated to Grandma's Home Cooking

TROOP TRAINS came through Glade Spring, Virginia three or four times a day, packed with young men being sent to places they couldn't even pronounce. These young men were a constant source of concern to my great-grandmother, whom we called "Mammy". Each of those boys, she said, was "some mother's son".

The troop trains had no dining cars. Mammy knew most of the boys would be hungry. So each day, as long as the war lasted, she walked to the depot with home-cooked food for those soldiers. Eager hands reached out the windows for her tenderloin and sausage biscuits, gingerbread cookies and corn cakes—whatever Mammy had the means and time to prepare.

Throughout the war, cards from all over the globe traveled to Glade Spring for "Miz Ida", and she wrote back.

Her motherly love reached across the miles to many a lonely boy aching for the comfort of his own mother. Some of those boys continued corresponding with her for years, right up until her death.

Once Mammy boarded a crowded train in Glade Spring to visit a sister in New York. A young serviceman named Bruce tried to give her his seat, but she refused. "Son, you're going away to protect my children and me," she told him. "The least I can do is give you a seat."

When another passenger left the train, Mammy sat next to Bruce. They became fast friends, and wrote to each other for months afterward. When Bruce later died on a faraway battlefield, this kindhearted woman mourned him as if he were her own.

—Martha Phillips, Glade Spring, Virginia

Creativity Provided 'Butter' for Teatime

DURING RATIONING, we could get only a small amount of butter, and the only other spread was a tasteless white block that looked like lard. One company added a small "dot" of liquid that could be added to the spread to give it a buttery color.

My mother, who came from England, and I loved "afternoon tea" with buttered bread, but hated that white spread. So my father would patiently mix what little butter rationing provided with the white spread and the colored dot until it was the color of butter. Then he'd form it into a block and divide that into four sticks.

By the time Dad was done, it looked so much like butter that teatime again became a pleasure. —*Cathy Toole Reynolds, Georgia*

Film Gave Moviegoers Taste of Postwar Meals

WE ATE LITTLE meat during the war. Rationing coupons drove my mother to distraction—she always confused the "points" with the price.

As Catholics, we had no meat on Fridays, and then the government started "meatless Tuesdays". So we ate mostly chicken and fish.

One day at the movies, there was a short film titled *U.S. After the War Is Over*. A teenage boy came into the kitchen and asked what was for supper. "Steak," his mom said. The boy replied, "Oh, no! Not steak *again*!" The whole audience groaned! —*Bonnie Farnum Alexandria, Virginia*

DYEING FOR BUTTER. Butter was rationed, so cooks mixed white oleo with a yellow capsule that provided the look, if not the taste, of the real thing.

Everyone Played Role in Rationing and Recycling

RATIONING was a big part of our lives. Butter was rationed, but we all enjoyed playing "toss" after Saturday dinner with the bag of white oleo that had a capsule of yellow dye inside. There was always applause for the one who got the "goop" warm enough for the capsule to break, turning the white oleo into yellow margarine.

Sometimes I was sent to the store with our grocery list, tokens and stamp book. It made me feel so grown-up! One day I dropped a token between the store's floorboards, and I was panic-stricken. I knew how important those tokens were! The grocer finally retrieved it with a meat cleaver. I was so happy, I cried!

All of us kids turned into scavengers. We'd walk along the curbs, scuffing through debris in the gutters, looking for gum wrappers and cigarette packs so we could retrieve the silver.

We also collected newspapers, kept fat drippings for munitions, and flattened tin cans for recycling. Soap chips were put in a large jar with a little water. The resulting "slime" was used for washing dishes, hands and even laundry. And when we ran out of toothpaste, tooth powder or liquid tooth cleaner, baking soda mixed with a pinch of ground cloves would do the trick.

—*Marilyn Parker, Townsend, Delaware*

Victory Garden Handbook Offered Food for Thought

EVERYONE WHO had access to even a small plot of ground was encouraged to grow a "victory garden" to help alleviate food shortages. I well remember the handbook of the Victory Garden Institute. Its cover was red, white and blue, and the slogan was: "Have a victory garden; eat what you can, and can what you can't eat." —*Mary Wetmore Knoxville, Pennsylvania*

Meatless 'Sausage' Won Rave Reviews

IN 1944, I was earning my college room and board by cooking for a faculty member's family. With rationing, meat was in short supply, so I developed a recipe for meatless "sausage" patties.

I served them once for a faculty dinner, since we didn't have enough meat stamps to serve a large crowd. The dinner was a huge success, and one man told me the patties were "the best pork sausage he'd had in a long time".

You should have seen his expression when I told him the patties were made with oatmeal! He quickly recovered from his shock—and asked if he could have another!

Here's the recipe:

SAUSAGE PATTIES
    1 cup rolled oats
    1/2 teaspoon salt
    1/2 teaspoon sage
    2 eggs, beaten
    2 tablespoons butter
    1 beef bouillon cube

Mix the oats, salt, sage and eggs; form into four flat patties. Fry in the butter until browned on both sides. In a kettle or saucepan, boil 1 qt. water and add bouillon cube. Pour mixture over patties; simmer, covered, for 30 minutes. **Yield:** 4 servings.

—*Kathryne Jean Moeller Easton, Pennsylvania*

Girl's Wave to Mom Started a Stampede!

DURING RATIONING days I was a student nurse living at school, and one memorable time I returned home for a visit on an overnight pass.

When it came time to return to school, it was imperative that I made the right trolley connections to get back on time. Back in those days, there was no acceptable excuse for being late for class.

SMALL VICTORY. **Dorothy Page of Peoria, Arizona had a victory garden —and so did her daughter Suellen, 3.**

Mom had already left for the butcher shop, so I raced downtown to tell her good-bye. I looked in the door of the shop just as my trolley was approaching, so I caught Mom's eye, gave her a big wave and hopped on the car.

When I turned to sit down, I was amazed to see a dozen women running from the butcher shop to the grocery store a few doors down.

After I returned to school, I called Mom and listened to a very amused lady describe how everyone else had misinterpreted my wave as a signal meaning the butter deliveryman had arrived at the grocer's! The stampede was on, and Mom—who knew what that wave *really* meant—went from the end of the butcher's line to the front!

—*Mary Harominek Mahopac, New York*

RATIONED OUT. Items that were rationed could be purchased only with books, stamps or tokens (right) plus cash. The restricted goods included meat, fat, sugar, coffee, butter, cheese, shoes, metal appliances and gasoline. Car owners were limited to 3 gal. of gas a week.

Memorable Ditty Warned Citizens About Hoarding

OUR TOWN near the Pacific Coast had to prepare for blackouts by covering our windows at night. The radio kept us informed, and warned everyone not to panic or to hoard things.

One ditty I've never forgotten was sung by two men, one in a falsetto: "You're out of order, Mrs. Hoarder. Uncle Sam's gonna be mad at you." I never knew who those singers were, but they certainly got their message across! —*Lenoa Stoneman, Elkton, Oregon*

Mom Got Money's Worth Out of Sausage Purchase

MOM WAS VERY protective of our ration stamps, especially those for meat. Once she found a fantastic bargain—barbecued sausage that required no stamps! She bought some, brought it home and couldn't wait to cook it. Much to her dismay, that sausage cooked almost completely away!

As Mom surveyed this fiasco, she suddenly cheered up. While there was virtually no sausage left, she did have a skillet full of grease. What a bonanza! Shortening was as hard to find as meat, and now she had enough to fry several chickens—the most delicious we ever ate! —*Barbara Moore Page Weatherford, Texas*

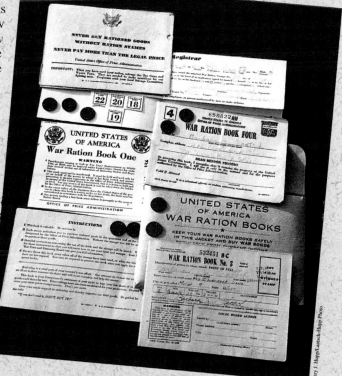

STOCKINGS FOR UNCLE SAM. Women donated thousands of stockings that were converted into military items.

One Woman Tried to Rent Silk Stockings for Church!

IN THE WAR YEARS, silk stockings seemed even more scarce than hen's teeth. This ad appeared in the newspaper in Sterling, Colorado: "Wanted to Rent: 1 pair silk stockings, for 1 hour, every Sunday morning; to wear to church." —*Mary Ann Kunselman Longmont, Colorado*

Scouts' Hosiery Drive Netted 600,000 Pairs

AS A TEENAGER, I helped collect silk and nylon hose to be recycled for parachutes and gunpowder bags. This was a project of our Girl Scout troop, and our goal was to collect one or two pairs a month from every home in Wichita, Kansas.

We must have done a good job, because we collected 600,000 pairs and got our picture in the local paper! I was proud to do my part to help the war effort. —*Peggy Brown Garringer Wichita, Kansas*

Leg Makeup Solved Hosiery Shortage

THE BIGGEST problem for me and my friends in Washington, D.C. was hosiery. Nylons were almost nonexistent. Department stores sometimes sold "service weight" stockings, which were so heavy they made the shapeliest ankle

BOARD OF REVIEW. Women visited the local rationing board for their allotment of stamps. An "A" stamp was good for 3 gal. of gasoline.

look thick and stodgy. The only alternative was to go bare-legged.

Then some enterprising manufacturer brought out leg makeup—thick, tan-colored liquid with a dauber applicator and a pencil for drawing on the "seams".

It was a novel idea, but had its drawbacks. We had to shave our legs daily for a smooth application. Rain made the makeup run like cheap mascara, and I often washed the stuff off my shoes. Still, for the summer, we hailed it as a lifesaver.

Unfortunately, the makeup couldn't protect us from Washington's winter weather, and we all had to go back to dowdy "service weight" stockings. —*Ruth Carpenter, Norman, Oklahoma*

Teen's Ingenious 'Zippers' Kept Tires Going

MY DAD died during the war, making me, at 15, the "man of the house". Of all the responsibilities I faced, keeping our 1936 Pontiac Chieftain running was among the toughest. Tires were the main problem.

In those days, there were no steel-belted radials. We had inner tubes instead, and blowouts were common. When a tire blew, we could only hope the hole was on the side, where it could be fixed. A hole in the bottom usually spelled doom.

I fixed our tires by drilling holes all around the area of the blowout and lacing

it up with wire. At first the lacing didn't hold, but with experience I got better at it. When I was finished, the tire looked like it had a zipper in it, and sometimes the seam was more than a foot long. A reliner or strong "boot" was added to prevent undue pressure on the weakened tire.

By war's end, the Pontiac had three "zippered" tires on it, so driving was always an adventure! We never drove faster than 15 mph, tires clunking the whole way. We didn't do any pleasure riding, either—not on 3 gal. of gasoline a week, which would take us only 45 miles. But whenever there was an emergency, we had transportation, and I'm proud to say that the car lasted us through the war! —*Marko Lulich Bellevue, Michigan*

Rationing Clerk Knew Just When to Say 'Yes'

THE FIRST registration for rationing was done by schoolteachers like me. I started the day after school was dismissed, for $105 a month! I intended it to be a summer job, but stayed for over 4 years.

My favorite task was issuing a rationing card for a new baby. You could usually tell just by the proud look on a man's face what he was going to ask for!

Sometimes, though, we had to refuse requests. Someone once told me, "Young lady, you have said 'no' to so many people that you won't be able to say 'yes' when the right man comes along!"

After the war, all the servicemen came in for their shoe, sugar and gasoline stamps, and I was quite able to say "yes" when the right one did come along! We just observed our 46th wedding anniversary. —*Mary Ellen Blatchford York, Nebraska*

Oh, Fudge! Rationed Sugar Made for Sweet Memories

SUGAR RATIONING is what I remember best. When it was almost time for new coupon books to be issued, Mom would give us four kids 2 cups of sugar—if we had that much left—to make fudge. That was the only time we were allowed to touch the sugar jar.

Whenever Mom went shopping, she left my older sister in charge and warned us not to use the sugar. "I'll be able to tell when I come back," she said.

Once Mom was out of sight, we'd rush into the kitchen. Somehow, my sister knew how to reduce the recipe on the cocoa box to make just enough fudge to fill a saucer. We'd cut that saucer of fudge into four equal pieces and eat it very slowly so it would last a long time. It was delicious, and turned out perfectly every time.

When Mom got home, she'd head straight to the jar and ask, "You kids didn't get into the sugar and make candy, did you?" We all said no and ran off, giggling.

Years later, I asked Mom if she knew. "Of course I did!" she said. "I only had to run my hand over the cabinet to feel the grains of sugar you missed when you cleaned up. Plus, I could smell it and hear you giggling."

"Why didn't you punish us for lying to you?" I asked. The answer was simple. "Times were so tough then," she said, "and everything was so uncertain in the world with the war. I didn't want to spoil the enjoyment you kids got out of sneaking to make fudge!"

—Anna Lee Fevang, Xenia, Ohio

'Chocolate-Sardine Fudge'... Memorable—and Inedible

OUR FAMILY was very poor during the war, so we never ate beef or chicken, although we occasionally could afford canned salmon or sardines.

When rationing started, the worst deprivation for my sisters and me was sugar. We loved fudge, and craved it all the time. Our mother had to hide what little sugar we had to keep us from depleting it in a fudge-making frenzy!

One evening, Mom put some groceries on the table for us to unload. Someone—we never knew who—absentmindedly laid a bag of sugar on a platter of sardines that had been placed on the table for supper. By the time we

GROCERY SHOPPING could be a challenge during the war. Food shortages and rationing forced cooks to revise their menus and recipes. Some hoarded ration coupons, saving them up for special meals.

discovered it, the sardine juice had seeped into the bag. But since the sugar smelled only faintly of fish, Mom suggested we use it to make a batch of fudge.

With great excitement, we mixed up a huge batch and put it on the stove. After about 5 minutes, a strange odor began rising from the pot, and it kept getting worse. By the time the candy was done, the house reeked of chocolate and fish.

But my sisters and I loved fudge, so we bravely bit into it—then fell over each other scrambling for glasses of water so we could rinse out our mouths. What a disaster!

I can't begin to describe the flavor other than to say it was absolutely dreadful. The house smelled so bad we threw open all the windows and doors, but the odor lingered for several days.

—Dawn East, Jarrell, Texas

'Making Do' at Christmas Produced Beautiful Tree

WE TRIED HARD to make Christmas special during the war years, but it was hard. There were no fancy ornaments for sale, no tinsel for the tree and very little sugar for baking.

One year I went to my aunt's farm for the holidays, and she cut down a huge cedar tree in the woods. The tree was so big we didn't have enough orna-

ments to decorate it, and the one string of Christmas lights didn't work. All we had was a dozen cardboard balls covered with foil.

My aunt and I went to the woods and collected pinecones of every size, and dipped them in gold and silver paint. Then we found some silver candle holders with candles that had never been used. We decorated the tree with the 12 silver balls, silver and gold pinecones, and the candles that would be lit only on Christmas Eve. It was one of the loveliest trees I ever saw! *—Gwen Medcalf, Hagerstown, Maryland*

Rationing Changed Their Coffee-Drinking Habits

WHEN UNCLE SAM rationed coffee, it was just about the last straw for my Norwegian sister-in-law and me. We usually walked our 2- and 4-year-olds to the park after their naps, then ambled back to her house or mine for a cup of coffee.

Rationing cut down on our afternoon coffee klatches. We solved that problem by making "Roosevelt coffee", adding more water to the same grounds over and over. It was sort of brown, sort of tasted like coffee and didn't keep us awake at night! *—Alma Wheaton, Seattle, Washington*

'We Built Mount Scrapmore!'

By Frederick Chesson
Waterbury, Connecticut

AS A 12-YEAR-OLD seventh grader, I was eager to do my part on the home front. Sometimes I'd gather with my parents and other air raid wardens under the circle of light cast by a shielded street lamp, and I'd proudly help enforce air raid drills and blackout alerts.

A more concrete contribution was gathering scrap metal, like iron and brass, to be recycled into bombs and cartridge casings. Our first neighbor-hood scrap drive was like a rehearsal, with little piles appearing in the gutters outside each house on our street.

Our cellar was mined of such vital metals an an aluminum agitator from a defunct washing machine, and an an-tique bronze lamp base.

The "big show" came later, when a vacant lot across from our house was posted with a large sign designating it as an official U.S. scrap depot for the entire neighborhood. Every day, the col-lection grew, and we gave it the name "Mount Scrapmore"!

The variety of salvage was remark-able, ranging from the usual garage and cellar castoffs like bike frames and old sewing machines to such exotic items as dented silver-plated cocktail shakers. Living so close to the heap, I performed daily "inspections" of its contents. I was occasionally tempted to

---

"Our cellar was mined of vital metals like a bronze lamp base..."

⭐

"swap" my nearly intact erector set for some treasure like an antique bear trap, but I never gave in to temptation be-cause there was a war on.

In fact, when the driver of a fish market van stopped and tried to take an old lawn mower, we guardians of Mount Scrapmore threatened to call the police.

After several weeks, word came that city dump trucks were on the way to pick up the scrap so it could be recycled into B-17's, Sherman tanks and battle-ships. My friends and I posed atop our salvage trove before the trucks arrived. Within an hour, it was gone, the vacant lot reclaimed by grasshoppers, golden-rod and poison ivy.

In 1949, a house was built on that lot. Now only "old croakers" like me recall its glory days, when we were young and eager to be part of "the last good war".

Scrappy Students Rewarded for Metal-Collection Drive

IN 1942, our government launched a national scrap drive, with each school collecting as much metal as possible. I worked very hard in that drive, using my red wagon and a shovel. When the drive ended, our small school had collected an average of over 5,300 lbs. of scrap per pupil—more than any other in the state of Oklahoma!

One day, our teacher asked each of us to write down the name of the student who'd worked the hardest during the drive. When she tallied those "votes", I had won! Three other Oklahoma students and I would go to Washington, D.C., meet President Roosevelt, tour all the monuments and help christen a ship, the *SS Will Rogers*!

I was the one chosen to christen the ship, but the Women's Christian Temperance Union objected to having a small boy handle liquor. So Mrs. Will Rogers did the honors instead, with me standing next to her. I still remember the champagne splashing on me!

By the way, we didn't get to meet the President—he'd gone to Paris to meet with Charles de Gaulle—but we did see the sights and have dinner with Irving Berlin. I can honestly say that the whole experience was the most important event of my childhood. —*Jack Terry*
Konawa, Oklahoma

WINNER Jack Terry single-handedly collected 2,122 lbs. of scrap metal!

Kids Pitched in To 'Ax the Axis'

OUR CHILDREN knew all about the war effort. They knew about food stamps and rationing, sacrifice and sharing, and they were eager to do their part.

Each day, they rolled out their little red wagon. With patched knees and twice-soled shoes, our little patriots turned into pack rats, tramping the alleys, vacant lots and junk piles in search of scrap metal. They returned bruised and dirty, but thrilled with their latest wagonload of loot.

My husband and I supplied a huge metal oil drum for their finds. They chattered excitedly as they filled it with broken toys, andirons, car bumpers, tail pipes, grates, stove parts, wheels, pails, pans, doorknobs, gasoline cans, trash cans and springs.

Their father, a professional sign painter, made them a 2- by 5-ft. wooden sign to display at the curb: "AX THE AXIS, FROM PATRIOTIC CITIZENS ON THIS BLOCK".

The children's collection soon filled the drum to overflowing, calling even greater attention to their all-out efforts. How very proud they were of each other! And how proud we were of them!

—*Emma Shafner, Dayton, Ohio*

"BUY BONDS!" **Ernestine Jarvis of Quinton, Virginia shared this photo of her brother, who sold war bonds.**

POD COLLECTOR. Ronald Baertsch learned that children had a role to play in the war effort, too. In addition to helping tend the victory garden on his family's Wisconsin farm, he also collected milkweed pods. The fluffy white substance inside the dried pods was used to make life preservers for the Navy.

Child's Milkweed Pods May Have Saved Sailors

THE BIGGEST PART I played in the war effort was going through all the fields and pastures on our farm to gather milkweed pods. The fluffy white stuff inside was being collected for use in life preservers for the Navy.

I walked and ran all over the fields, gathering every pod in sight, putting them in old onion sacks. Then I hung the sacks on the clothesline to dry.

It made me feel very good to help out because our next-door neighbor had a son in the Navy, and I liked to think I was helping him directly. I've often wondered if those pods collected on our farm might have saved a sailor from drowning.

—*Ronald Baertsch Huber Heights, Ohio*

Students Proud to Buy War Bonds and Stamps

IN KEEPING with the patriotic theme of the war years, our sixth-grade teacher encouraged all of us to bring money to school every Friday to buy a war bond or savings stamps.

We would all stand and, on cue, start marching toward her desk to make our purchases, singing *Remember Pearl Harbor*. How proud we were!

—*Jo Ann Cox, Vallejo, California*

Scrap Drive Efforts Gave Him '15 Minutes of Glory'

MY FATHER was a hired hand during the war, moving from farm to farm. One-room schools were all I'd known, so when we moved to a farm near a big city, the huge school was very scary to me.

But that's where I got my 15 minutes of glory.

The school started a scrap-iron drive, and the student who collected the most would get a war bond. When I asked my father's employer for scraps, he pointed to a huge horse-drawn roller that was used to crush the dirt before planting! Dad hitched the horses to it and pulled it to school for me.

Needless to say, I won hands down and was announced the winner during an assembly. I'll never forget the clapping and cheering! I was helping with the war effort, and getting a war bond was a dream come true.

A few days later, my dad pulled the roller through cheering crowds in a parade. I guess he got his 15 minutes of glory, too!

—*Arnold Rossell La Fayette, Illinois*

Telegram Deliveries Brought Sorrow *and* Joy

By Albert Bazzel
Turnersville, New Jersey

I WAS a teenage telegraph messenger for Western Union in Trenton, New Jersey during the war. Without meaning to, I struck fear into hearts as I rode my bike along the streets of my hometown. Everyone knew that the War Department notified relatives of war casualties via telegram.

Each messenger was sent out with one to three of these messages every evening. All began in the same frightening way: "We regret to inform you that your [relationship and name] was killed/wounded/missing in action while serving his/her country…"

Of course, nearly everyone who received such a message was distraught, and it wasn't easy for me to be the bearer of bad news.

Trenton had many new immigrants who could not yet read much English.

One evening I was sent to a household where the serviceman's mother, a recent emigrant from Poland, asked me to read the message to her. I read, "We regret to inform you that your son John is missing in action…"

On hearing the news, the woman began pacing her front porch, wringing her hands and sobbing, "My Johnny! My Johnny! What has happened to my Johnny?" The scene is as vivid to me as if it happened yesterday.

Several weeks later, through sheer luck, I delivered a second message to the same address. I then had the profound joy of reading: "We are pleased to inform you that your son John is safe in allied hands…" John's mother again paced and wrung her hands, but this time she cried tears of joy.

My experience with this very patriotic woman, and with so many other brave relatives of American GIs, taught me lessons I've never forgotten.✪

War Bonds
ARE CHEAPER THAN WOODEN CROSS
BUY MORE THROUGH PAY ROLL SAV

MODEL MP. Russell Reiter of Montross, Virginia was the model for this war bond poster. "I was stationed at the northwest gate of the White House as a military policeman with the 250th MP Company," Russell recalls. "Sgt. Ardis Hughes took a picture of me holding the crosses and shovel, then painted it for the seventh war bond drive."

"BONDS FOR BABIES". Bette Duncan, now of Sun City, California, vividly recalls the war bond campaign that went by that name. In May 1944, she was the first employee of the Los Angeles Department of Water and Power to purchase one of those bonds. She bought it from Mrs. Spencer Tracy, and that's Mrs. Tracy handing the bond to Bette's daughter Patricia, who was 2 at the time.

This Patriotic Girl Went to Great Lengths 'Knittin' for Britain'

THE RED CROSS' "Knitting for Britain" project provided mufflers to keep the troops warm and snug against the cold English winter. Volunteers received a skein of gray yarn, along with instructions for the scarf's width. The length was determined by using up the whole ball of yarn.

What a thrill it was for me, a high school senior, to be doing my part! The work went quickly, and I soon came to the end of my skein.

As I unrolled my handiwork, the muffler grew longer...and longer...and longer. The serviceman who received that scarf was probably the warmest soldier in the Army. It was long enough to have wrapped around his entire body!

I was happy to be knittin' for Britain —and it's a good thing the Red Cross hadn't asked me to knit socks…after all, "Big Foot" was unheard of back then!
—*Jacqueline Brown, Titusville, Florida*

Defense Worker Was Thankful

By Estrella Montgomery
Inverness, Florida

MY HUSBAND and I both served our country during World War II. He was in Europe with the merchant marine. I worked stateside in naval ordnance, assembling shells and inserting nose fuses into bombs.

Along with our two children, I lived in a federal housing project for defense workers and families of servicemen.

One Thanksgiving during wartime stands out quite clearly in my memory. I had to work on that holiday—there was a war going on and shells were urgently needed.

During our shift, one worker let a bomb slip through her hands—*and its nose fuse was in place!*

When she fumbled that bomb, by some miracle of God, it landed lengthwise on her shoe tops—not on the hard concrete floor.

A Marine who was on duty instantly grabbed the round and put it back on the conveyor line. White-faced and shaken, we all bowed our heads and recited the Lord's Prayer.

Ammo Depot Spared

Had that bomb hit on its nose, the building and most of the entire Ammunition Depot surrounding it would probably have gone up in a gigantic explosion!

Soon, we were sent home for the day. A blizzard was raging, and on the way home, our bus went into a slide that wedged it crosswise on a bridge. There was nothing to do but get out and trudge 2 miles through drifting snow to our

BRAVE WOMEN contributed greatly to the war effort, whether serving overseas or tackling difficult jobs at home. Many, like the author of this story, recall working in defense plants while taking care of their families.

homes. I opened the door to cozy warmth and the delicious smell of baking gingerbread. My son Billy said, "I warmed everything up, Mom, and I made gingerbread from a mix."

With tears streaming down my face, I embraced my precious children. We had a wonderful dinner of roast chicken with vegetables that we had grown in our victory garden...and warm gingerbread for dessert.

I told the children about the bus accident, but never told them about the bomb which nearly made that Thanksgiving Day my last. I've never felt more thankful than I did on that day.✪

To Children, War Seemed Unreal

WORLD WAR II had been raging for a couple of years, but for kids like me it was unreal—pictures we saw on a newsreel at the movies, or an idea for a new game.

But that late spring day when I saw my grandmother holding a telegram in her shaking hand, I saw for the first time the dark side of war—on her anguished face.

"No...no," she repeated over and over. "It's not true..."

My grandpa stood opposite her, looking stunned, tears streaming down his cheeks. Scared, I ran to Grandma. She took

my hand and led me to the couch. We sat there in silence for a moment. Then she looked at me, her face filled with an awful pain I'll never forget.

"Your Uncle Eddie's not coming home," she said. "He's never coming home. He's been killed in action."

We sat there with Grandpa, crying and hugging and comforting each other, for a long time.

Looking back, I'm impressed that no one seemed bitter about my uncle's death. There was great grief and sadness, but also much pride. We knew he died for what he believed in, for what we all believed in, and we honored him for that.

—*Dianne Price, Indian Rocks Beach, Florida*

'Ordinary People' Created Work Force Second to None

WHEN A defense plant was built just 6 miles from our home back in the '40s, I applied immediately, despite some apprehensions about working around ammunition. Little did I know that the job would be top secret, too!

If I agreed to continue, I would be working in an area where a new, very secret weapon was being made. We would be sworn to absolute silence; not even our families could know where or with what we were working. Our home telephones might even be monitored! Each of us had a chance to back out if we thought we couldn't handle the secrecy and restrictions.

Those of us who agreed to continue took intensive classes about the new weapon, which would later be known as the antitank missile. All our notes were collected at the end of each session, since no written materials could be taken from the building, and we were often searched. Security was extremely tight.

The plant ran 24 hours a day, and everyone took turns working different shifts. Many of us became close friends; I'm still in touch with two of my co-workers from those days.

Many of the workers were women, and almost all were untrained. Yet we, and others like us all across the country, came together to create a work force second to none. We were dedicated, ordinary people doing a job that had to be done.

Wonderful people from all walks of life, of all races, creeds and colors, worked day and night to produce whatever our country needed. We presented a united home front for our fighting men overseas, and made memories to last a lifetime.
—*Gladys Waddell
Decatur, Illinois*

'The Work Was Hard, But We Did It for America'

I WENT TO work in a defense plant in Richmond, Virginia so a male employee there could join the service. I worked three different shifts, but the hardest was midnight to 8 a.m. Believe me, it was hard getting out of bed at 10 p.m. to go to work when everyone else was asleep!

Many times I didn't get enough sleep during the day, and the *clack-clack* of the machines winding fiber for parachutes and airplane tires would lull me to sleep on my feet.

Times were hard, and so was the work. But we were doing it for America. It was a thrilling, exhilarating feeling to walk out of the plant at 8 a.m. and hear the rousing strains of *Praise the Lord and Pass the Ammunition* coming from the loudspeaker.

That put a spring in our slow steps and straightened our tired backs. We pulled together and won!
—*Bernice Simon, Richmond, Virginia*

At Defense Plant, Small Errors Were Big Trouble

LIKE THOUSANDS of other women, I joined the war effort by working in a defense plant—one that tested and furnished steel for artillery guns. My job was to run a machine that tested the strength of the steel. My husband was with an artillery unit in Europe, so this work made me feel a little closer to him.

A friend of mine, also a soldier's wife, worked in the office upstairs. One day we both made mistakes—she made a slight error in her books, and I made a miscalculation on my machine.

Our boss gave both of us a long lecture, telling us we were traitors to our husbands. In fact, he labeled us "The Sabotage Twins"! It was a sermon we didn't soon forget, and unfortunately the nickname stuck. You can be sure we made no more mistakes!
—*Elizabeth Alaskey, Troy, New York*

HOW MANY PEOPLE did it take to build a military plane? This many! All these folks worked on this C-47 transport at Douglas Aircraft in Long Beach, California. Riveter Bea Romey of Templeton, Iowa sent the photo. She's in the center of the front row, wearing dark coveralls with a white collar.

GRANDMA WAS A MACHINIST. When the U.S. went to war, women became skilled at countless industrial tasks. Some, like in this story, toiled long hours in home machine shops. The four grandmothers above were hired to work at a shipyard. They are (from left) Agnes Algar, Madeline Stelling, Florence Denton and Lizzabell Decker. All lived in New Jersey.

Couple Ran Machine Shop—in Their Basement!

By Margaret Sayers
Vancouver, Washington

MY HUSBAND and I did our part to help win the war by opening a machine shop in the basement and employing our neighbors!

John had heard about another man who'd organized about 150 "home front" workshops and decided it was a good idea. In April 1942, he quit his job, invested $1,000 in six electric drill presses and started hiring our friends and neighbors to drill holes through the heads of aircraft bolts and then "de-burr" them. By June, it seemed the whole neighborhood was working for us!

At 8 a.m., eight of my friends from the PTA would show up to start their shifts. At 6 p.m., they were relieved by their husbands. These men already had put in long hours at their daytime jobs, but they were doing their part for the war effort—they worked for us until midnight. We provided cots for rest breaks, and everyone chipped in to provide refreshments.

Eventually the business outgrew the basement, and John and a friend opened a bigger shop with 50 drill presses. But what I recall most is those early months, when a newspaper reporter came by to write a story about our little shop and the people who worked there. My husband proudly told him, "These are the people who will win the war."✪

Co-Worker's Prank Left Her Blue in the Face!

AFTER MY husband joined the service, I went to the local trade school, took a 6-month machine course, passed with flying colors, and went to work for a local firm's machine tool department. As the only woman there, I was something of an oddity.

One day I was running the lathe, using Prussian blue ink to mark lines on the piece I was handling. A lot of Air Force brass were there that day, and since I was the only woman, they apparently decided I was the one to watch.

They started laughing and snickering, and I got so annoyed that I shut down my machine and went to the ladies' room to cool off.

I looked into the mirror to straighten my hair and saw why they'd *really* been laughing. My nose, forehead and cheeks were covered with that blue ink!

It turned out a co-worker had put a tiny dab of Prussian blue on every handle of my lathe, so each time I touched my face, it just kept getting bluer! We all had a good laugh about it, and as time went along, everyone in the shop became fast friends.

—*Grace McNulty*
New Milford, Connecticut

POWs' POWER was used for farm labor in U.S. during the war years. Encamped in Kentucky, these POWs worked on Ewing Galloway farm in Henderson County.

German POW Taught Boy a Lesson

By Cal Lambert
Lancaster, Wisconsin

IN 1944, the Japanese occupation of the Philippines had choked off this country's regular source of hemp, which was used to make rope.

Since hemp for the rope mills was in high demand, it became a big cash crop for Iowa. One 16-acre hemp field paid the full rent for our 200-acre farm.

I was 14 then, and my most vivid memory is of the German prisoners of war who worked in our hemp fields. I didn't know where their camp was…all I knew was that for 2 or 3 days a week, two big olive-drab U.S. Army trucks with canvas tops would rumble in, raising a cloud of dust.

Out would jump 20 or 30 POWs to work our fields for a few hours. They bundled and stacked the cured hemp, which was a back-breaking job. Even so, they seemed to enjoy the work. Sometimes they'd holler to one another and laugh; other times, they sang.

An American Army sergeant watched over them, just one man for the two truckloads of prisoners. He spoke their language, and usually left his carbine in one of the trucks. Once I even saw him hand his rifle to one of the POWs as he climbed through a fence! I guess those Germans weren't about to try to run away. Where could they run to?

One day I went through the fields to get the cows for the evening milking. Just because the field was full of POWs didn't make this day any different.

I was looking down, trying not to step on the sharp hemp stubble as I made my way along. Suddenly, when I looked up, I found myself face-to-face with one of the prisoners!

He was dressed in khaki pants, work shoes and a blue shirt with "POW" emblazoned across the back in big black letters. The blond young man said something to me, but I couldn't understand his language.

"What?" I said.

He tried again, this time more slowly, but I still didn't have a clue what he

---

"I was face-to-face with a prisoner…"

---

was saying. The American sergeant came over to us and smiled.

"Was ist, Hans?" he asked the POW.

Again the POW spoke.

The sergeant turned to me and said, "Hans wants to know why you aren't in the Army."

"I'm only 14!" I blurted, as I started to blush. Did he think I was a coward?

"Hans is 15," the sergeant said. "He was wounded and captured when he was your age."

The sergeant said something else to Hans, who answered, *"Danke schoen"*.

I guessed that meant "thanks", and not knowing what else to do, I said, "Welcome", and stuck out my hand. Hans looked at the sergeant, who nodded. Hans grinned, took my hand and shook it, twice, real hard.

"I've got to get the cows," I said, and hurried off.

Fourteen! In the Army at 14…and shot!

Ever since Pearl Harbor I had dreamed of getting into the fighting. How I'd wished I could take on those Japanese or Nazis. For the first time, though, war didn't seem like all that much fun to me. And it took a former Nazi soldier to teach me that.✪

'I Was Helping Our Troops Win the War'

AFTER I graduated from high school in 1945, I traded in my poodle skirts and saddle oxfords for denim pants and steel-toed shoes. As a production clerk in a munitions plant, I was helping our troops win the war. At 18, I was making as much money as my father, who'd been working for a refinery for 25 years!

Tractors pulled gray-green shells and thousand-pound bombs past my desk every day. My job was to count them. Every hour, I reported to the main office how much ammunition had been processed.

I worked a different shift every week. The graveyard shift was hardest. There was a railroad car outside the plant's paint shop, and when I got my "lunch break" at 4 a.m., I'd crawl inside it and sleep on inch-thick cardboard for half an hour. Those short naps helped get me through the long nights.

I never dreamed during that difficult time that someday love and friendship would wipe away the war's bitterness. More than 4 decades later, my Japanese pen pal's son, Shin, visited us and got to know our grandson.

Their grandfathers had fought on opposite sides during the war, and now those veterans' grandsons were friends. We couldn't have asked for a happier ending. When Shin said good-bye and thanked us for a beautiful visit in America, we all cried.

—Lila Morgan, Pratt, Kansas

Beloved Youth's Death Broke More Than One Heart

By Olive Huisman
Waldorf, Maryland

MY FATHER was a pharmacist, and I spent many hours in his drugstore. On summer nights, I'd wait for him to close up and walk me home from band concerts in the park. In winter, I'd do my homework at the big rolltop desk behind the counter. I got to know all the staff, but my favorite was Alex Peterson, whom we called Pete.

Pete was in high school when Dad hired him to do janitorial chores. But Dad quickly realized Pete's warm smile and polite manner would make him a good clerk. Pete soon was helping customers find everything from toothpaste to foot powder. Dad felt as though he had a goodwill ambassador on the payroll.

Most boys his age never would have given a little girl a second glance, but Pete always had time for a chat. He'd ask me about school and share secrets about my teachers. I didn't have a brother, but if I could've chosen one, it would've been Pete.

Everyone admired Pete, including his peers. This only child, whose father had died several years before, was an Eagle Scout and president of his church youth group.

But no one admired Pete more than his mom. She was a seamstress at a department store, and Pete was always finding ways to make her life a little easier. He'd buy a day-old pastry from

GOLD STAR in the window indicated a family had lost a son in the war.

the bakery so she wouldn't have to make dessert, or insist on carrying her packages home when she stopped by

the drugstore after shopping. Her eyes lit up whenever she looked at him.

When Pete graduated, the war was in full swing, and he was drafted. It was impossible to picture such a good-natured boy with a rifle in his hands, but patriotism was a powerful force. Pete had no choice but to do his duty. Mrs. Peterson seemed to age quickly after he left. Dad helped her as much as he could, but there wasn't much he could do when she told him Pete was being sent overseas.

No more than a month later, Dad came home unexpectedly early. He fell heavily into a kitchen chair and stared down through his tears at the hat in his hands. Pete had been sent to an island in the South Pacific, he said. Only minutes after stepping into the dense jungle, he was shot by a sniper. Pete was dead.

Until that moment, "war" had been sort of scary, but exciting at the same time. It meant victory rallies at school, collecting tinfoil and tin cans, sitting through newsreels at the theater.

Now I knew its real meaning. It was going past Mrs. Peterson's house and seeing the gold star in her front window, the symbol of the ultimate sacrifice.

War Years Shaped Lives Of Those Back Home, Too

I DON'T recall much about the battles that were won or lost during World War II. What I remember most is my dad.

When Pearl Harbor was bombed, Dad was 28—just the right age for the draft that would start soon. But he was in "war work", building materials needed for the war effort, so he got a deferment. He suffered many questioning looks from people on the street wondering why a young able-bodied man wasn't in uniform.

Dad was serving where he was needed most, working 50 hours a week or more with no overtime pay, walking to work with his lunch wrapped in newspaper and tied with string. My brother and I didn't see him much during the war—something Dad still regrets. But such sacrifices were part of the war effort.

Even though Dad was never drafted, those years helped shape his life. His courage was forged not in hand-to-hand combat, but in sticking to his job, working long hours in a factory that was too cold in winter and too hot in summer, seeing his kids too infrequently—and, through it all, providing the best for his family that he could.
—*Janet Zoellner, College Corner, Ohio*

LONG HOURS were common for able-bodied men who worked factory jobs to supply war materials. Though they didn't wear uniforms or earn medals, these factory workers were heroes all the same.

HOME FRONT SISTERS. Sarafina, Josephine and Theresa Rachiele (from left, in photo at right) built planes for Republic Aviation. When Tommy Dorsey entertained for bond drive, they posed with him. Theresa is at Tommy's left, and her sisters are above him.

Three 'Sister Rosies' Met Big Band Legend

By Josephine Rachiele
West Babylon, New York

I WORKED at a coat factory until August 1943, when I decided it was time to do something for my country. I applied for a job as a mail girl at Republic Aviation Corp. in Farmingdale, New York—but was hired as a "Rosie the Riveter"!

In no time at all, I went from sewing buttons on coats to drilling holes and riveting parts for the famed P-37 Thunderbolt. What a switch!

My sisters, Sarafina and Theresa, worked for Republic, too. We were referred to as the "home front sisters".

One day in 1944, Tommy Dorsey and his band, with Buddy Rich on drums, put on a show in one of the hangars to boost morale and spur interest in a bond drive. What an evening! It was especially memorable for my sisters and me, because we had our picture taken with Tommy right by the wing of a P-47!

Then came the day in 1945 when a vice president climbed onto a workbench and announced the war was over. I can still hear the cheering that surrounded me as my eyes filled with tears.

We were all laid off then, but I returned 1-1/2 years later and stayed with Republic until my retirement in 1986.✪

Emergency Vehicles' Blue Lights Resembled Jewels

MY MEMORIES of the war always include a beautiful glow of aquamarine blue. The police cars and emergency vehicles of the day were equipped with blue headlights to help distinguish them from other vehicles at night. I used to look at lines of headlights on hills and count the "blue jewels". I thought it was some kind of magic.   —*Pat Mariner Bustamante*
Cupertino, California

Champion Welder Was Pride of the South

By Roberta Graham Powalksi
Baton Rouge, Louisiana

JACKSON COUNTY, Mississippi is a land of many legends, but one of them is true—that of a young woman known during World War II as the country's best female welder. I know, because I worked with her!

Vera Anderson was working in a garment factory when she heard Ingalls Shipbuilding Company in Pascagoula needed female welders. She signed up for night school to learn the trade while she continued to work at her day job.

After 104 hours' training, the petite 19-year-old was hired and quickly gained a reputation as Ingalls' best female welder. (She was better than some of the men, too!) "Miss Vera" became a legend across the South, raising the spirits of many women whose menfolk had been called to war.

Before long, Miss Vera was famous nationwide. In 1943, an Oregon shipyard challenged her to a contest with *its* best female welder. The two women, dressed in overalls and welding helmets, stood in the hot Louisiana sun as they raced against the clock to weld pieces chosen by the judges.

Before half the allotted time had expired, Miss Vera stepped back, pushed her helmet from her face and smiled shyly. The Pride of Mississippi had already finished! The crowd cheered as the Movietone News cameras rolled.

Her "Christening"

Later that year, a group of my co-workers won a bond sales contest, entitling us to christen a new ship. We named the ship *Seahawk* and chose Miss Vera to christen it. The crowd went wild when Miss Vera and her 12 "maidens of honor" appeared to do the honors in work coveralls instead of frilly tea dresses! Miss Vera wore an arrangement of war stamps instead of a corsage. After the christening, she smiled at her maids and said, "Girls, let's get back to work."

In January 1944, Miss Vera bested another competitor, a champion welder from California. After that, no one again challenged her skills. A media favorite, she was entertained several times by congressmen and senators in Washington.

Vera later became a welding instructor, married a man named Harrison N. McDonald and, as far as I know, lived happily ever after. I often wonder if she tells her grandchildren she was years ahead of women's liberation!○

WELL DONE! Women trained as welders became so good at their jobs that some of their employers hosted competitions for them.

Training Turned Mom into Drill Operator

IN THE spring of 1943, a defense factory opened in a small village near our home in upstate New York. Nearly everyone who applied was hired and given on-the-job training. Finally, a chance to pay off the Depression-era bills we still owed! My mother offered to care for our two children, and I applied. I was hired for the night shift at 55¢ an hour.

I'll never forget how scared I was the first night I walked into that factory. I'd never seen the inside of a machine shop, let alone understood what all that equipment was for. I was ready to turn around and walk out when a nice man greeted me and told me to follow him. He led me to a row of 15 drill presses and said I could work there.

The first drill press I was to work on had a very fine drill. "You'll need a gentle touch with these babies," the boss said. "They break real easy."

That night I broke 11 of those babies. I definitely did not have a gentle touch!

I figured by the end of the shift, I'd be fired. But to my surprise, the boss just said, "See you tomorrow."

The next night I broke only three drills. The boss said I was "catching on fast". By the end of the week, I wasn't breaking a thing. For me, it was quite an accomplishment to go from housewife to drill press operator in 1 week's time!

After about a year, the hand drills were replaced with automatic drills, which did 10 operations at once. They turned out to be tailor-made for the way I worked, and I was assigned to run one.

My husband and I not only paid off our old bills but bought some war bonds for the future. When the war ended in 1945, I quit my job and went back to being a housewife and mommy, and everyone was happy.

Rosie the Riveter I wasn't. I never touched a rivet throughout the whole war. But I drilled lots of holes in rocket nose cones, and as I did, I thought, "This is for you, Hitler or Hirohito—I hope it makes a hit where it hurts and puts an end to this insanity soon."

—*Viola Groot, Largo, Florida*

SHIPSHAPE. Ann Cottrell of Lexington, Kentucky has fond memories of her work as a welder. She helped build LSTs in Jeffersonville, Indiana, and later worked at a shipyard in Tampa, Florida. She was photographed with fellow workers in Tampa in 1945. She's in the center of the front row, standing next to the man holding his hat at his side.

Welding Was Best Job She Ever Had

I'M ONE OF the women who worked in a shipyard all through the war, from 1942 to 1945. First I worked in Jeffersonville, Indiana, where LSTs were made. These were the boats that took the soldiers right up to the shoreline.

Later, I went to Tampa to work as a welder. It was the most satisfying job I ever had. I loved welding, even though it left me with a few burns on my arms!

The women were really needed for those jobs then. The day the war was over, though, we all got our pink slips.
—*Ann Cottrell, Lexington, Kentucky*

Drill Skills Came In Handy Years Later

I WAS one of many "Rosie the Riveters". After 2 weeks' training, I was sent to a plane assembly plant to work on wing panels. We drilled the panels first, then put in the rivets.

Riveting made your whole body shake—good for reducing, only I didn't need that. I was thin to start with, and the longer I worked, the thinner I got.

Finally my boss said, "Evelyn, I'm going to put you to work in the tool crib, handing out rivets and tools. You're getting so thin I'm afraid someday you'll go right in with the rivet!" So there I stayed until the war was over.

Handling a drill came in handy years later, when I helped my husband build our house. I drilled every hole in the hardwood floors before the nails were put in, and my husband was very proud of me!
—*Evelyn Robinson South Bend, Indiana*

Her 'War Sacrifice' Was A Pain in the...Stomach!

IN 1943, while my husband was serving overseas, I went to work at the Port Newark shipyard in New Jersey. I was assigned to drill holes on sheets of metal, using a radial automatic drill that stood well over my head.

This task sometimes exposed my stomach, because I had to reach up so high that my shirt would come untucked.

One day, as I drilled a hole close to the edge, I noticed the drill was forming a spiral of hot metal. The spiral kept getting longer and heavier and finally fell off—onto my bare stomach! I didn't want to ruin that whole sheet of metal—materials were costly and scarce, and we'd been warned to be careful—so I kept working, wiggling my body frantically to try to shake off that hot spiral. My co-workers must have thought I was a belly dancer!

That was my sacrifice for the war effort, and I'm still proud of it!
—*Josephine Juliano Toms River, New Jersey*

Lady Welder Did Her Work in Tight Spaces

I STARTED working as a welder in Bethlehem Steel's San Francisco shipyards in 1943. My first job was welding in the chain locker in the bow of a destroyer escort.

I was small, so I inherited all of the jobs in tight spots that a bigger person couldn't crawl into. I wasn't a pretty sight, though, in the leather pants and jacket, heavy boots, gloves and helmet I had to wear!

I was proud to be a journeyman welder and stayed on the job until V-J Day, when all the women were terminated. Once we were no longer needed, our jobs once again became "men's work". But I was happy because I'd had a chance to do my part.
—*Irene Wheat Fuentes, Cooper, Texas*

Welder Penned Poem To Cheer Her Sailor Son

MOTHERS of servicemen did whatever they could to keep their sons' spirits high. This anonymous poem, written for a sailor son, was printed in a Navy magazine with a photo showing a female welder at work, her face hidden behind a welder's hood.

The poem was submitted by Norma John of Vancouver, Washington, who also was a welder during the war.

Dearest Son,

I'd like to see you at this moment,
I'd like to hear your merry shout,
Though I know you must be puzzled
Wondering what it's all about.
But if you'd lift that little window—
I mean, if you only could—
You'd be surprised, my son, to find
Your mom—behind the hood.

You have often heard the lauding
Of the man behind the plow,
Who's behind the fighter with the gun,
And he deserves it, I'll allow.
But someone else is helping
And I'll have it understood
And in her own way fighting,
Namely, Mom—behind the hood.

There's no time for idle fingers,
There's so much work to do.
And you may rest assured
That we'll see you carry through.
Oh, my work, it's not fancy,
But you know I never would
Fold my hands and yell "I'm quitting"
'Cause I'm your mom—
*   behind the hood.*

How I'd like to be there with you
But it cannot be, I know,

WORKING WOMEN. Defense industry jobs helped many women feel closer to the sons and husbands who had joined the fighting overseas.

So I'll do my best right here, dear,
And may God bless you as you go.
Just remember this, my laddie,
Be you faring ill or good,
That in thoughts I'm right beside you.
Love, your mom—behind the hood.

This Riveting Rosie Built B-29 Bombers

By Helen Kosierowski
Upland, Pennsylvania

I APPLIED for a job in 1943 at the Philadelphia Navy Yard. My patriotism must have been running awfully high back then, because I would be working as a riveter on the midnight to 8 a.m. shift.

An instructor taught me and my co-workers how to use a rivet gun. It was tough at first, but when he thought we could handle the job, he sent us to rivet together the B-29 Flying Fortress.

BOMBER BUILDER. Helen Kosierowski (left) tells above role she played on home front during World War II. One of her pay stubs from 1943 (right) shows she cleared 92¢ after deductions, which included $3.75 for war bonds.

The rivet guns were not only noisy, they were tough to hang onto, and some of us were afraid of them at first.

You had to grip your gun very tightly as you worked. If the gun got away from you it would fly all over the place, making everyone jump for cover until someone shut it down.

But handling the gun was only half the job, because you needed a partner to "buck" (or flatten) the rivets. That person would stand inside the plane, holding an iron bar against the metal being fastened. If the bar wasn't held tightly against the metal, the rivet wouldn't be properly flattened.

Bucking rivets was draining work, and my partner and I would switch off when either of us got tired.

When my partner and I arrived to work on the B-29, we were astounded at the size of the plane. It was *huge*. The tail, of course, was the tallest part of the plane, and my partner and I had to stand way up high on a plank to rivet together the tail section. When we started the rivet gun, the whole plank shook like mad.

After our shift was finished, inspectors would come through and red-circle any rivets they wanted done over. When we returned to work the next night, we always checked for any circles the day shift inspectors had left for us.

I guess we did all right, though. Those B-29 bombers sure seemed to fly okay in action. And one, named *Enola Gay*, eventually dropped the bomb that ended the war.✪

						GROSS EARNINGS		DEDUCTIONS		
EMPLOYEE NUMBER	MO.	DAY	TREASURY CHECK NUMBER	AMOUNT OF CHECK		5	6	RETIREMENT	BONDS	VICTORY TAX
287025	10	3	1272475	00.92		0.42	04.64	0.24	03.75	0.15

STATEMENT OF YOUR EARNINGS, DEDUCTIONS AND NET PAY
FOR PAY PERIOD ENDING AS SHOWN BELOW IN COLUMN 2
THIS RECORD WILL BE OF VALUE IN THE PREPARATION OF YOUR TAX STATEMENT AND SHOULD BE RETAINED FOR THAT PURPOSE

GROSS EARNINGS { COLUMN 5 = EARNINGS NOT SUBJECT TO RETIREMENT FUND DEDUCTION
COLUMN 6 = EARNINGS SUBJECT TO 5% RETIREMENT FUND DEDUCTION
AMOUNT OF CHECK = SUM OF COLUMNS 5 AND 6 MINUS SUM OF COLUMNS 7, 8 AND 9

Ads Stressed Patriotism

ADVERTISERS quickly capital-
ized on the nation's patriotic
fervor in the 1940s, using like-
nesses of service personnel to sell
everything from food to cigarettes.

Some corporations, like air-
craft-builder Bendix (below),
emphasized their direct contribu-
tions to the war effort. A Purina
Mills ad (opposite top) included
information on local feed dealers
who'd signed up for active duty.

Many ads also included re-
minders to buy war bonds.✪

Widow's Grief Taught Child Poignant Lesson

By Mary Chandler
Rancho Santa Fe, California

I CAN STILL hear the keening of that beautiful young woman, even after all these years.

Before then, World War II meant only adventure. To help the war effort, I collected and smashed tin cans for recycling. I peeled strips of foil from gum wrappers, wadding them into ever-expanding silver balls, and deposited them in collection bins.

I saved my dimes and quarters and bought savings bonds at school, on the installment plan. My second-grade class sent CARE packages overseas. Each of us chose a pen pal. I chose Dorothy, a dimpled girl from Great Britain who wore her hair in pigtails, just like me.

At home, I substituted honey for rationed sugar, and I stirred yellow dye packets into oleo, trying to make it look like butter. I walked everywhere.

Saturday matinees were my entertainment. Between double features, I watched newsreels, waiting for a glimpse of Adolf Hitler. Going home, I'd goose-step.

Sometimes I played "kamikaze", diving then crashing into raked leaves.

But that was before.

Two of my uncles enlisted in the Navy. One came back in a coffin.

I remember the long car trip with Mother and the solemn funeral where another sailor sang *My Buddy*. I remember the graveside gun salute and the lump that kept choking me.

An Odd Feeling

Later, inside Grandfather's house, the grief was palpable. I felt uncomfortable, out of place. I quietly opened a closed door.

Pictures of my uncle covered the walls: a young sailor with curly blond hair and sparkling brown eyes in his crisp dress whites; a smiling farm boy driving Grandfather's tractor through the golden wheat fields; an oval-framed portrait taken when he was a little boy, with his arm around the shoulder of his youngest brother; a handsome 21-year-old groom with his new bride.

His laughter and playfulness surrounded me. I could almost hear him again, telling tall tales, scary ghost stories, funny accounts of farm animals. I found myself listening, waiting.

I thought, too, about the time he had held his dying dog, "Rascal", in his arms, whispering soothing words and nuzzling against the animal's blood-soaked body.

My newest aunt did not see me at first. She sat on the edge of the bed, holding a folded American flag. She lifted the flag to her face and cradled it there, her long flaxen hair shrouding the red, white and blue. Then she began to cry. Great sobs shook her body.

Shyly, I walked over and stroked her hair. Taking me onto her lap, this young war widow I scarcely knew began to rock me, back and forth, back and forth, her arms encircling me, her face buried against my cheek.

I knew then the meaning of war—of grief, of love, of loss—and how precious, fragile and fleeting are the moments of our lives. ✪

"V" FOR VICTORY dress pins were popular among women with a loved one at war. These were saved by Ruth Bon Fleur of Port Orange, Florida, whose collection of pins numbers more than 250.

CHAPTER FOUR

Our Proud Women in Uniform

Our Proud Women In Uniform

BRAVE WOMEN served in the military during WWII in unprecedented numbers, helping defend their country at home and on foreign soil.

W omen have gone off to war for a long, long time. Before World War II, they mostly served as nurses or American Red Cross volunteers. Even a few were spies.

But World War II was a different matter. More than 300,000 women volunteered for service, and this time for almost every job you could name. They were airplane mechanics, airplane pilots and flight instructors.

Some were secretaries or journalists, and others played in military bands or worked as air traffic controllers. Some chauffeured generals, others drove supply trucks. Name it and they did it, in the Air Corps, Army, Navy, Coast Guard and Marines.

Did Patriotic Duty

Why did they volunteer to be placed in harm's way? Plain and simple patriotism, for the most part. Every woman in the service freed up another man for combat duty. Many enlisted because their husband or sweetheart had already joined up. And for others, a few years in the military sounded like a grand adventure—a chance to see new places, meet new people and experience a little excitement.

I saw my first "lady soldiers" at the induction center in Des Moines, Iowa. Soldiers in skirts! What next?

They proudly marched by in perfect formation, ignoring the wolf whistles and cries of "You'll be sorry!"

Just like the men, they had to endure boot camp, make do with ill-fitting uniforms, survive the medical officers' pokings and proddings and shots, run obstacle courses, clean latrines, scrub barracks floors on their hands and knees, be rudely awakened long before the sun came up and live by the old military rule: "If it moves, salute it; if it doesn't move, pick it up; and if you can't pick it up, paint it."

Make no mistake, World War II was every bit as real—and dangerous— for many of these women as it was for any man. Torpedoes, bombs and bullets were gender-neutral.

Showed Their Bravery

Whether in Europe or the Pacific, a considerable number of women worked within earshot of battle. The very first, of course, were the incredibly brave nurses working with dwindling supplies in Malinta Tunnel during the siege of Corregidor.

Military service wasn't for the squeamish, especially the women who served in the South Pacific, where creepy-crawly critters (as well as many that slithered) were in abundance. They skittered around on walls and ceilings, took up residence in your shoes overnight and buzzed annoyingly inside your mosquito netting.

Antimalarial tablets turned a peaches-and-cream complexion into an unappealing yellowish tint. And, while I'm not really sure, it must have been tough to feel girlish wearing olive-drab undies.

The old warriors had a tough time accepting this new breed of soldier at first, but by war's end, the WACs, WAVEs, SPARs, WASPs, Women Marines, nurses and others had earned the respect and admiration they deserved.

—*Clancy Strock*

PLANE JANE she wasn't! Jean Talcott flashed a winning smile back in 1943, when she served in the U.S. Navy as an Aviation Machinist Mate, Third Class. Now Jean Wicks, she lives in Omak, Washington.

Army Bugler Found Her Calling

By Helen Reed Trobian
Johnson City, Tennessee

WHEN THE Army announced in 1942 it needed a tuba player for the WAAC band in Daytona Beach, Florida, I headed straight for the recruiting office. The recruiter was delighted with my credentials and assured me I'd be in the band. I was overjoyed at the thought of helping to keep up morale. What a worthy enterprise!

When I arrived for training, an officer told me, "Why, you couldn't possibly play in the band. You haven't had professional experience!"

I wasn't even allowed to try out, and the fervent fires of patriotism began to dwindle in me. The Army had hidden my talents under a bushel!

One evening, the commanding officer said the company bugler was leaving, then asked, "Can anyone here blow a bugle?" It was a far cry from the tuba, but I could play cornet. When no one else volunteered, I timidly asked to try it.

That evening, I sneaked the bugle down to the beach to try it out all alone. The first few sounds were awful, but they soon improved.

Next morning, I tried to blow *First Call*, and it bore no resemblance to a military bugle call. But no one could have possibly stayed in bed after hearing it, either!

Socked It Out

My company was soon sent to Philadelphia, and we were housed in a hotel. I practiced bugling in my room, stuffing socks into the horn so that I wouldn't disturb anyone. When the CO heard about it, she decided to do away with the first sergeant's wake-up whistle and have me blow my muted bugle instead. So, every morning, I opened the door of each hotel room and did the best I could with a bugle full of socks!

When I wasn't bugling, I was working in the regimental offices with the enlisted men. One afternoon, after the men left to stand retreat, their major came in and said, "Where's that WAAC they told me could blow a bugle?" His bugler was gone; could I blow *Retreat*? He gave me a quick briefing, and off we went.

Women had not yet been fully accepted in the Army, and each chance we had to show how able we were was looked upon as an opportunity. As I waited to sound *Retreat*, I felt as if the future of all women in service depended on my performance.

I marched to the flagpole and looked out over a sea of GIs as my fellow WAACs watched from the windows. It seemed a long time, but the command to sound *Retreat* finally came. The bugle sounded perfect, with a sharp, clear tone.

I ran into the major afterward. My salute was halfway up when he said, "Lady, you got yourself a job!" From

PRACTICE PERCH. Corporal Helen Reed practices her bugle calls on the roof of the Clarendon Hotel in Daytona Beach, Florida in 1943. The hotel had been stripped down for military use and her unit was billeted there.

> *"Buglers weren't always popular…especially in the morning…"*

then on, I bugled for retreat, and we rarely heard another whistle.

Later, after the WAAC became the Women's Army Corps, I boarded a train with 500 other women headed for England and then Germany. We found our seats and sat in silence, some of us near tears. An officer saw my bugle and asked me to play some songs. I did, including *You're in the Army Now*. That got everyone singing and the heavy mood lifted.

Buglers weren't always popular— especially in the morning. But people often told me how much they enjoyed hearing *Taps* in the evening, or the calls at retreat.

I like to think my bugling made military life a bit more pleasant. Today I believe more than ever in music as a universal language that elevates the human spirit.✪

Military Service Kept Pilot Flying High

By Florene Miller Watson
Borger, Texas

WHEN I TOOK MY first airplane ride at age 8, I never dreamed that someday I'd be one of the first women to fly for the U.S. military, piloting everything from fighter planes to transports—and even teaching men how to fly!

I was one of the 25 original members of the WAFS, female pilots who delivered planes, passengers and equipment for the military. From 1942 until our group was deactivated in 1944, I flew almost two dozen different types of military planes.

I'd loved flying ever since I was a child, when my father took me for rides with barnstormers. Later, when I was in college, Dad bought a plane so the whole family could learn to fly.

My father, two brothers and I all got pilot's licenses, and I began giving lessons. In 1941 I signed on as a war training instructor. Each of my classes had 50 men.

In September 1942, the government's Ferrying Command decided to form an elite group of 25 female pilots to deliver military planes from factories to airfields and shipping points. I volunteered, was accepted, and became one of the first members of the WAFS, the Women's Auxiliary Ferrying Squadron. (Later, as our ranks grew, we were renamed the Women Air Force Service Pilots, or WASPs.)

We were sent to Delaware to learn Air Force procedure and learn to fly military training planes. These planes had no radios or navigational devices, but we successfully delivered them to destinations all across the nation.

One memorable trip took us to Great

UP, UP AND AWAY was Florine Miller, as she flew fighters like the P-51 at top, and trainers like the AT-6 above.

Falls, Montana in December. The temperature was well below zero and we were flying open-cockpit planes. We wrapped ourselves in sheepskin jackets with heavy pants, boots, gloves and helmets to stay warm, and covered our faces with chamois masks to keep our skin from freezing.

In January 1943, I was sent with several other WAFS to Dallas' Love Field to start a base. I was named commanding officer.

Most of my flights went off without a hitch, but there's one I'll never for-

get. It was November 1943, and I was learning to fly a P-47, our largest and heaviest fighter.

As I approached the runway to land, I was blinded by the setting sun shining directly in my face. I hit a telephone pole, knocking out the field's runway lights and radio.

The impact tore up the plane, nearly flipped it over and I barely missed flying into a hangar. The plane was flying just above stalling speed. If I could gain enough altitude, I planned to bail out.

After experimenting a bit, I thought I might be able to land, although the instruments were vibrating badly. As I turned toward the airport, I still had no radio contact. And since it had turned dark there was no airport in sight—because I'd knocked all the lights out!

I finally made contact with a man who was working on airplane radios at the airport. He called the tower by telephone to get a few cars parked at the end of a runway. Guided by their headlights, I landed just moments before the plane ran out of fuel.

Afterward, I learned the plane was in even worse shape than I'd thought. Part of the elevator was gone, part of a propeller blade had melted off, and much of the plane's belly was torn.

Despite that close call, flying for the military was wonderful, and it gave me the chance to realize a dream. I'd wanted to fly a P-38 since 1940, when I first saw one of those sleek planes. Its beauty made a lasting impression on me. Thanks to the WAFS, I did learn to fly a P-38. And when my service ended, it was the last plane I flew.✪

General Treated WACs to R & R On Capri

By Dorothy Weirick
San Clemente, California

FOR MERITORIOUS service in Italy, my WAC platoon received the Fifth Army Plaque with Clasp.

General Mark Clark decorated a group of us with ribbons and bronze stars, then made arrangements to fly us to Naples in his private C-47 plane. We were headed for the Isle of Capri for a few days of R & R, and we couldn't believe our good fortune!

We boarded the plane for Naples, and Jeeps met us there, taking us to a strip of beach and a waiting motorboat. We waded out to the boat, and a bearded old Italian fellow helped us aboard.

After an hour or so, we docked on the Isle of Capri. A charming woman named Maria met us at the pier and led us up a narrow path to the center of the village. Children gathered around us, singing, as we walked.

We followed Maria along a quaint street filled with the scent of flowers. Bright red bougainvillea climbed over

GENERAL MARK CLARK decorates Dorothy Weirick for meritorious service in Italy. He then sent Dorothy and four other WACs on an unforgettable trip.

the balconies, rooftops and even along the streets. Finally, we arrived at the old enchanting house that would be our home for the next 10 days.

Maria prepared marvelous meals, and even made ice cream for us! A boatman named Luigi took us to the sea for daily swims in the famous Blue Grotto. Sunlight would reflect in the cave of the grotto, mingling the brilliant blue of the

Mediterranean Sea with breathtaking red coral. It was delightful!

Later, we would walk to the piazza for chats at open-air cafes with the American airmen who were resting after their missions. We drank in the fragrance of the flowers, the friendly faces and the singing of children. For those 10 days, the world seemed a safe and friendly place in spite of the war.✪

Admirals' Cordiality Impressed Young WAVE

WHEN I was in the Navy, the men's rain gear included a rubber hat cover that came down over the bills of their hats, obscuring the golden "scrambled eggs" worn by captains and admirals.

One rainy day shortly after I started a secretarial assignment at Commander in Chief Headquarters in Washington, D.C., a tall Navy man wearing one of these rubber hat protectors joined me as I walked into the Navy Department building. We chatted amiably until we reached the third floor, where we entered the same door and all the officers snapped to attention.

It was only then I realized the man I'd been talking with so easily was the commander in chief, Admiral Ernest J. King— the man who was to the Navy what General Dwight D. Eisenhower was to the Army!

About a year later, I was assigned to type some reports for Admiral Chester Nimitz and told him he looked very much like my father. He gallantly told me that if my father was as handsome as I was attractive, he was very flattered! He was a charming man, and a brave hero of the war in the Pacific.

—*Anna Marie Shinn, Atlanta, Georgia*

ERNEST KING, Commander in Chief of U.S. Fleet, was one of two high-ranking admirals Anna Shinn met.

Pacific Tour of Duty Filled with Surprises

By Midge Brubaker Ahrendt
Calabasas, California

I WAS ASSIGNED to Far East Air Force Headquarters in Hollandia, New Guinea. When we shipped out of San Francisco, we didn't know where we were headed, so this was a surprise—especially since we'd been issued nothing but winter clothing, most of it lined with fur. Now we were in the jungle!

The only non-winter clothing we had was a pair of fatigues each, and we'd been washing them in salt water for 27 days, so they practically stood up by themselves. But the quartermaster had no khaki clothes for us. We were told to ask the GIs in the recreation hall if they could spare some of theirs.

We met the GIs that night. All the time they were talking to us, saying how happy they were to see American girls, we were sizing them up to see if their clothes would fit us! After a few days, my tent mates and I managed to scrounge a few used shirts and pairs of pants. At last we were out of those smelly fatigues!

The WACs lived four to a tent, with

DRIVIN' HOME. The then Midge Brubaker (right) and her Army friend Bobbi Gerlack posed for this shot when these WACs arrived stateside in 1946.

WRONG, ROSE! Midge reached the Philippines in 1945—though Tokyo Rose predicted her WAC unit wouldn't make it!

outhouses and showers down the hill at the edge of the jungle. The monkeys, birds and exotic animals made such strange noises that none of us made the walk alone at night. And darkness fell early and abruptly in Hollandia—at 4 p.m., with no twilight.

After about 4 months, New Guinea was secured and we moved on, boarding a plane for Tacloban in the Philippines. During a stopover on another island, "Tokyo Rose" interrupted Armed Forces Radio to say the 25 girls from Hollandia wouldn't make it to Tacloban! We were immediately assigned barracks and told to be prepared for takeoff at any time.

When we finally flew out, at 2 a.m. a couple of days later, Japanese planes were spotted. We were ordered to line up and prepare to parachute out if necessary. You could practically hear our hearts pounding over the roar of the engine! After several hours, we landed in Tacloban, but the airstrip was being strafed! We rolled out of the plane and crawled away on our stomachs.

Our new home was bordered by jungle at the back and beach at the front. It could have been a beautiful resort area in another time, but we were at war. Foxholes were dug next to each tent and

outside the officers' headquarters and rec hall, and we needed them. The Japanese shelled us day and night.

Later, we moved to the outskirts of Manila. We got permission to visit the city, but there was one catch: All the bridges had been bombed out, so we'd

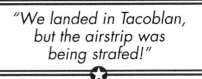

"We landed in Tacloblan, but the airstrip was being strafed!"

have to walk across a hanging bamboo bridge. It was quite an experience; I hate heights, and the river was 1,000 ft. below. I ended up crawling most of the way across!

But I'm glad I made that trip—that's when I met my future husband! One of my friends already knew him and was hoping he'd ask her out. He asked me instead, and we were married when we both eventually returned to the States.

When the Japanese surrendered, I was jubilant to be going home, but sad, too. I was leaving behind not only my friends but the man I planned to marry. Still, when I first caught sight of the Golden Gate Bridge, I couldn't wait to get my feet back on U.S. soil. ✪

When Duty Called, Army Nurse Answered

By Doris Gregory Beccio
Mariposa, California

I WAS BORN 3 years after the end of World War I. My parents were hoping for a boy to name after my uncle, who died in that war. "Oh, well," said Mother, "at least *she'll* never have to go to war." Wrong!

Early in 1943, I joined the Army Nurse Corps and requested overseas duty, hoping for Europe—maybe even France, where I could visit my uncle's grave. Little did I know what the Army had in mind!

Two months later I was at Camp Stoneman, California, ready to ship out. We boarded a small troop ship, which had seen better days as a Dutch freighter, for what would be a 30-day trip. As the ship sailed out under the Golden Gate Bridge, we wondered about our destination.

Accommodations were Spartan—six nurses sharing each tiny cabin. It was a tight squeeze. The food, though mediocre, was served in grand style on linen tablecloths with gleaming silver by Indonesian waiters in white jackets. Enlisted personnel had the same food, but Army-style—they had to stand in chow lines and eat from mess kits.

As we sailed south, balmy breezes caressed us, and we delighted in watching silvery fish skim the blue water. Tropical nights under the Southern Cross sparked more than one shipboard romance. This was heady stuff for a 22-year-old from Wisconsin!

On our 12th day out, we saw a reconnaissance plane. Was it ours or the enemy's? Apprehension mounted when a torpedo alert sounded. Soon we spotted pieces of wreckage floating in the distance. That night, we were ordered to sleep fully dressed, with life jackets nearby. Few of us actually slept.

For the next 14 days, we followed a zigzag course and eventually landed in New Guinea, a place most of us had

JUNGLE HOME. Lt. Doris Gregory posed for this photo in New Guinea during 1943.

never heard of. We spent a year on the island, which was more than enough, with the swamps, crocodiles, snakes, giant bats and bigger-than-life insects. Most of our patients weren't wounded; more often, they were suffering from tropical diseases, "jungle rot" and boredom.

In January 1945, we moved to Leyte Island in the Philippines. Now we began seeing battle casualties and nightly air raids. Weeks later, we landed on Luzon, where we watched the battle that liberated Manila. Our hospital soon overflowed with severely wounded men, and we worked day and night, nonstop.

After about 4 months, the area was secured and we saw fewer casualties. Now we were treating some of the emaciated POWs who had been held at Santo Tomás for more than 3 years.

Finally, we got a chance to explore Manila, or what was left of it. We still had to take cold-water showers, but it was a taste of civilization after living in grass shacks or tents with dirt floors.

There were some good times, too, like being able to occasionally hobnob with the rich and famous. Mrs. Douglas MacArthur, Jack Benny, Gary Cooper and John Wayne were among the luminaries who visited our hospital and dined in our mess hall.

On September 2, 1945, while the surrender was being signed on the *USS Missouri*, our unit came ashore at Inchon, Korea and stayed for almost 3 months. Then, at long last, we came home—just in time for Christmas. ✪

Job with Nurse Corps Took Plenty of Drive

ARMY NURSE Wilma Hawkins helped organize the Cadet Nurse Corps in Washington, D.C. in 1943.

I HAD spent 2 years as educational director of nursing at a Chicago hospital, and had no thoughts of leaving until I received a letter from the head of the new Cadet Nurse Corps. This federal program would dramatically increase the number of registered nurses as part of the war effort. It was too good a challenge to pass up, and St. Luke's granted me a year's leave to work with the corps in Washington, D.C.

There was just one complication. I had just bought a car, but I didn't know how to drive. I didn't want to leave the car in Chicago, and I would need it in Washington. So, with a friend's help, I learned to drive before I left, practicing in the parking lot at Soldier Field!

My friend then found a teenage girl who not only could drive but wanted to visit Washington, and off we went. The girl drove most of the way, but I got a chance to practice my new skills on the backroads.

—*Wilma Hawkins*
Carlsbad, California

Lady Marine's Lessons Have Lasted a Lifetime

By Frances Liney Morris
Santa Fe, New Mexico

DURING THE early years of World War II, when everyone was doing whatever they could to help with the war effort, I decided to enlist in the Marines. I was a sheltered only child, not yet 21, but my parents reluctantly gave their blessing.

I was a petite young woman whose endurance had previously been tested only by being a Girl Scout, so boot camp was hard for me. We slept in barracks, prepared for endless inspections, ate the "chow" or went hungry, and did predawn calisthenics.

We didn't know what to expect—and we expected the worst. The worst thing for me was standing at attention for what seemed like hours in the freezing cold and scorching heat.

But we also learned to work together and help each other, and developed a kind of camaraderie we'd never known before. There were no class distinctions in boot camp, and no young men to distract us or cause rivalries. When we made it through basic training, and most of us did, we were very proud of ourselves.

Looking back, the funniest thing that

> "We developed a kind of camaraderie we'd never known before..."

happened to me was when it was my turn to drill my platoon. I was trying to sound like a proper drill instructor, making no mistakes, while a company of male Marines marched by, grinning from ear to ear at the sight!

When the war was finally over, I had the satisfaction of knowing I'd done all I could, and the sense of humor and self-discipline I acquired have helped me all my life.✪

WOMAN MARINE Frances Liney worked in recruiting in Richmond, Virginia (above), then was assigned to a quartermaster's office.

Brief Leave Led to Lifelong Commitment

By June Cook Northrop
Owego, New York

I'D BEEN working on P-41 fighter planes in Buffalo, New York when I decided to enlist. I soon was sworn in as a SPAR, a female member of the United States Coast Guard.

I went to boot camp in West Palm Beach, Florida, then on to pay and supply school, and finally was shipped off to San Diego, California, where I relieved a fellow Coast Guardsman for sea duty.

On my first leave home, I met a sailor who also was on leave. He had been wounded in the Solomon Islands and his ship, *The Vincennes,* was sunk. He and I spent a grand total of only 3 days together, but before he left for his next station, he asked me to marry him!

While we were apart, we got to know each other by writing many letters, and on our next leave, we were married. We're proud to have served our country, and we'll always be grateful that those difficult years brought us together.✪

SPIFFY SPARS above included June Cook, third from left. Before June enlisted in the Coast Guard, she riveted fighter planes.

MacArthur Honored Army Nurses

IN DECEMBER 1944, General Douglas MacArthur had this to say about the role of the Army nurse:

"The Army nurse is the symbol to the soldier of help and relief in his hour of direst need. Through mud and mire, through the murk of campaign and battle, wherever the fight leads, she patiently—gallantly—seeks the wounded and distressed. Her comfort knows no parallel. In the hearts of all fighting men, she is enshrined forever."✪

This WASP Flew Right into a Blizzard

By Ruth Tompkins
Mountain View, California

DURING THE WAR, I was a member of the WASPs—Women Air Force Service Pilots. We were the Army Air Force's first female pilots, flying missions within the United States to free male pilots for overseas duty.

Ours was an elite group. About 25,000 women applied when the WASPs were started in 1942, but just over 1,000 of us graduated from the 7 months' training and earned our wings.

One day a group of us were in Montreal with our AT-6 planes, ready to fly to Newark, New Jersey, where the planes would be crated and shipped overseas.

When we got takeoff approval, we took off into the wild blue yonder. Before long, I ran into a unexpected white wall of snow. I couldn't see anything ahead or below. Since we had to navigate visually, I made a 180-degree turn to head back out of the storm.

I spotted another plane just as its pilot spotted me, and recognized she was one of my classmates. Communicating with hand signals, we headed back north, looking for a safe place to land. When we reached an Army field with an unplowed runway, we decided to try to land there.

I circled while my classmate landed on the snow-covered runway. To my horror, her plane tipped up on its propeller and stayed there! I continued circling as military personnel came to

---

"As I circled the field, I waggled my wings to them..."

⭐

---

her rescue and helped her out. Once I saw she was okay, I continued flying north, looking for another airport.

I eventually found an airport that wasn't being used. The runway had only a light covering of snow, and I landed safely. Before long, people

appeared from everywhere. You should've seen the surprise on their faces when they saw a 120-lb. girl in uniform climb out of the cockpit of that large military plane!

After recovering from their astonishment, they put my plane in a hangar, took me to town, put me up in the only hotel, found me a place to eat and helped me contact my superior to relay what had happened. Later, I learned that

most of my classmates hadn't reached our destination. Three had crashed, but none of the pilots were injured.

The next morning was beautiful, and the town sent snowplows to clean off the runway so I wouldn't have any problems taking off.

As I circled the field, I waggled my wings to thank the many people who'd helped me in what could have been a very unpleasant situation.✪

WOMEN WITH WINGS. Ruth Tompkins, second from left, was one of 1,830 female pilot applicants accepted in the WASPs. The female gremlin logo at left was a design donated by Walt Disney.

Fifinella

W.A.S.P.
WOMEN AIR FORCE SERVICE PILOTS WWII

Little Cake for Max Baer Gave Army Cook Big Trouble

I WORKED as a baker in the Women's Army Auxiliary Corps, and one of my toughest assignments was to bake a birthday cake for boxer Max Baer—the former heavyweight champion of the world!

Max was stationed at the same place I was, working as a physical instructor for the men. He wanted an old-fashioned chocolate cake just like Grandma used to make.

Making a small three-layer cake was harder than it sounds, because I was accustomed to baking for hundreds. Trying to cut down a gigantic

Army recipe to make just one little cake was quite a task, but the big boxer seemed plenty pleased with the result!

Another funny incident occurred while I was in Des Moines, Iowa for basic training. The streets often were covered with snow and ice, and once I met an officer while crossing an icy street. I saluted—and promptly fell flat on my rear! I turned to look for the officer and saw he had fallen, too. I don't know which of us was more embarrassed! —*Oleta Bogard*
Kansas City, Kansas

CHAPTER FIVE

Cherished Photos

Cherished Photos

LASTING IMAGES of World War II linger in the collective conscious of America, thanks to legendary photos like the flag raising at Iwo Jima. Most family-album pictures may not hold such drama, but they present a far more personal side of the war—as experienced by real folks who lived through it.

WAR BRIDE. Anna and Floyd Winn met when Floyd's unit took over a bakery to make bread for troops occupying Anna's hometown of Foggia, Italy. Married in 1945, they now live in Haines City, Florida. "They're devoted to their family and each other," says Palma Davis, who sent her parents' wedding photo. "Theirs is a beautiful love story."

We've been trying to preserve images of our wars for as long as there have been wars. The Egyptians did it 5,000 years ago. The Greeks, the Incas and Mayas and the American Indians all left pictures to record their feats in battle.

Most of the pictorial history of the Revolutionary War consists of romanticized paintings that now hang in art museums.

Our images of the Civil War were preserved by Mathew Brady and a tiny handful of other commercial or press photographers.

The photos of World War I give us a little better overall picture of that period, even including some jumpy, scratchy motion picture footage.

But by the time World War II came along, most Americans owned a decent camera, and many of these went off to war with a soldier, sailor, airman or Marine.

The family cameras that remained behind helped record what life was like for folks back home, pulling together in whatever little ways they could to help carry their country to victory.

Literally millions of photos are stored away in albums or desk drawers, and they add up to an incredibly detailed personal history as it was lived by our fathers, grandfathers, uncles, aunts and neighbors.

A Priceless Picture

I especially treasure a snapshot taken just before I boarded a bus for basic training at Jefferson Barracks, Missouri. It wouldn't impress you a bit—just a gawky 18-year-old standing beside his dad. But to me, that photo represents a special moment because it was the first time I ever saw Dad cry. In that brief instant I suddenly understood a bookful of things I'd never known or suspected about him, including the fact that he did, indeed, love me.

There's another photo of me standing amid the bombed-out ruins of a 400-year-old cathedral built by the Spaniards in Manila. It was my first personal confrontation with the hideous ability of war to destroy not only lives but also the beautiful things we create to prove that we are civilized people.

We've all seen the memorable photos taken by Margaret Bourke-White and other brave and talented combat photographers. You won't find many combat photos in our own albums and desk drawers, because Grampa or Dad were a little preoccupied with other things during the heat of battle.

Their photos are of their buddies. And the places where they learned to become soldiers. And of the strange and exotic new places where they served.

Meanwhile, the photos taken by their loved ones back home detail determination…through scrap drives, bond drives and victory gardens. They reveal profound hope, as mothers and small children pose with their biggest smiles for their husbands and fathers so far away from home. And they depict the deepest love, when after the war, these families were united once more.

To see World War II through the eyes of the men and women who lived it, just turn to the pages that follow.

Our special thanks to all those who entrusted these priceless photos to us, so we could share them with you.   —*Clancy Strock*

1. Rally 'Round the Flag

1. PATRIOTIC FEVER swept up even the youngest of children. Betty Cogg Baughn of Burlington, North Carolina sent photo of her three young cousins, who kept their flags flying even while playing.

2. POETIC REWARD. When Lois Thut sent a poem about war hero Jimmy Doolittle to *The Story Hour* radio program, the host forwarded it to the general himself. Two weeks later, Doolittle sent Lois a personal letter and an autographed photo. "I often reflect on the kindness of a busy Air Force general who took the time to write to a 9-year-old girl," says Lois, now of Oakville, Connecticut.

3. YOUNG BOYS looked up to the brave men fighting the war, and Larry Vance was no exception. He was mighty proud to have his picture taken with his Uncle Tom Vance, when the sailor came home on leave. Tom's niece, Trudi Bellin of Franklin, Wisconsin, provided the photo.

2. Write on, Lois!

3. Role Model

4. Tater Time

5. Bombs Away!

4. KP DUTY generally involved peeling potatoes—and plenty of them! Mrs. Willard Becraft of Greensburg, Indiana sent photo of her husband, who was peeling spuds along with fellow GIs at Fort Lewis, Washington in 1942. Willard is at the rear of the group.

5. LOVED ONES' NAMES often graced the bombs that were loaded into B-29s on Tinian Island, says Grace Taylor of Cheswick, Pennsylvania. This bomb happened to have her name on it! Her husband, Albert, is riding the cart pulled by his buddy Frank. "All the fellows got quite a kick out of writing their family members' names on the bombs they loaded on the planes," Grace explains.

6. STAFFERS at O'Reilly General Hospital, Springfield, Missouri, posed for a group portrait in 1946. Tech. Sgt. Myrtle Baxter Frederick of Waukesha, Wisconsin worked with plastic surgeons who were treating GIs. She's fifth from right in the front row. "We felt as though we were really doing something there, instead of just sitting at home," Myrtle recalls. "It was a great time to serve our country. I enjoyed every minute of it."

6. WACs at Work

7. Buy War Bonds!

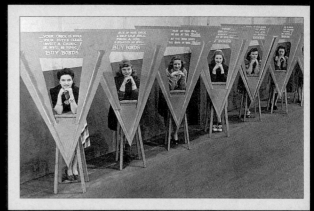

9. "V" for Victory

8. Thrifty Threads

10. Army Nurses

7. YOUNG WOMEN rode a float promoting war bonds at a 1945 company picnic at Wisconsin State Fair Park. Nell Zietlow of West Allis, who sent the photo, is seated at far left on float.

8. FEED SACK FASHION. Clothing shortages and tight funds kept feed sack dresses popular. Rosa Lee Schultz of Dunwoody, Georgia says the photo her husband took originally appeared in *Collier's* magazine.

9. CHECK, PLEASE. Payroll workers at a West Allis, Wisconsin firm distributed checks from V-shaped stands and encouraged co-workers to buy war bonds. Nell Zietlow is second from left.

10. WHITE HATS and starched dresses weren't part of nurses' attire—not during Army basic training. Elise Smith of New Albany, Mississippi sent shot taken at Camp Forrest, Tennessee.

11. Dog Show

11. *POOCH ON PARADE.* "Judo" was adopted by Fritz Schaupp and his Army unit. He traveled with them and appeared atop Fritz's tank in military parades. Fritz's daughter, Candace Slaterback of Pittsburgh, Pennsylvania, sent the photo.

12. *TENTMATES* at Ft. Dix, New Jersey seem to be sharing one mess kit. Ned Doll of San Jose, California (far left) sent this photo.

13. *LETTERS FROM HOME* always brightened a soldier's day. This Marine waited for his mail at "post office" on Saipan in 1944. Wesley Loveall of Bakersfield, California provided the photo.

14. *TODDLER TWINS* Lamont and Laura Peterson got soldier outfits from their grandparents. Mom Virginia of Rock Island, Illinois sent the photo.

12. Who Gets the Plate?

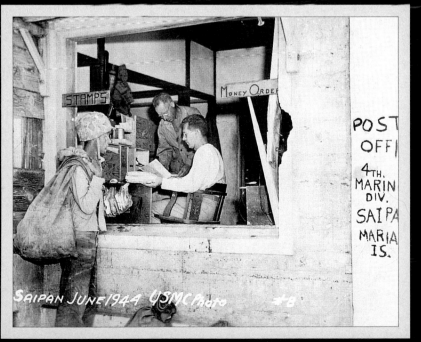

13. Local Post Office?

14. Little Soldiers

15. Times-Square Meals

16. The Ties That Bind

15. *COAST GUARDSMAN* Wally Pelchen was stationed in New York City. Wally, now of Brookfield, Wisconsin, regularly met his uniformed friends at the Pepsi-Cola building for free soda and hot dogs.

16. *EARLY ENLISTEES* got their uniforms only in bits and pieces. John Willard of Randolph, Massachusetts sent photo. He's second from left in back row.

17. *AMBULANCE DRIVER* Woody Ostland shed shirt in the heat at Williams Field, Arizona. Today, Woody lives in Phoenix.

18. *FIX IT!* Jeanne Lever of Perrysburg, Ohio says shoe shortage kept her dad's repair shop busy throughout the war.

18. Shoes Soled Here

17. Hot Work

19. Brothers in Arms

19. *SEVEN BROTHERS* from the Sondeno family of Turlock, California served their country during the war. Gunnar, George and Milton are in front row; Joseph, Fredolf, David and Philip are in back. Fredolf served in occupied Japan after the war and returned later as a missionary.

20. *NAVY TRUCK DRIVER* Saxon Morris of Cave Junction, Oregon worked in Oakland, California, driving everything from pickups to semis. The photo shows one of her simpler tasks—driving a station wagon for Navy officers. "We got an easy assignment about once a month," she says.

21. *PRETTY PICTURES* of his daughters back home in Milwaukee, Wisconsin kept Raymond Anderson's spirits up while he served overseas. One daughter, Elaine Carson, now of Millsboro, Delaware, especially likes this shot of herself (far right) and sisters in homemade WAC uniforms.

20. "Need a Ride?"

21. "Hi, Daddy!"

22. Back to the Gay '90s

23. "The Quiet Boys"

24. Relatives Reunited

22. *REST AND RELAXATION.* When Sally Zorge of Glenview, Illinois got off the late shift at Douglas Aircraft, she and two co-workers joined some sailor friends for a "gay '90s party" at Chicago's La Salle Hotel. Sally—second from right—helped build C-54 airplanes.

23. *CORDIAL TENTMATES.* Corporal Ernest Weber of Ottawa, Illinois snapped this photo while stationed in Italy. He dubbed the group "The Quiet Boys of Tent No. 1". The photography buff took many photos during the war. This one was submitted by Trudi Bellin of Franklin, Wisconsin.

24. *FANCY MEETING YOU HERE!* When a ship delivered supplies to the front lines in France, Staff Sgt. Ernie Kraus (left) realized his nephew, Bob Michel, was on board and paid him a surprise visit. The skipper gave Bob, of Fayetteville, Pennsylvania, the day off to spend with his uncle. They had this photo taken in Nice to commemorate their unexpected reunion.

25. To Mom with Love

25. *SPECIAL VALENTINE.* Walter Ribeiro of Pennsauken, New Jersey wanted to send his mother a valentine but couldn't find one on base. So he drew this heart and sent a photo of it.

26. *ITALIAN VILLAGERS* befriended Ernest Weber while he was stationed in their country. Trudi Bellin of Franklin, Wisconsin shared this photo.

27. *UNIVERSITY OF IOWA* band became "girls only" after young men left for war. Member Jacquelyn Piez of Peace Dale, Rhode Island sent photo.

26. Making Friends
Far from Home

27. All-Girl Band

28. MARINE'S HOMECOMING in 1945 reunited him with the daughter he hadn't seen in 3 years. Bette Duncan of Sun City, California cherishes photo of her husband, Stew, and daughter Patricia.

29. DEATH OF A PRESIDENT. Franklin Roosevelt's unexpected death April 12, 1945 stunned the nation. F.R. Vogel of North Fort Myers, Florida was photographed as he read a story about the President's passing in *Stars & Stripes* in Paris, France.

30. POKER PALS identified only as "Babcock", from Maine, and "Bishop", from Alabama, were snapped somewhere in Italy by buddy Ernest Weber of Ottawa, Illinois. Trudi Bellin of Franklin, Wisconsin provided the photo.

31. SUNBATHING on a troop transport might not have been what these WACs expected! They wore denim coveralls and the mandatory life vests while en route to Allied headquarters in North Africa. The picture's from Lori Reese of Brooklyn, New York.

29. A Nation Mourns

28. Welcome Home

30. Ante Up!

31. You're in the Army Now...

CHAPTER SIX

Memories
From
The Field

Memories from The Field

AMERICAN BOYS got to see the world when they put on GI green or navy blue. Their experiences across the seas left them with many impressions, happy, sad and humorous... and those strong impressions have lasted a lifetime.

B ack in the '40s, relatively few Americans had set foot outside the United States. For that matter, few of us had been more than a few hundred miles away from the place where we were born. If you grew up in the heartland, chances were that you had never seen an ocean. The only foreign language taught in our schools was Latin.

And then one day you found yourself aboard a troop ship or on an airplane headed...somewhere. Wherever it was, it was across an endless ocean.

My journey across the Pacific took 34 days. One morning, standing at the rail, I remarked to the man standing next to me that the ocean sure was big. "Yes," he said, "and there's a lot more underneath it."

Destination Was a Mystery

In the middle of all that water we had no way to communicate with the rest of the world, and we weren't told where we were going. All we knew was that we were near the equator and headed west.

And when we finally got there, we didn't know where we were. Natives in canoes came out to greet us. Where were we? "Leyte," they said. The only problem was that no one on the ship quite knew for sure where Leyte was, except that it was part of the Philippine Islands.

It was evening by the time the 1,200 men on board were taken to shore on barges. We were loaded onto trucks and hauled through the night. Oil lamps flickered in thatched huts nestled under palm trees. Smallish brown people standing alongside the dirt road waved to us. The air was heavy and smelled of rotting jungle vegetation.

It sure wasn't Illinois.

My experience was duplicated by hundreds of thousands of other Americans. Some landed on the shores of North Africa. For others it was England or Australia or the Aleutian Islands or China or India.

Wherever, it sure wasn't anything like home.

A Whole New World

Usually the language was strange. The food was strange. How many lira or pesos or pounds were there to the dollar? Things in stores and shops didn't have price tags, so you had to learn the art of bartering.

The locals drove on the wrong side of the road. The druggist was called a "chemist", and cars had "bonnets" instead of hoods. Farmers plowed with water buffaloes instead of John Deeres. You could mortally insult someone without even realizing what you had done.

On the other hand, you were one of the wonderful Americans who had come to set things right. You were more than welcome, you were a hero, even if you had never heard a shot fired in anger. Families adopted you. Young ladies were eager for your company. Everyone was anxious to get to know these strange young men from across the water. Were we really cowboys? Or gangsters? Or movie stars?

What an experience!

That's not to say there wasn't mud and rain and cold and terror and close friends who would never come home. That came later. That was war.

But for those who did come home, the experiences that went with being overseas left us with a lifetime of memories and a zest for seeing the rest of the world. No one on the planet would ever be a stranger again.

—*Clancy Strock*

BEANS AGAIN? American soldiers cooked dinner on a GI stove at the foot of the World War I Memorial in Verdun, France. A sense of brotherhood and camaraderie helped many soldiers keep their spirits up during difficult times.

THE YANKS ARE COMING! After suffering months of devastating bombing in the German Blitz, Britons were thrilled to see American GIs "invade" their shores. Yvonne Kent, a "native Brit", says the English remain grateful to the Americans for their help to this day. "Without them," she says, "we would not have survived."

British Welcomed 'Yankee Invasion'

GREAT DAY in the morning! The Yanks are coming!

When the first Americans landed in Northern Ireland in January 1942, great cheers rang throughout Great Britain. The World War II "invasion" of the U.K. by 2 million American servicemen had begun!

The bad guys had practiced their goose-step for 5 long years, giving the whole world a super kick in the behind.

As a British citizen, I'd watched in the autumn of 1940 as valiant Royal Air Force fighter pilots won the Battle of Britain by the skin of their teeth. We suffered terrible casualties in bombings of our cities, and huge Royal Navy losses (the *HMS Hood* had three survivors out of a crew of 1,400). Now we feared being cut off from the outside world if Hitler invaded.

So when the GIs arrived, it was as if they'd offered an outstretched hand to the drowning. We greeted them happily. The quiet little kids were especially pleased to see them, hanging around the soldiers to ask, "Any gum, chum?" and then saying, "Ta", for "thank you". The soldiers were very generous with everyone, sharing food and cigarettes, too.

British servicemen rather resented those sweet-talking Yanks swiping their girls, though. Those freewheeling Americans felt we were fair game, and they were so cheeky!

They loved dancing to Glenn Miller's *In the Mood*, and they taught us

By Yvonne Kent
Middleburg Heights, Ohio

to jitterbug—a dance our older citizens considered "quite unruly". They also loved the sociable British pubs, but not the beer, which was served warm.

The GIs were told not to wave their money around, but that didn't stop them from doing it. Those on leave in London liked the Underground subway and Madame Tussaud's Wax Museum. They had their pictures taken with the pigeons in Trafalgar Square and next to the boarded-up statue of Eros in Piccadilly Circus.

The GIs had their own newspaper, *Stars and Stripes*. Ernie Pyle wrote about how the American pilots liked to listen to the RAF members talking to

---

"GIs' arrival was like an outstretched hand to the drowning..."

⊛

---

each other in the air over North Africa: "I say, old chap, there's a Jerry on your tail." The warned pilot's reply: "Quite so, quite so. Thanks very much, old man."

In 1943, I was hired by the London American Red Cross Headquarters as secretary/accountant for the Aeroclub at Middle Wallop. I was one of four women living on the American Air

Force base amid thousands of GIs. They talked with us and spent lots of time in the Aeroclub, showing photos of their wives, girlfriends, families and dogs. They were terribly homesick.

They worried about heavy casualties in their Air Force. They told us what Ernie Pyle had written about the stalemate in Italy, where men "had to be half beast to survive". They worried about the Marines in the terrible Pacific fighting. And they wanted to go home.

Liberated Europe

Finally, great things began to happen. On June 4, 1944, the Americans liberated Rome. Two days later, on a brilliant moonlit night, the long-awaited invasion of Europe began. The noise was indescribable! The sky was full of planes flying low over the English countryside. We stayed up all night watching. It was both wonderful and terrifying.

General Eisenhower's message to the troops had been "Godspeed", and they needed all the help they could get.

The invasion took hold on that 60-mile stretch of Normandy. Freedom for Europe was costly, and took longer than expected, but finally the war was over. At last, the GIs could go home.

I know the British people were, and still are, immensely grateful to their American allies, without whom we would not have survived. When the GIs left, they were greatly missed.

In April 1946, I left, too—to join the U.S. Army Air Force man I'd married.

Sub Rescued 58 Americans from Philippines

By Mary Sevilla
South Lake Tahoe, California

IN MARCH 1944, an American submarine, the *USS Angler*, was directed to Panay Island in the Philippines to rescue 58 American men, women and children who had eluded Japanese troops for several years. I was one of those children.

My family had lived a nomadic existence since December 1941. Our goal was simple: Elude the enemy by moving frequently from one remote area to another. After my father was killed, our survival often depended on the Filipino people, who befriended us by sharing food and shelter whenever they could.

News was scarce; we had little or no information about the war beyond our island. We did not know that General MacArthur's forces in Australia were planning an offensive to recapture the Philippines, nor that a growing network of guerrilla forces was involved.

All that changed in March 1944, when a small group of well-armed guerrillas located us. Their orders were to escort us to a safe place for the duration of the war. My mother, now a widow with four children, had no idea where we were going, but she knew this offer meant the difference between survival and possible capture by the enemy. We swiftly packed our meager

belongings and set out that same day.

Our trek across the island took 2 weeks. We followed our escorts through the jungles and over mountains, valleys and streams. Finally we arrived at a small camp where, to our astonishment, we met dozens of other Americans who also had eluded the enemy for years. We were all excited, but nervous and fearful we might still be caught. The camp was close to the provincial high-

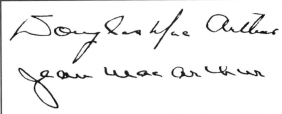

GEN. MacARTHUR and his wife signed Mary Sevilla's autograph book after the General's planning and Filipino guerrillas rescued her family.

way, and Japanese troops patrolled the area frequently.

At dusk the next day, several soldiers escorted us across the highway into coconut groves near the beach. They helped us board several outriggers. In darkness, we paddled out to the empty sea. Suddenly, a submarine surfaced

right next to us. The hatch opened silently and crew members urged us to board quickly and quietly. Within 15 minutes, all 58 of us were aboard, and the submarine prepared to submerge. We were stunned!

The commanding officer told us our destination was Darwin, Australia. The journey would take 11 to 12 days. *Angler* would travel under water during daylight hours, and we were told we might have difficulty breathing because of the lack of oxygen. To conserve oxygen, movement would be restricted.

Although fresh water had to be conserved, the meals were generous. Most of us had trouble readjusting to a rich diet. We hadn't tasted milk, much less butter, for years. What a miracle! We couldn't believe our good fortune.

When we arrived in Australia, the officers and crew lined up on deck to say farewell. Our gratitude to them would last a lifetime. From Darwin, we were flown by Army transport to Brisbane, where staff officers under MacArthur's command greeted us.

A few days later, Gen. MacArthur himself signed my autograph book, as did his wife. I still cherish that signature. He was the one who made it possible for 58 refugees to survive, despite the most difficult odds.✪

Ewing Galloway

Chaplains' Service Enriched Many Lives

By Howard Lee, Dallas, Texas

SOME OF THE most pleasant memories of my 3-1/2 years in Europe involve three chaplains who were assigned to our combat logistics headquarters. One was a Catholic priest we called "Padre", one was a Jewish rabbi named Joe, and the third was a Baptist minister named Steve.

The three lived and worked together in the field for more than a year after the invasion of northern France, working with front-line soldiers of all faiths. The Army gave each chaplain a kit that could be set up on the hood of a Jeep for Christian or Jewish services.

A few Bibles and Jewish books had been provided by congregations in the states, but there wasn't much else. They all improvised as necessary.

After Allied forces recaptured the French port of Cherbourg from the Germans, I was told a plush German naval officers' club had been found. The major prize was four truckloads of fancy cheese, canned sardines and the finest liquor available anywhere.

While I was distributing the loot back at headquarters, Padre said he wanted a single barrel of sweet red wine for "official business". The wine was repackaged and sent to the field for use in Christian communion and Jewish Passover services, courtesy of the German navy.

Another time, Padre said he needed some eggs in their shells for a special Jewish service. We ate Army-issue powdered eggs and hadn't seen a real egg in months. Padre and I spent several days in the surrounding farm towns, trading, buying and even "liberating" several dozen fresh eggs to send to the front. We also opened a local bakery to make the matzohs needed for the service.

Military Decorations?

A week later, Rabbi Joe asked for some crepe paper so he could put up decorations for our observance of Easter. He worked most of the Saturday night before to put them up, and we all thanked him.

In December 1944, German attacks caused heavy casualties, and the field hospitals were overloaded. Late one night, a call came from an aid station where a dying soldier was asking for a

FULL HOUSE greeted the Catholic priest who said Mass on the *Birmingham* before the ship was returned to active duty with the American fleet. Many servicemen say the military chaplains were among the war's unsung heroes.

priest to give him last rites. Padre and Steve had left for another hospital, so Joe went. The medic told me Joe performed the rites perfectly, and that young soldier died peacefully.

The next morning, I asked Padre if it was a problem to have a rabbi perform the last rites. He said Joe knew what to do, and he didn't intend to tell anybody about it until the war was over. "The bishop would throw a fit, and the Vatican would be upset," Padre said with a smile. "But the big man upstairs will understand."

These three chaplains were never promoted, and they received no medals or citations. But many of us will always remember them.✪

Savvy Sailor Knew 'Parts Is Parts'

AFTER THREE DAYS at an invasion site in Salerno, Italy, our assault transport, the *USS Samuel Chase,* started back to Algeria. That night the Luftwaffe found us and we underwent an intense raid. Just as the attack subsided, one of the 40mm guns malfunctioned. At daybreak, the gunner's mates discovered a broken part.

There was no replacement part to be found in Algeria; we'd have to wait until we got back to the States. In Bayonne, New Jersey, we were surprised to find we still couldn't locate the part.

The word went out all along the East Coast, but we kept getting the same response: No part.

Finally, a seaman who had observed this fiasco said, "I think I can find that part." In a most unmilitary way, he was given cash, a car and a driver. He returned within the hour.

"Did you find one?" he was asked.

"Yes."

"How much was it?"

"Five bucks," the sailor said, "so I bought four."

"Where on earth did you find them?"

"Montgomery Ward."

—*Russ Jacobs, Higginsville, Missouri*

Humorous Times Made Chaplain's Job Easier

I WAS PASTOR of the First Foursquare Church in Long Beach, California when the war broke out. Two years later, I was on my way to chaplain school at Harvard University.

I was assigned to a dormitory room with two other chaplains. One morning the school commandant entered our room for a surprise inspection. I was the first one to see him and immediately cried out, "Attention!"

One chaplain was dressing and had just started to pull up his pants. As he snapped to attention, his pants fell to the floor.

The colonel inspected the room without cracking a smile, then turned to leave, saying, "At ease, gentlemen." None of us will ever forget that morning!

When my training was completed, I went to Europe. I had my share of harrowing experiences, including some with an infantry division at the front, but the many humor-

FAUX PAS embarrassed Chaplain Howard Rusthoi when he met a French mayor.

ous moments helped keep things in balance.

Once I conducted a service for a group of soldiers in Laigle, France, and they told me about a chateau fire that had broken out a few nights before. A caretaker rode his bicycle to town to report the fire. Town officials sent another man back, on another bicycle, to see if a fire engine was needed.

The engine finally arrived an hour after the fire had started, and the firemen all had to shake hands and exchange greetings before going to work. They also wanted cigarettes from the soldiers first. What a way to fight a fire!

Another time, I was walking on the street in Dreux, France and saw the mayor approaching. When he tipped his hat to me, I wanted to be polite and greet him in French. To my horror, I said, "Bon jour, madam!"

The mayor stopped dead in his tracks, his mouth open. He muttered something in French that I couldn't understand (which was probably best), and I left as fast as I could without running.

—*Howard Rusthoi*
Alameda, California

Army Had Heart as Well as Purpose

By Donald Walters
Clifton Springs, New York

IN 1943, my Army unit was camped in a large olive orchard in a picturesque part of Sicily. Many small farms surrounded us, with winding paths leading to country cottages nestled against the hillsides. It was such a peaceful place that the war seemed very far away.

But the impact of the war was obvious. Most of the able-bodied men were gone, leaving behind only women, children and old men. The women made a little extra money by doing our laundry. (I still remember going to pick mine up and seeing a woman hanging homemade spaghetti on the clothesline to dry!)

The farms had no electricity, and the only local mode of transportation was donkey carts. I guessed the villagers here were living much as they had in the 1890s.

One Saturday afternoon, a young boy was traveling on a lane through our orchard to the main road. His donkey was groomed to perfection, complete with a flowered straw hat with ears poking through. The cart was beautifully painted and freshly washed, and the boy was dressed in his Sunday best, singing at the top of his voice.

Suddenly there was silence, then many voices. I went to see what had happened and found the donkey lying

in a puddle of water, and the boy crying his heart out.

Our unit carried a portable power generator, and the donkey had stepped on a cracked, wet wire and was killed.

Learned the Story

A member of our unit spoke fluent Italian, and we learned the boy, who was about 14, had been on his way to visit his girlfriend and take her for a ride. We also learned his beloved donkey was a very important part of his family's livelihood. The boy was heartsick at the thought of going home and telling Mama their donkey had died.

Our old sergeant immediately took over. "Okay, you guys," he said. "Are we gonna let this kid go home and tell his ma we killed their donkey? Or are we gonna do something about it?"

Before anyone had a chance to answer, he went on. "I'll tell you what we're gonna do. We're gonna dig down deep in our pockets. Then we're gonna take this kid and his donkey and his cart home and tell his ma we're sorry, and give her *at least* enough money to buy another animal. Now get moving."

I never found out how much we col-

lected, but I know it was more than enough to replace that beloved animal.

I was sad we had brought sorrow to that struggling family, but proud to know the Army had a heart as well as a purpose. ✪

A FAIR TRADE. GI Donald Walters traded cigarettes and candy with Italian villagers in exchange for an armful of melons and tomatoes.

Bugler's Ragtime Melody Was Music to Troops' Ears

IT WAS DAWN on a summer day in 1944 at the Seabees' Camp Endicott, Rhode Island, and I was a regimental bugler. As I stood at the flagpole, waiting to play *Reveille*, I saw a long line of men shuffling down the street. Their eyes were on the ground, their chins hung low on their chests and their shoulders drooped. These battle-weary heroes were what was left of some broken battalions returning from war. What could I do for them? What could anyone do?

I raised my hand slowly and turned on the PA system, then on impulse swung into the *Bugle Call Rag*. The men stopped. Then they clapped and cheered. Tears rolled down their cheeks. They were home!

Since no one complained and the popular tune was more fun to play than *Reveille*, I repeated it often.

A few weeks later, after another rendition of my not-by-the-book bugling, I did my about-face and found myself nose to nose with a highly respected admiral! As I snapped off my smartest salute, I wondered how fast I could dig a hole and pull it in behind me. Or would I spend the rest of the war in the brig?

But the admiral was smiling. "I heard about you," he said. "So I made a special trip from Washington just to hear you play. Keep it up. The men like it. It boosts their morale."

He certainly boosted *my* morale that day.   —*William Swoboda*
Battle Creek, Nebraska

Eruption Nearly Blew Their Cover

EIGHT OF US from the 138th Infantry Regiment were on outpost duty at Amak Island, a tiny hump in the Bering Sea. The unit that established the outpost had dug a 10-ft. by 12-ft. hole in search of drinking water, but never found any, so we used it for a garbage pit.

One morning we found the hole filled with snow. We continued throwing tin cans and trash on top of the snow, and quickly built up quite a mound. Two of the men decided to dig a hole under the snow cap, pour in airplane fuel, and light it so the snow would melt down and we'd have our garbage pit back in action.

They splashed on the fuel, allowing plenty of fumes to build up inside

REGIMENTAL BUGLER William Swoboda admits he didn't play "by the book". At this 1945 Memorial Day ceremony in Joliet, Illinois, he used a trumpet instead!

the pit. Then they tossed in a torch.

You guessed it—the contents of the pit blew sky-high, spewing several months' worth of garbage all over, and splattering our quonset hut.

Thank goodness the Japanese weren't flying over at that moment, because every one of us was out in the open, having a lot of fun policing up the area.   —*Edward Prokopf*
Shreveport, Louisiana

He 'Stacked the Deck' In Favor of the U.S.

AS A DRAFTSMAN for the signal corps, I spent 18 months developing radar at a deserted golf course in the swamps of Florida. I'll never forget the day we discovered our radar triangulation really worked.

A test plane suddenly disappeared from our scopes one afternoon and could not be picked up again. In a few minutes, we received word from our ground observers that the plane had crashed. Later, we learned the plane didn't really crash—it had landed in a swamp.

The pilot was using an old biplane with four gas tanks, and one of them had run out of fuel. He didn't realize all he needed to do was turn on another tank!

When the radar project was completed, I was transferred to the air base in Orlando, Florida as an illustrator. One of my most important tasks was "stacking" bomber formations, positioning each plane so that its bombs could be released without hitting other planes in the squadron.

I also had to position the planes to direct as much machine-gun firepower forward as possible. The German fighters had learned to fly head-on into our bomber formations, because most of our guns were not positioned forward. To remedy this, our bombardiers were later given machine guns.

It was a memorable day when our office heard that Hitler had lost a huge portion of his fighter planes in just a few hours. The bombardiers had picked off his planes before word of our new weaponry reached German headquarters.   —*Harry Brown Jr.*
Wyoming, Michigan

'Childhood Pal' Got Soldier Past Crisis

By Jean Baker, Weatherford, Texas

THE BALDWIN Locomotive Works turned out thousands of steam locomotives, and while they all looked alike, each had one distinctive feature—its whistle. No one whistle was like any other. Like the sound of a loved one's voice, you never quite forgot it, even across a span of many years.

One of those trains, Old Number 5, was part of even my earliest memories. It awoke me in the morning as it came pounding down the hill, rattling windows and shaking the house. About noon it repeated the performance on its return trip. It was as much a part of our daily lives as the sunrise. Old Number 5's beautiful, melancholy voice was part of my youth in Texas, synonymous with home, love, happiness and security.

My civilian life ended November 7, 1942, when I was called to active duty. I marched down to the railroad tracks with hundreds of other soldiers to take a train to Florida.

A string of coaches sat waiting, and there at the head of the line was Old Number 5, ready to take me on a sentimental journey through the only part of the world I had ever known. Each mile brought back memories. It was as if Old Number 5 was giving me one last look at a happy, carefree childhood, soon to be gone forever.

Off to Battle

After months of training, we eventually became the first Americans to land in occupied Europe. Historians have described the campaign that followed as the hardest-fought of the entire war.

We landed in Italy in September, but winter soon descended. The cold rains fell in torrents, turning the valleys into seas of mud. Every yard we gained was bought with the precious blood of young men just like me. Each of us wondered when we'd forfeit our own lives for a few yards of nameless clay.

The cruel winter seemed to last a lifetime, with death stalking us every moment. Every mountaintop, river and crossroad became a strong point to be wrested from the enemy, and beyond each strong point lay a stronger one. We were afraid and exhausted. For over 100 days we went without a hot meal, a change of clothes or a bath.

At last our division—what was left of it—was relieved. I spent my birthday at a rear area, where we'd rest and draw replacements. When we regained our strength, we'd go back into battle.

One night I was electrified by a sound that brought me bolt upright in bed. I could hear my heart pounding as I waited to hear that sound again. At last came the long, lonesome wail of a steam locomotive—not the shrill scream of an Italian engine, but the deep, full-throated call of a Western Baldwin.

My heart stood still. It wasn't just any old Western Baldwin, but Old Number... "No," I told myself. "It

---

"Why couldn't this be my old friend?"

★

---

couldn't be. My exhausted mind must be playing tricks on me."

Next morning, I didn't know what to make of the experience. I'd seen men with combat fatigue. Could it be happening to me?

I took a Jeep and drove in the direction the sound had come from. After a few miles, I came to an Allied marshalling yard with a number of switch engines. I parked alongside the road, walked to the tracks and sat down to watch. I was so homesick!

Then it happened. Down the tracks from Naples she came, dragging a string of boxcars. If it wasn't Old Number 5, it was her twin. Like me, she was wearing the olive drab of the U.S. Army, and

her gold-leaf lettering was gone, but it *had* to be her! I knew the Army had purchased a bunch of small steam locomotives to work European tracks. Why *couldn't* this be my old friend?

A Homesick Boy

When she drew alongside me and blew her whistle, I began to cry. Big, uncontrollable sobs shook me and tore at my heart. Suddenly I was a little boy again, scared and so very tired. I wanted my mama, and the feel of Daddy's hand on my shoulder. I cried for my wife and the son I'd hardly seen, for an unfair fate that had me born during the Depression and would now probably kill me in a far-off place, and for all the helpless people who were caught up in this dreadful war.

I have no idea how long I lay there. At last, control returned and I noticed, for the first time, tender shoots of green grass showing through the gray leaves. The long, cruel winter was over at last. *And I had survived.*

As I drove back to camp, I remembered a time when Mama was staying with a very sick relative. When she came home, she told Daddy the patient had passed the crisis. When I asked what that meant, she explained, "The worst is over. Now she will get well."

As I turned into the motor pool parking lot, I realized I had passed *my* crisis—and somehow I knew I would live. Although I'll never know for sure, I'll always believe it was Old Number 5 that triggered my outpouring of tears that day. I think she saved my sanity and maybe even my life.✪

LONESOME WHISTLE of a familiar steam locomotive moved one tired, homesick soldier to tears—and helped him realize that the worst days were behind him.

CASH BOXES. Clark Cowburn was in charge of disbursing boxes of "invasion currency" (left) to GIs in Normandy. At one point, Clark (lower left) stood guard over the entire $2 million under an apple tree in a French orchard!

rifle a dozen times, only to put it back on again. What if it was one of my own men? My hair was standing so far on end it could've lifted the hat off my head.

Just then, a big old black cow pressed her nose against me and I must have jumped 3 ft.! The sound had been nothing more than the cow eating grass.

—*Clark Cowburn*
Ulysses, Pennsylvania

Close Call Changed Pilot's Attitude About Flak Suits

ARMY AIR CORPS Lt. Frank Hathaway had little faith in flak suits or steel helmets. They were heavy and awkward—just more baggage to look after and carry. He was a fatalist: If you were meant to get hit, you would.

Frank was piloting our B-24 over enemy territory near the North Sea. Antiaircraft guns are very mobile, so their latest locations were not always on our maps. Suddenly, we were fired upon, and shrapnel hit the plane. It appeared to be minor.

Frank asked his co-pilot to relieve him, which was not unusual, because flying formation was hard physical work. I was the navigator, and from the nose of the plane I could see Frank's legs and the bottom of his seat. One look at the twisted metal told me his seat had been hit.

Over the intercom, I asked, "How bad are you hit, Frank?" No answer. I could see him exploring a hole in his flying suit, but didn't see any blood. Finally Frank said, "I'm not hit." The shrapnel had entered and exited his flying suit without even touching his winter underwear!

When we landed, Frank picked up the cushion that was part of the pilot's seat, and there lay a flak suit, placed there by some other pilot. After that, Frank never talked about flak suits or steel helmets, but he always wore them.

—*Ron Bradley, Annawan, Illinois*

Guarding Invasion Currency In France Had Him Cowed

I WAS ASSIGNED to the Army's Finance Department during the war. Around June 1, 1944 we received a truckload of suitcase-sized wooden boxes marked TOMCAT. It was invasion currency, for the coming invasion of Normandy, and all finance personnel were sworn to secrecy until we were to disburse that money. We shipped out for France early in July, dragging TOMCAT along with us.

Our first night in France found us in an apple orchard with about $2 million in invasion currency stacked under an apple tree. I decided to post a guard at dark, and took the first shift myself. It was the blackest night I ever saw, and lights of any kind were a no-no.

As I sat atop TOMCAT with my rifle, I heard what I thought was someone crawling toward me on the ground, but I couldn't see a thing.

I must have taken the safety off my

Chance Meeting Reunited GI Brothers in Germany

IN FEBRUARY 1945, my infantry division moved to the town of Hurtgen, Germany, which had been virtually destroyed by artillery fire. One day, a mechanic returned from another town about 6 miles away and said he'd seen my brother, Harold, with an engineering battalion there! I was dumbfounded, but eager to look him up.

As soon as I could get away, I raced to town in a Jeep and started looking for his work detail. I found Harold in a truck loaded with gravel, ready to start some road repairs. He was so excited to see me that I thought he might fall out of the truck! After we talked for a while, he got permission to come back to my battery for the afternoon.

Every now and then we'd just look at each other and shake our heads in amazement. With millions of American servicemen scattered around the globe, the chance of running into each other so far from home seemed unreal.

—*Richard Vantine*
Middleton, Massachusetts

REUNITED. Brothers Richard (left) and Harold Vantine never expected to run into each other overseas, but did, in Germany.

Ice Left Bomb Crew 'Up in the Air'

By James Mund, Bedford, Texas

IN 1944, our bomb squadron, based in southern Italy, was dispatched to bomb a German armament factory in Austria. As we approached the target in formation, the pilot told the bombardier to open the bomb bay doors. It couldn't be done. Our B-24 had taken off in rain, and as we gained altitude, the doors had frozen shut!

This presented a problem. We typically didn't carry enough fuel to give a heavy payload of bombs a round-trip to the target, then back to base. That left few options.

We could stay in formation and drop our bombs anyway, hoping that they would rip the doors open. But then the doors would flap in the 160-mph slipstream all the way home, making the plane slower, harder to fly and more fuel-hungry.

The only other possibility was to drop to lower altitude so the ice would thaw—not an attractive option over enemy territory, where a lone bomber would be easy prey for enemy fighters.

Our formation was already attracting antiaircraft fire, so the pilot decided not to travel all the way to the target area and rejoin the formation later on its way back. Unfortunately, we lost sight of our squadron.

We spotted another formation and flew toward it, but they were in the process of dropping their own bombs and were attracting heavy flak. We dropped out of that formation, too, heading south toward the Alps.

Heading for Home

Now our pilot just wanted to get out of enemy territory as fast as possible. "Pilot to navigator," he called. "Give me a heading home." Our navigator, who was on his first combat mission, did not answer.

"Pilot to navigator. GIVE ME A HEADING HOME!" Still no reply.

The exasperated pilot tried again. "Pilot to navigator. Do you know where in blazes we are?"

The reply came through loud and clear: "No, sir."

All we knew was that we were over the Alps. We zigzagged across northern Italy until we spotted the Piave River, which we knew emptied into the Adriatic Sea. *Now* the navigator could get a fix on our location!

Once over the Adriatic, we dropped to a lower altitude. The ice thawed, and we jettisoned our bombs into the open sea.

We were the last plane to return to base. The rest of the squadron sustained some flak damage, but there were no injuries—except for our navigator's bruised ego.✪

FROZEN SHUT. When B-24 Liberators took off in wet weather, their bomb bay doors often froze up—which complicated a bombing run for one crew over Italy!

Latrine Duty Really 'Burned Him Up!'

MY COMBAT unit was set up on a small island in the Pacific, and each day my pal, Collier, would maintain our latrine. Part of his routine was to pour a small amount of gasoline down into the two-holer and light a fire.

One day after pouring in a little more gas than usual, Collier found he had no matches. He left to look for some. While he was gone, a buddy of ours stepped inside to use the facility.

Sometime while he was in there our buddy emptied the live coals from his pipe down one of the outhouse holes.

When I heard the explosion, I thought the Japanese had scored a direct hit. Not only was our two-holer blown sky-high, but my buddy had to sleep on his stomach for quite a while—and at the mere mention of the name "Collier", he'd reach for his rifle!

—*James MacInnis*
Sault Ste. Marie, Michigan

South Pacific Soldiers Battled Monsoons, Mud

THE SOUTH PACIFIC may sound like a paradise, but those of us stationed there knew it had its drawbacks—namely monsoons, mud and mildew.

When the monsoon season started, we were in for a very uncomfortable 3 or 4 months. In addition to constantly slogging through the mud, which was everywhere, we had no way to dry out garments or shoes. Every man did his own laundry with a galvanized bucket and scrub brush, which was fine when clothes could be hung in the sun to dry. But during monsoon season, there was no sun for weeks on end. Anything that got wet, stayed wet.

We solved this problem by washing everything in 100-octane aviation fuel, which was highly refined and contained no lead. Clothing and bedding washed in it would dry quickly, with no odor, and no soap was needed. We even washed our mess kits in the stuff!

Mildew was another problem. Anything that wasn't used or worn daily would mildew, so we were always trying to scrub it away. And some species of fungus glowed in the dark—we could see it on the jungle floor on moonless nights. The same phosphorescence glowed on the coral walls of our bomb shelters. Such was our life in "paradise"!

—*N.B. Kell*
North Fort Myers, Florida

Soldier Cherished Moment Of Calm Amid War's Storm

AFTER THE Marines took Guadalcanal, U.S. forces began hopscotching north toward Japan. During one such "skip landing", we took Biak Island in Dutch New Guinea in a battle with little fanfare. We then were ordered into what was expected to be a major conflict at Wardo, 40 miles up the coast.

As it turned out, no enemy troops had been there. The natives told us the enemy was at Kinindi, 15 miles away. After our evening meal, the natives took one of our boys out for a boat ride. The boat returned as the sun was setting, with coconut palms swaying in the gentle breeze. I called out "Tobea", a native salutation. From all over the island, native men, women and children called back, "Tobea...Tobea...Tobea".

Later that evening, the islanders surprised us by singing Christmas carols in their native tongue. For the first time in my 26 months on New Guinea, beauty and calm had replaced conflict.

I turned to a fellow GI and said, "If I ever get home from this war, I'm going to build a cottage and call it Kinindi." And I did—in honor of the moment in August 1944 when the war stopped for one day.   —*F.W. Sawyer*
Winthrop, Massachusetts

His Shipboard Hobby Put Rings on 'Rosie's' Fingers

DURING MY STINT in the Navy, I learned how to make rings from U.S. quarters—something many did to pass the time at sea. This hobby kept me alert when I was alone on the midnight to 4 a.m. watch in the engine room!

To make a ring, I held the quarter between thumb and forefinger and slowly rotated it while pounding the outside edge with a tablespoon. It took quite a few hours of pounding to get the coin to look like a ring. The last step was the toughest—whittling out the center of the quarter with a penknife. The finished product looked like a shiny wedding band.

I sent a few rings to family members, but most went to "Rosie the Riveters" working on fighter planes at the General Fireproofing plant in Youngstown, Ohio. My cousin Dottie worked there, and after I sent her a ring, all her co-workers wanted one, too. I'll bet their rings still shine brightly!

—*Michael Lacivita, Youngstown, Ohio*

ENIWETOK ALL-STARS. This fast-pitch softball team composed of Navy men stationed on Eniwetok, the Marshall Islands, held the title of "all-stars" for 32 months. Richard Cronce of Voorheesville, New York (far left, back row) sent the photo. "Our pitcher, Harry James (second from right, back row), made as many as 17 strikeouts in one game," Richard recalls. "I was 18 and thought a guy 36 years old was too old to play. Boy, did I find out differently. Harry could hit, too!"

MASTER STRATEGIST. One soldier recalls that General Douglas MacArthur's clever tricks kept the enemy guessing about troop movements and numbers.

Gen. MacArthur's Guile Kept Enemy in the Dark

CAGEY GENERAL MacArthur had a few tricks up his sleeve for confounding the enemy. Early in the war, he had only one squadron of fighter-bombers. Each time that squadron landed, the planes' engine cowlings would be painted different colors as the bombers were being refueled and rearmed.

That way the Japanese thought the general had about six times as many planes as he actually had!

Some bombers that were used to attack Japan did not have tail gunners. But the Japanese never knew that. MacArthur had a black broomstick with a wide black strip attached to each plane's tail to mimic the movable tail guns.

The general also had a helicopter crew that located down planes, disassembled them and flew them back for repairs.
—*Harry Brown Jr.*
Wyoming, Michigan

Ernie Pyle Told Sailors He Foresaw His Own Death

ERNIE PYLE had a premonition that he was going to die while covering World War II. I know, because he told me—and several other sailors.

I met the award-winning war correspondent a short time before his death.

After he was killed by Japanese machine-gun fire on Okinawa, I wrote to my mother about our meeting:

"I suppose you've heard of the death of Ernie Pyle. I met him a little while back. He was a wonderful guy, Mom. He told us fellows who were shooting the breeze with him that he did not think he would come out of this war alive."

When the war ended, I felt lucky to have survived. But I couldn't help thinking of Ernie Pyle and so many others, wishing their luck had held out so they could go home, too.
—*Thomas Fusner, Fort Myers, Florida*

Bartering for Souvenirs Brought Tasty Reward

THE SPOILS of war made great souvenirs, and the front lines on Okinawa were great places to pick them up. We had plenty of room in our tanks to stash Japanese rifles, flags, pistols, swords and helmets.

U.S. naval vessels of all types were offshore, and many sailors made their way to shore to hunt for souvenirs. They quickly learned we tankers had plenty of booty, and that if they brought something to barter with they could return to their ship with a nice souvenir.

One day a sailor approached with a package and asked if we had an enemy rifle we'd like to trade. I just happened to have a Japanese sniper's rifle I'd recently pulled from an overrun gun emplacement. When I asked what he had to offer, he opened his package—a whole slab of smoked bacon!

I quickly jumped into my tank and grabbed that rifle! The sailor went away happy, and my crewmates and I enjoyed fried bacon for quite a few days.

—*Joseph Petti, Bayonne, New Jersey*

COURAGEOUS CORRESPONDENT Ernie Pyle (above) won a Pulitzer Prize for his reporting from the front. After he was killed by Japanese machine-gun fire, the 77th Infantry Division erected a monument in his honor (right) on Ie Shima, an island near Okinawa.

Artwork Sketched Out His Life as Pilot and POW

By George Procak
Phoenix, Arizona

I MET MY future wife in June 1942 at a USO barn dance in Newburgh, New York. On our first date, I asked her to marry me. Soon after we got married, I learned my application for the Aviation Cadet Corps had been accepted. In a few days, my new wife and I were parting at the ferry terminal with promises to write every day.

Like all pilots, I wanted to be like Lindbergh and fly over the Atlantic. Instead, I crossed on the "Lizzie", the converted *Queen Elizabeth* luxury liner. She carried at least 10,000 servicemen on that 5-day passage, and was unescorted, but that didn't matter—she could outrun anything afloat! I continued to send my wife letters and illustrated stories of my adventures.

My stay in England was short. I was shot down over Germany after only 2 months and became a prisoner of war.

As a POW, I was allowed to send only three letters and two postcards home each month. A Catholic priest assured me he could get my drawings and extra letters home through a secret pipeline, but I decided against it. There had just been an assassination attempt on Hitler, and there was so much turmoil that I didn't want to risk having my innocent drawings endanger the padre or me. I'd just sweat out the war and carry them home.

I continued writing and sketching as I listened to geese honking their way north, accompanied by the steady rumble of Russian guns to the east. Little did I know that they were only a few days away!

On May 1, 1945, the Russians arrived at our camp to liberate us. The tommy-gun-toting Russians rolled up in horse carriages and through an interpreter, told us we were free.

Then they gave us the option of tearing down the fences and destroying the guard towers ourselves, or we could wait for their tanks, which would simply run over them. It was something we were happy to do ourselves.

In about 20 minutes, with two or three guys pushing back and forth at each leg, all the towers came down, and down with them tumbled the power of the Third Reich.✪

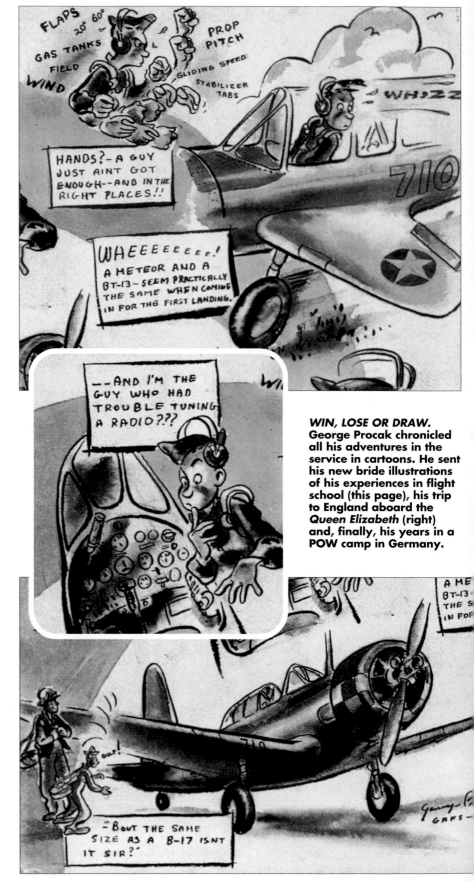

WIN, LOSE OR DRAW. George Procak chronicled all his adventures in the service in cartoons. He sent his new bride illustrations of his experiences in flight school (this page), his trip to England aboard the *Queen Elizabeth* (right) and, finally, his years in a POW camp in Germany.

ARMY MAGICIAN Ralph Lewis Jr. (above) often entertained troops who'd just returned from bombing missions. He brought many a smile to weary fliers, but grieved for those who never came back.

Emptiness Haunted Ramps of Planes That Never Returned

AS A SERGEANT in the Army Air Corps, Ralph Lewis Jr., now of Erlanger, Kentucky, supervised several entertainment troupes touring Army camps in Italy. His troupes often were on hand to lend moral support when bombers returned from battle missions. But as he told his parents later in this letter, it was the planes that never returned that made the biggest impression on him.

August 28, 1944

"Whenever I watched a group of bombers depart on a mission, I wished them Godspeed and all the luck in the world. The sight of those mighty planes made me feel proud to be an American. Sometimes we were there when the men came back, too, their planes riddled and their nerves on edge. But the worst was the silent emptiness of the ramps and crews for the planes that would never come back.

"During our shows, we'd look out into the audience and see faces that were angry and sad…angry at the enemy that had cost them their closest friends, and sad that those friends were now gone. Yet they were eager to be entertained. I felt good if I could make them forget, if only for a few fleeting hours, that tomorrow it might be their turn.

"These men know they must continue to fly and fight and even die—not for any reason an armchair patriot back home might give, but because they know the quicker they knock out the enemy, the sooner we can all go home.

"Newspaper accounts tell very little about a bombing mission. They simply say a tremendous force of planes blasted some enemy city, overcoming slight opposition and doing great damage.

"What they don't tell about is the shattered nerves of those who survived, and those who didn't make it back at all.

"They don't show you the dejected faces of the ground crew members whose planes don't return, or the way they keep scanning the sky, hoping that somehow, some way, their ship will struggle home."✪

Humor Helped Ease Soldiers' Fears

HUMOR WAS absolutely necessary during the war. As the weeks and months progressed, humor helped us overcome the fear, danger, sadness and sheer monotony.

One of my favorite stories involved a friend who served with the Seabees in the Far East. They were building a new runway, and my friend was operating a road grader with adjustable wheels that slanted to negotiate the slope of the terrain.

When a brand-new second lieutenant came to the work site and noticed the acute angle of the front wheels, he called my friend down from his seat.

"Private," he barked, "before you drive that machine any farther, get it into the maintenance area and get those front wheels straightened up!"

Another story involves an old friend who joined the service as a naive 17-year-old, completely ignorant of Army regulations. Standing at attention at his first formation, he was chewing gum, and the corporal in charge was quick to notice.

"Do you have enough of that gum for the rest of the men, private?" the corporal shouted.

"No, sir," my friend replied. "But I can run over to the PX and get more!"

—*Robert Miley*
Marion, Ohio

German Thanks 'GI Joe' Who Spared His Life

Dear GI Joe,

I don't know your name, but if Alsace-Lorraine, October 1944 and the U.S. Third Army ring a bell, read on.

We met at an intersection not far from Metz, France. It was before noon; you always attacked in the morning. I wanted to go southwest to my outfit, and your plans involved real estate to the east.

Someone on your side shot holes into my black Citroen and the staff car behind me, so I found myself in a grenade crater between a ditch and the pavement. It was crowded; there were three of us.

Your armored car stopped right above us, almost within reach. You were careless, GI Joe—you climbed on top of your vehicle to look for us, not even knowing we were huddled there below you.

As a comrade behind me was pulling on my Luger, you kept looking into the distance. Nothing there. You

---

"We met at an intersection near Metz, France..."

⭐

---

thought the three German soldiers picked up by your buddies were all there were, so you relaxed.

I was watching you trying to find a resting place for the butt of your carbine. After the second try, you instinctively looked down and saw us. Your carbine flew up. You looked pale and scared, like me. And with a quivering high-pitched voice, you screamed for us to reach for the sky. You could have pulled the trigger, or one of us could have beaten you to it.

What would it have mattered? A couple more wooden crosses, one with an olive-green helmet and one with an Iron Cross, to add to the thousands that marked the trail from Normandy to our intersection.

We only met for a very short time, but I think I know you—a combat soldier a few years my senior, drafted to do a job for your country, anxious to get it over with, willing to do what survival demanded. You had carried your buddies off the battlefield, but you hadn't lost your values. Now I thank my lucky stars that it was you standing on that armored car on that October day in 1944. I hope life has rewarded you.

With kind regards,

The German Soldier You Made a POW
—Alfred R. Wittig
Baldwin Park, California

P.S. The odds of your reading my letter are somewhat small, but if you do, you might be interested to know that I was a guest of your Army for nearly 2 years. In 1949, I brought my wife and our 20-month-old daughter to the United States. We are all U.S. citizens, involved in community affairs, conscientious voters and thankful for the opportunities given to us and the rewards our efforts have brought us. ✪

GERMAN POWS moved through chow line en route to work camps in the United States. One such POW, his life spared by an American GI, is now thankful to be a U.S. citizen.

He Was 'Texas Proud' of Lone Star State

THE TEXANS in our South Pacific Marine Corps squadron were proud of their state and liked to brag that it was the biggest and best of the 48. Everything in Texas was bigger, better and more colorful than anywhere else.

I was from Kansas, but became friends with several of these fun-loving characters. My friend Wesley was a typical Texan. We were issued one .45-caliber pistol each, but Wes somehow managed to obtain and wear two of them.

When I asked Wes why he wore two .45s, he replied, like a true Texan, "Because they don't make .50s, Ace." —*Carl Crumpton, Topeka, Kansas*

ROAD BUILDER. Army engineer Bill MacRobbie was stationed in Iran for over 2 years, supervising construction of highways and airports.

Brush with Bristles Drove Chief Hog Wild

MY ARMY ENGINEER company was stationed in Iran for 26 months during the war. My job was employing and paying several hundred Iranians to help build highways, airports and other facilities. The people were from a nomadic tribe headed by a likable chief named Khan.

One day Khan was in my tent office when the mail clerk brought me a package from my mother in New York. Khan asked if he might open the package, and I agreed. Among the cookies and other goodies was a clothes brush—my mother's response to my complaints about the desert's devastating dust storms. Khan soon raised a dust storm of his own, vigorously brushing his very dusty felt hat.

When Khan finished, he asked what the printed words on the brush handle said. When I told him they said, "100% Pure Hog Bristles", he slammed his hat to the floor, stomped on it and strode out without a word.

Too late, I realized I had insulted Khan's religious beliefs. Muslims are taught by the Koran that the hog is an unclean animal and must not be touched.

It was 3 or 4 days before I was able to apologize to Khan and regain his friendship. I vowed then and there to learn more about Moslem beliefs and customs!
—*Bill MacRobbie*
Coconut Creek, Florida

Commanding Officer Was Victim of His Own Orders

MY ARMY UNIT in Brisbane, Australia operated the signal air warning system on one floor of an office building. If there was ever a red alert, the guard on duty was under strict orders from the commanding officer to lock the building's doors at once. No one could leave or enter until the alert had passed.

No one really expected a red alert, but one afternoon the radar showed an aircraft without an IFF (Identification Friend or Foe) signal. The controlling officer on duty ordered the aircraft intercepted by Australian fighter planes. We were on red alert. The sirens sounded, and the guard closed and locked the doors.

Seconds later, someone began pounding on the door. "Let me in!" he shouted over and over. "Let me in!" The guard wouldn't budge.

When the Australian pilots identified the plane as one of our B-24s, the alert was lifted. The guard finally opened the door, and there stood our commanding officer, red-faced with anger. "I'll have you court-martialed!" he shouted at the guard.

"No, you won't," the officer in con-

HOMETOWN BUDDIES. Kenneth Kolb (right) was stunned to run into Russell Druckenmiller, a longtime pal from back home, in New Guinea.

trol replied. "He only acted on your specific order, and I think he should be commended!"

The rest of us thought it quite humorous that the CO was a victim of his own orders!
—*Kenneth Kolb*
Coplay, Pennsylvania

'Flying Cobra' Had Flying Tiger Baffled

MY BROTHER, Herschel Smith, was a member of the 14th Air Force's Flying Tigers squadron during the war. While Herschel was stationed in India, there was a sudden air raid and each man scrambled for his foxhole. Just as Herschel got settled in, he looked up to see a king cobra snake go flying overhead, right across the opening to his foxhole! Could he actually have seen such a thing, he wondered, or was he cracking up?

When the "all clear" sounded, Herschel ran to his buddy's foxhole to see if he was all right and ask if he'd seen the snake, too. He had.

"Well, Smith," his pal replied, "when I jumped into my foxhole, that snake was already here. I knew one of us had to leave, and it sure wasn't going to be me, so I just reached down and threw him out!"
—*Christine Hamilton*
Fort Worth, Texas

FLYING TIGERS. Herschel Smith (kneeling, on right) poses with buddies from the Air Force's famed Flying Tigers squadron in India.

Sandstorms Slammed Troops in North Africa

ONE OF THE toughest adversaries for troops fighting General Rommel in Egypt was sandstorms. Norman Schuth of Spencerport, New York shared this letter from his brother, D.H., who, with the rest of the 85th Fighter Squadron, weathered a vicious storm in 1943.

Still in the Middle East

January 3, 1943

"Dear Norman:

"Tonight started like any other night, and at 7 I retired to my warm, comfortable Army cot. I'd noticed a brisk wind earlier. Now, unable to sleep, I lay there trying to identify the noises made by things rattling in the tent.

"Around 10 o'clock there was a drizzling rain that stopped suddenly. That's when I first noticed the dry taste of the air. Dust—the worst thing in the desert—was starting to fly. We were in for another bad sandstorm. After checking the tent's ropes and stakes, I tied the front flap shut and went to bed.

"When I woke at midnight, the tent was being pulled and tugged by a mighty wind, and everything was covered with dust. After checking the ropes and stakes again, and plugging up holes with sweaters and jackets, I went back to bed—this time with a towel wrapped around my head. The sand sounded like hail rattling on a window. Above the howling wind, I heard someone pounding stakes. His tent must have broken loose in the darkness.

"The next morning, the wind and sand still were trying to tear my tent from the ground. When I moved to get up, a thin stream of sand ran to the floor from the folds of my blankets. I had to shake my clothes to identify them.

"After breakfast at the mess hall, I felt better. The food was gritty, but we ate it anyway. I filled my empty canteen and returned to my tent. It had weathered the storm, but others were leveled or had broken poles.

"Now it's 3:15 and there's still no sign of a letup. Twenty hours of continuous sand and wind! It must end sometime. Will finish this after it's blown itself out."

January 5

"About 4 p.m. I peeked outside. To my amazement, it was raining, and I was able to breathe fresh air. Except for the sand dunes piled up everywhere, one never would know we'd had a 2-day storm.

"It was dark when I washed off the last remains of the storm. I started up an oil fire and put on about 3 gallons of water for a hot bath. It was cold outside, but that was a minor detail.

"I went to bed feeling thankful for the last 2 days. Now I can really appreciate the good days we are sure to have in the future."✪

DESERT BATTLE. Troops stationed in the Middle East weren't fighting just the enemy. Sandstorms kept them pinned down for days. Fierce winds sandblasted their tents, snapping poles like matchsticks.

Archive Photos

Ewing Galloway

PROUD BATTLESHIPS made an imposing sight in fleet formation. One sailor believes the most distinguished of them all was the *Pennsylvania*. She was the only ship to take part in every amphibious battle in the Pacific, and fired more ammunition than any ship in history.

Sailor Recalls Years on *Pennsylvania* with Pride

I JOINED the Navy as a frightened country boy of 17 before the start of World War II. For the first 10 months, I was on an old destroyer, the *USS Welles*, in and around Panama Canal and Guantanamo Bay, Cuba. After that ship was turned over to the British Navy, I was transferred to the battleship *USS Pennsylvania* in Pearl Harbor.

I was on the top deck at 7:55 a.m. December 7, 1941 when I saw the Japanese bombers roar out of the overcast sky, and I raced to my battle station. The *Pennsylvania* was one of the first in the harbor to return fire, acting even before the call to general quarters was issued. After that attack, we served in a seven-battleship task force. We participated in campaigns in the Aleutian Islands, the South Pacific, Guam, and so many other islands I can no longer remember all their names.

Just before the war ended, a Japanese plane launched a torpedo that struck our ship, causing extensive damage. A

large steel plate was welded over the hole so the *Pennsylvania* could return to the states. She limped into the navy yard at Puget Sound, a crippled but proud ship.

From her first action at Pearl Harbor to the end of World War II, the *Pennsylvania* steamed almost 150,000 miles and fired more ammunition than any other ship in history. She was the only battleship to take part in every amphibious combat operation in the Pacific.

Although hit at Pearl Harbor and again at the very end of the war, the "Pennsy" had a career between those disasters so distinguished it'd make any man proud to number himself a member of her crew.

—Leslie Blair
Downey, California

He 'Held' Pal's $20 Across 6,000 Miles

IN 1945, I met a fellow soldier on a train. We'd grown up in the same town, attended the same high school and ended up in the same barracks in Boston

while waiting to ship out. One day my new friend had liberty and gave me $20 to hold for him so he wouldn't lose or spend it.

Two days later, my orders were posted and I said good-bye to my friend as I marched out. His $20 marched right out with me. I had forgotten it! Now what? I didn't know his assignment or serial number. My ship returned to Boston a week later, but by then my friend was gone.

Some time later, as our ship was on its way to Panama, I received a light message from an incoming ship: "Where's my $20?" I sent an answer, and my friend promised to catch up to me in Honolulu. When he sailed in, I hitched a ride on a mail boat to return his $20—several weeks and 6,000 miles later!

—Leonard Bulwicz
Whippany, New Jersey

They Made Ice Cream In Washing Machine!

OUR COMBAT unit lost all its equipment when our ship sunk, and we were moved to the South Pacific island Espiritu Santo. When the 1st Marine Regiment joined us for a rest and recreation break, we found they had plenty of equipment, including luxuries like washing machines.

We all longed for ice cream, so one night we swiped the Marines' washing machine to make some! We scrubbed it for a whole day, then filled it with a mixture of chocolate, dried milk and other ingredients. We pushed it into our freezer, turned that washer on and went to the movies.

When the movie was over, we retrieved the machine and ate every bite of that frozen mixture—even if it did carry the faint taste of dirty socks.

—*James MacInnis*
Sault Ste. Marie, Michigan

Sailor Quickly Learned Value of Fresh Water

AS A NAVY sailor, I really came to appreciate the importance of fresh water. We'd fill the ship's fresh-water tanks while in port, but whenever the supply ran low, we had to shower with salt water. It was so sticky we felt like we hadn't showered at all!

The ship was commissioned in July 1944 and the insides of the water tanks were freshly painted. Unfortunately, the paint hadn't dried completely before the tanks were filled, because for the whole 18 months I served on that ship, the water tasted like paint! I finally bought a gallon of Coca-Cola syrup and added a little to each cup of water to mask the taste.

—*Michael Lacivita*
Youngstown, Ohio

Ship's Mascot Made a Monkey Out of Skipper

MY MOTHER saved all my "Dear Mom" letters from the war, thinking I might enjoy reading them later. This excerpt is from a letter written aboard the destroyer *USS Bell*, somewhere in the South Pacific.

"The ship now has a mascot. One of the crew had the nerve to bring a monkey aboard. And it is a character. About all he lives on is chewing gum. He smells the gum before he unwraps it, chews until the flavor is gone, and then either spits the gum out or gets it gummed up in his tail.

"The other night they were showing movies, and in the middle of a dramatic and serious part the monkey put on a show of his own behind the screen. The light from an open hatchway was shining on him in such a way that all we could see was his silhouette jumping around and swinging in the doorway.

"I can't believe the monkey will be with us much longer. If he isn't killed first by accident I believe the captain will throw him overboard, as he isn't too pleased. The monkey got into a can of lye mixture, which is bad enough, but he also prowls the muzzles of the 5-inch guns.

"He was extremely lucky one of the signalmen, instead of the skipper, discovered his monkeyshines the other day. He got into the captain's cabin on the bridge and was scrubbing himself with the captain's toothbrush when the signalman found him. Everybody on the ship has heard about it except the skipper, and he won't be censoring this letter."

—*Lawrence Helsel*
Raytown, Missouri

Harold M. Lambert

SHIP, AHOY! Time could go slowly at sea, especially for new recruits. Some developed hobbies to pass the long hours. One crew even adopted a monkey, who promptly got in trouble by brushing his teeth with the captain's toothbrush!

Army Cook Kept His Troops Well Fed

ARMY COOK Mel Peters checks evening chow. Everything was made in huge quantities, even Mel's cookbook (below right)—10 by 13 in.!

By Mel Peters, Tomahawk, Wisconsin

BASIC TRAINING at Camp Davis, North Carolina was over, and I was waiting for my orders to ship out. Then one of the cooks in the training unit got sick, and I was asked if I wanted to give that job a try.

I did, I liked it and stayed for 18 months, feeding the "90-day wonders", as the men coming out of officers' training were called.

Next I was sent to Camp Hulen in Texas and started training with an antiaircraft unit. I was just about to ship out when an ordnance company needed a cook. I shipped out with them instead, cooking in a boxcar on the way to Boston Harbor, then working in the butcher shop in the hold of our ship.

When we finally landed in France, the beach had been reduced to several inches of mud. Our first night, we put our raincoats down in the mud and pitched pup tents on top of them. Luckily, we were on field rations, so I didn't have to try to cook there!

We finally set up shop in Reims, France, where I cooked for soldiers who were repairing heavy automotive equipment. We were bombed by the Germans during the Battle of the Bulge, and it was an anxious time. Some of the German prisoners worked with us in the kitchen, and they occasionally got

cocky, so we had to wear sidearms while we cooked.

We worked from a 96-page Army cookbook that included recipes for everything from sweet rolls and cherry pie to pork chops and fried chicken—all in quantities to serve 100 hungry soldiers. Here are a couple of recipes from that book.

WHITE BREAD

      15 pounds flour
   1/3 cake yeast
      7 mess spoons salt
      1 pound sugar
      1 pound lard
      1 14-ounce can evaporated milk
      4 No. 56 (quart) dippers water

Dissolve all ingredients except flour and lard in water. Add flour and lard and mix well. When mixed, dough should be smooth and elastic. A 10-minute mixing period is required. Keep dough out of drafts. Allow to stand for 2 hours until fully risen. Punch well and allow to stand 20 minutes. Cut into loaves of desired size; mould them evenly and place in greased pans. Proof (let rise) to double volume. After proofing, bake at 425°, approximately 30 to 40 minutes, depending on loaf size. Makes about 20 loaves.

DEEP-FAT FRIED CHICKEN

      50 chickens,
         weighing about
         2 lbs. each
   Salt and pepper to taste
   Flour
   Egg and milk dipping
         mixture
      20 eggs
         1 No. 56
            (quart) dipper
            evaporated milk
         1 No. 56 (quart)
            dipper water
   Bread crumbs

Disjoint and wash chicken. Salt and pepper well. Roll in flour. Dip in egg and milk mixture. Cover with bread crumbs. Fry in deep lard starting at 350°, and allowing temperature to drop to 325°. Fry for 15 to 20 minutes. Note: Unless very small young chickens are used, it

is best to precook by simmering in water until tender.

HAM CROQUETTES

      5 pounds ham, cooked and
         chopped fine
      3 mess spoons salt
      2 mess spoons pepper
      1 mess spoon mace
         (optional)
   1/2 cup chopped parsley
         (optional)
      2 pounds lard
      30 eggs
      5 pounds onions, chopped fine
      2 pounds flour
      5 No. 56 (quart) dippers ham
         stock
      5 pounds bread crumbs
   Eggs and milk mixture
      10 eggs
         1 14-ounce can milk
         1 14-ounce can water

Season ham with salt and pepper. Fry onions in lard until tender and brown. Mix in flour. Add stock and cook a few minutes. Remove from fire and mix in eggs and bread crumbs. Add chopped ham and refrigerate until ready to use. When mixture is cold, shape into croquettes. Roll in flour. Dip in egg and milk mixture. Roll in crumbs. Fry in deep lard at 350°, until brown, about 12 to 15 minutes.

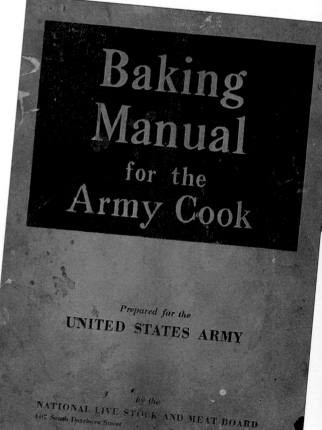

Baking Manual for the Army Cook

Prepared for the
UNITED STATES ARMY

by the
NATIONAL LIVE STOCK AND MEAT BOARD
407 South Dearborn Street
Chicago, Illinois

CHRISTMAS SPIRIT became more important than ever to the men and women who were serving overseas. No matter where they were stationed, most found some way to make the holiday memorable. One GI who spent Christmas in England recalls a dance in a huge ballroom that "looked like an old-fashioned English postcard".

GIs in England Planned Christmas to Remember

By Charles Bodnar
Bergenfield, New Jersey

AS CHRISTMAS approached, every American serviceman in Britain felt the same: We were all looking forward to the yuletide season with childlike anticipation.

Our company was given permission to have a Christmas party in the ballroom of Northington Grange. Truckloads of holly and fir boughs were gathered and hung on the walls. An 8-ft. Christmas tree lit up one corner, decorated with nuts, hard candies, apples, oranges, pears and other edibles, some of them wrapped in colored paper. The room looked like an old-fashioned English postcard come to life.

Logs were placed in the massive fireplace, and a four-piece unit from our regimental band provided music. The kitchen prepared a spread of cheese, roast ham, potato salad—and the inevitable dish of frankfurters and beans.

Each man donated some or all of his goody package from home. We had cookies, glazed fruit, pound cakes, chocolates, hard candies and assorted nuts—all worth at least a month's ration stamps.

We invited the girls from the Army Territorial Service, similar to the U.S. Army's WACs unit, to join us at the party. American and British military police accompanied them, and some of our company officers served as chaperons. When they arrived, a fire was

"Each man donated some of his goody package from home..."

crackling in the 8-ft. hearth as the band played *We Wish You a Merry Christmas*.

Dance and conversation partners were chosen with little hesitation. The dancing started with a slow waltz, but the party warmed up as jitterbugging

and the hokey-pokey took over.

Our guests were thrilled with the party and decorations, but the food really was the main attraction. Hard candy, chocolates and tropical fruits were almost nonexistent in Great Britain during the war.

When the band finally struck up *Till We Meet Again*, almost everyone hummed along with deep regret that the evening was ending. Many dates were promised for the week after the holiday. We helped the girls back onto their transports amid shouts, laughter and waving as the vehicles pulled away into the darkness.

The party had lasted only 5 hours, but all our efforts were worth it. The memories of that night would stay with us forever when we left Britain.✪

'Germans Across the River Sang to Us...'

AS CHRISTMAS approached in 1944, my infantry regiment was spearheading the Battle of the Bulge. We didn't hear from home for 5 to 6 weeks at a time, and we had nothing but K-rations and C-rations to eat.

We spent Christmas Eve and Christmas Day 1944 sitting on the bank of the Ruhr River, and turkey sandwiches were brought up to us. To our surprise, as we began eating, the Germans across the river began singing *Jingle Bells* to us.

—Elmer Bishard, Cambridge, Ohio

'I Spent Christmas on the Siegfried Line'

By Norman Wood
South Hamilton, Massachusetts

I SAW MONTHS of front-line combat duty as an Army infantryman in Europe during the war. But one morning stands out in my mind above all the rest.

It was Christmas Day 1944, and my outfit had flushed the Nazis out of a small town in Alsace-Lorraine only 2 days before. We were dug into a field skirting the town, just 1,000 yds. from the Rhine River and the infamous Siegfried Line.

I climbed from my field foxhole and headed for my post in town. It was a snowy morning with lead-gray skies, and I buttoned the top button of my heavy overcoat so the wind-blown snow wouldn't get down my neck.

It had been daylight for nearly 2 hours as I walked toward the village, yet no smoke rose from the battered chimneys and there was no sign of activity. No gleeful cries of children greeted this morning...could it really be Christmas? Could war kill the spirit as well as the body?

Felt Lonely and Homesick

"Merry Christmas" seemed to be a hollow phrase as I trudged alone through the desolate village. The narrow, snow-drifted streets were free of footprints, and the drifts seemed to seal the doors of the houses tight. Except for irregular gusts of wind, there was no sound in the town. It was easy to feel sorry for myself, spending Christmas Day in what amounted to a deserted heap of bomb rubble.

From the middle of the street, I glanced through the frosted windows of the houses I was passing. I halted abruptly at what seemed to be an odd sight in the midst of so much destruction.

I saw a Christmas tree fully decorated, and around it were two women and three little children. One of the women noticed me, so she raised the window and invited me inside.

Though the house wasn't warm, it did provide shelter from the icy wind and blowing snow...and the sight of that Christmas tree warmed me from the inside out. One of the women offered me cookies and a hot drink, which I thankfully accepted.

"Today is Christmas," she said. "We are very happy you have driven the *Boche* from our peaceful town, and we are thanking God on this day. Only a few hours ago they were all around us, but since then we have decorated a tree and made some cakes. This is surely a merry Christmas for us.

"The thankful people of our little town are asking you Americans to please accept these baskets of fruit and nuts so that your Christmas will be happy, too."

Gifts of Gratitude

There, in the corner, were some bushels of apples and pears and nearly a bushel of nuts. Each villager had contributed what little he or she could.

When I left that tiny house to get to my post, I thought deeply about those kind people. By all physical signs they had seemed crushed and beaten. Their homes were torn apart, their food supply was nearly depleted, and they had been subjected to Nazi discipline and hate. Yet they still cherished the spirit of Christmas and humbly gave their thanks to God.

The streets no longer looked desolate and unfamiliar to me. They were part of a quaint village that suddenly seemed so very much alive. I realized then that this December 25 would be the most gratifying Christmas Day of my life. War did not have the power to dim the beauty and meaning of this holy day. ✪

GIFT RECIPIENTS. This Army outfit had its Christmas holiday brightened by villagers' gifts. Writer Norman Wood is third from left in back row.

'Lucky' Troops Celebrated Christmas in New Delhi

MY FIRST CHRISTMAS overseas was in New Delhi, India, where I was stationed with the Air Force's photo unit. I considered myself lucky; unlike those in forward areas, we had the supplies and facilities for a real celebration.

On Christmas Eve, the building was decorated with lights, trees and flags. The weather was warm and beautiful, so we gathered outside to sing carols and listen to the chaplain speak. Hindus and Moslems, some of them on camels, crowded around us to watch.

After church the next day, I enjoyed an excellent roast goose dinner. The Army cooks did a good job! That afternoon, Uncle Sam came through again, delivering Christmas packages from home—something we hadn't expected until February. The cards and letters reminded us that the world was a pretty fine place after all. —*R.D. Lichty, Vacaville, California*

Christmas Tree Provided Poignant Reminders of Home

IN 1944, I was serving on a Coast Guard patrol frigate off the coast of Newfoundland. It was difficult duty—we lost both men and equipment in terrible storms, and sometimes were pounded by heavy seas for a month at a time. On the worst days, we had to tie ourselves on deck so we didn't wash overboard, and no one got any sleep.

We knew we'd be spending the holidays on the ship, so when we put ashore for fresh water and food, we tramped into the hills of Newfoundland and brought back a stunted pine tree.

The executive officer gave us permission to put it on the mess deck. We suspended it overhead; the seas were too rough for it to stay put any other way.

We returned to submarine patrol, and as Christmas drew closer, more and more of our 300-plus crew members would stop to admire our tree. As the waves tossed our ship, the pine boughs would wave up and down like flapping arms.

To make the tree more festive, a cook contributed a dozen onions, which we hung as though they were pretty bulbs. We cut out ornaments from white paper and pasted them to the boughs, then used wires to hang a few Christmas cards.

From December 23 until Christmas, I didn't see a single man who wasn't misty-eyed. Silent groups gathered around that tree covered with onions and paper, listening to holiday music on the public-address system. Some were so overcome by emotion that they left for the privacy of their bunks.

There hasn't been a Christmas since that I haven't thought of those lonely days on the North Atlantic...and that tree full of bobbing onions.

—Richard Paugh
Columbus, Ohio

HEADIN' HOME! A U.S. Navy transport like this one carried Prentiss Johnson on the first leg of his Christmas journey back home.

9,000-Mile Journey Took Him Home for the Holidays

By Prentiss Johnson
Omaha, Nebraska

AFTER 18 months of crisscrossing the globe on a troop ship, we all began hoping our next orders might take us home. It was well into December. Wouldn't it be wonderful to spend this Christmas at home?

Just as we resigned ourselves to reality and started thinking "Maybe next year", we heard a click on the PA and our captain's voice. "Hold onto your hats, men!" he yelled. "We're headed for the States!" He was just as eager as we were to get home.

My train arrived in Omaha, Nebraska on Christmas Eve, and I found my hometown covered with a foot of new snow. I gave a cab driver directions to our home north of town, hoping he could get through the drifts. The farther we got from downtown, the less traffic we saw. Finally, about 3/4 of a mile from home, the tire tracks we'd been following disappeared. The driver stopped and said, "This is it, buddy. You'll have to hoof it from here."

Dressed in a summer uniform and low oxfords, I started trudging through the snow. The closer I got, the harder my heart pounded. Almost home!

At last I crossed our yard and stepped onto the porch, where I could see the lighted Christmas tree in the living room. I had traveled 9,000 miles to get home, and now I was afraid to knock on the door! My family thought I was in the Philippines, and I knew there'd be tears when that door opened.

I stood on the porch in the softly falling snow and watched everyone come into the living room, one at a time, to begin opening gifts. I was shaking when I finally knocked, watching as they all turned their heads to see who could be out on a night like this.

The gift-opening was delayed another hour or two, and for me, this was a night of miracles.✪

NOT SPAM AGAIN! These GIs named their camp in honor of the canned meat they ate so often. Since Spam needed no refrigeration, it was the perfect fighting man's food. About 100 million lbs. of Spam was shipped to feed Allied troops.

Creative Cookery Turned Spam into Holiday Feast

Editor's note: This story, submitted by David Dahlberg of St. Louis Park, Minnesota, originally appeared in the 8th Air Force News. The author is Harry Guinther.

I WAS IN our local supermarket when I realized I'd been standing in the same spot for some time, staring fixedly at an item on the shelf. Seeing it again after all these years brought back a vivid memory. It was no longer the 1990s, but Christmas Day 1944.

I was a prisoner of war in Germany, and my roommate Tony was particularly good at creating exotic dishes from unlikely ingredients. Several days before Christmas, we decided to make a Spam loaf for our holiday dinner.

We carefully fashioned a very effective stovetop oven from flattened powdered-milk cans, being sure to put the shiny sides on the inside of the oven so paint fumes didn't "season" our food.

Tony used orange marmalade, provided by the British Red Cross, to make the glaze. Two cigarettes slipped to a German guard produced a small amount of brown sugar. The guard, knowing

"We made Spam loaf for our Christmas dinner..."

what we were up to, surprised us by throwing in six cloves, too.

So far, none of Tony's preparations were that unusual, so I waited to see what innovative twist he'd use to make this dish special. Imagine my surprise when he unwrapped several sticks of Doublemint gum and swabbed the

Spam loaf with the powdered side of the foil wrappers! What a genius! It was a Christmas dinner I'll never forget.

I could almost taste that dish again as I stood there contemplating the supermarket's Spam display. I slipped a can in my cart and told my wife I'd make that night's dinner.

She was curious but doubtful as she watched me re-create Tony's recipe. In fact, she was watching me so closely that I couldn't bring myself to swab the Spam with the gum wrappers!

I've often heard that Mom's apple pie isn't really as good as we remember it. Such was the case with my version of Tony's Christmas Spam. Maybe it would have tasted better if it had been Christmas and the house temperature was 45°. I know it would've been better if we'd been hungrier, and maybe, if there had been that added hint of mint.

★ ★ ★ ★ ★ ★ ★ ★ ★ ★

CHAPTER SEVEN

Mail
Call!

Mail Call!

March 22, 1945
Leyte, Philippine Islands

Dear Mom and Dad,
  It's been nearly 9 weeks since I've heard from you. Every day at mail call I keep waiting to hear my name called, but no such luck. I'm beginning to wonder if I gave you the wrong APO number. Or is something wrong at home? Mail is very irregular over here, and I marvel that it finds us at all, considering how many men and women are scattered all over the world. Still, I can't help but start worrying when there's such a long silence. Are you sick? Has something bad happened?

  P.S.: Since writing the above we had afternoon mail call. Still no letters, but your Christmas presents arrived! I notice that you mailed them in early November, nearly 5 months ago. So I guess I know why I haven't heard from you in a while.

Highlight of the Day

Mail call. No, make that, MAIL CALL! Whether you were still in the United States or on a ship or on foreign soil, mail call was the major event of the day.

Mail call was just like Christmas morning—except that you didn't know if Santa had come until your name was called. More often than not it wasn't.

Mail seemed to arrive in bunches, or not at all. You'd go for days without a letter, and then your name would be called a dozen times. You'd hurry back to your bunk and sit there with the letters in your lap, like a squirrel with a hoard of fine acorns.

The first job was to arrange everything by date, reading the oldest letters first. This stack had letters from the wife or sweetheart, the next stack from Mom and Dad and Sis, and the third stack was from aunts, uncles and buddies back in the hometown.

Letters with pictures were a special treasure. Most people didn't realize how much you ached for pictures of your home, your dog, the family cat, your parents, even your kid sister. Snapshots were your reassurance that the things and the people you loved were still there, and just the way you remembered them.

Here at home, "mail call" was the daily visit by the postman. Our RFD carrier always blew his car horn so Mom and Dad would know that there was a letter in the mailbox from me. That sent Dad scurrying down the lane a bit faster than usual, with Mom waiting impatiently on the front porch.

Like most servicemen, I had worked out a "code" before going overseas, to let Mom and Dad know where I was. Of course, there were only three or four ways to do it (first letter of the first word in each paragraph, for example) and the censors knew all of them. So much for outsmarting the system.

In the service or at home, mail provided magic moments for us all. The soldier or sailor or Marine could, for a few minutes, go back home. He could smell cookies baking in the oven, hear his mother's voice, feel the comfort of his sweetheart's arms.

And here at home, the most important thing was not so much what the letter said, but the fact that it meant a loved one still was safe from harm.

—*Clancy Strock*

NOTHING MADE a serviceman's day like a letter from home. Soldiers savored even the tiniest tidbits of news from family and friends. Each letter, no matter how brief, was like a precious gift. It was a reminder that no matter how far from home you were, you hadn't been forgotten.

"ANY MAIL FOR ME?" Mail call on Navy warships was the highlight of the week for most sailors. They huddled close as mail was handed out, eagerly awaiting news from home.

Mail Gave Soldiers 'a Reason to Go on'

By Marcel Langlois
Tucson, Arizona

RECEIVING MAIL from home was the most important event in a soldier's life, especially if he was overseas. A letter from home boosted morale and gave the fighting man a reason to go on.

Despite Uncle Sam's best efforts, though, there were days when the mail never reached our unit. The accompanying photo shows my feelings of sadness when we got no mail, May 12, 1946, on Okinawa. We had landed there months before, but by this time the island was calm, and mail was the preoccupation of every GI there.

After the war ended, the Army found something else for us to do, so I was assigned to work as a stevedore in the Port of Naha. I had been an infantryman and knew nothing about unloading barges, but that was my new job.

The average workday was 12 hours,

SAD SACK. Marcel Langlois' sign explained his melancholy mood in this photo he sent home.

7 days a week. After a hard day's work at the docks, I would came back to camp to "enjoy" a cold shower followed by a cold meal of Spam and reconstituted potatoes. The only thing that made it all bearable was finding a letter from home.

Reading a letter took priority over eating, working or sleeping. And if the letter was from my wife, it made my day complete. It was enough to make me forget the 12-hour workdays, the cold showers, even the cold meals. The news wasn't always good. Sometimes the kids had misbehaved or gotten sick or hurt themselves, but good or bad, it was news from home—and it was welcome.

Before going to bed, I'd answer my wife's letter, telling her how much I loved her and the kids, and how much I wanted to be with them. I'd be lonesome and tired, but happy, able to get a good night's sleep, and know that I'd be able to face another day.✪

First V-Mail Letter Filled Mom with Fear

By Rose Lacquement, Quincy, Illinois

IT HAD BEEN weeks since we'd heard from my brother Bill. He'd been very good about writing—until he was assigned to a submarine tender. Worry became Mama's constant companion.

One day our mail included a small envelope about the size of a thank-you note. It looked strange, its edges tinged a murky gray, as though it had survived a fire. My parents' hand-printed name and address showed

V-MAIL. Army Cpl. Robert Zorge (above) sent V-Mail (left). His sister, Sally Conrad of Glenview, Illinois, shared photo and letter.

through a tiny window on the front.

Convinced that letter edged in black portended bad news, Mama wouldn't even open the envelope. Instead, she sent me over to fetch our neighbor, Maud. Maud took a deep breath, unsealed the envelope and began to read, "Dear Mom, Dad and kids..."

It was a letter from Bill! Mama's fearful expression slowly changed to a grin, then a broad smile and, finally, tears of joy and relief.

We soon became familiar with the new V-Mail, devised by the government to accommodate the huge volume of mail. It consisted of a single sheet of paper, 8-1/2 by 11 in., with the addressee's name and address printed at the top, then the sender's and then the message.

The finished letter was folded to make its own envelope. After it was posted, censored and microfilmed, it was somehow reduced to about half its original size, requiring only half the cargo space of ordinary letters.

Mama's reaction to that first V-Mail letter reminded me of President Roosevelt's words, "We have nothing to fear but fear itself." We certainly had nothing to fear from V-Mail!✪

Wife's Recorded Message Made Many Long for Home

By Charles Swanson
Coloma, Michigan

WHEN I WAS in the Army, my wife sent a recording of her voice at Christmastime. I couldn't find a record player, so in desperation I had it played over the public-address system. It was a lit-tle embarrassing to have the whole company hear it, but it made everyone long for home. Here's some of what she said:

"Merry Christmas, honey. Surprised? I'm so glad I have a chance to say hello to you this way on our first Christmas apart. Remember our first Christmas together? We were planning to be mar-ried. You were busy building our little home. We went to Mass together and dreamed of the Christmases we'd spend together in our own home.

"Little did we know we'd spend our next one in a little apartment in Oklahoma, with *Taps* and reveille instead of Christmas carols. But we'd made new friends, we were happy just to be together, and we had the best present of all on the way.

"Then last Christmas, God was good again and we were still together, but there were three of us now. Oh, we had fun! Little Lynne's face when we lighted the tree was a joy in itself.

"About our little girl…she has blonde curls, her daddy's bright blue eyes and sweet mouth, and a complexion anyone would envy. She is just big enough to fill my heart and strong enough to help Mommy bear this ache of loneliness.

"I never knew how much I'd need her while you were gone. Sometimes when I'm lonesome and a tear falls, she puts her little arms around my neck as if to say, 'Never mind, Mommy, I'm here.' Her dearest treasure is her daddy's picture. It's all marked with tiny hand prints, and the glass is always cloudy from so much loving and kissing.

"I'm hoping you'll be listening to this on Christmas Eve, somewhere over there, your heart full of hope, faith and courage, knowing each day will bring that next Christmas together 1 day nearer. Lynne and I are going to Mass, praying for that tomorrow and offering our communion—not selfishly, but for all the daddies in the world to come home."

Wife Needed Two Boxes to Send His Shoes Overseas

ONE LAUGH WE had during the war was over a package I sent to my husband in Newfoundland.

He had asked me to send a pair of his favorite shoes, but his feet were so big that only one shoe would fit in the size of box we were permitted to send. So I used two boxes, one for each shoe, and then stuffed some goodies around them.

When I got to the post office, I was told I could send only one box. After much explaining and entreating, both boxes were accepted. They went out together. How-

ever, they didn't arrive at the same time.

When my husband got the first box, he was more interested in the goodies than his shoes. After he checked over all the "extras", he turned his attention to the shoes, but, of course, found only one. He set about looking under his bed because he thought he'd somehow lost it.

After some time, he realized only one was sent, and he thought I'd flipped my lid! Fortunately, the second box arrived a few days later and my reputation was saved.
—*Ruth Atchison, Winter Haven, Florida*

Archive Photos

Wife of MIA Kept Writing, and Hoping, Day After Day

FAITHFUL WIFE Marcella Sedlak wrote to her husband, Joe, every day, even after he had been reported missing in action.

By Marcella Sedlak
Hennessey, Oklahoma

MY HIGH SCHOOL sweetheart enlisted in 1942, and I wrote to him every day. In 1944 he came home on furlough and we were married. When he returned to his base, I kept writing.

His letters seemed to come in bunches. They were marked "FREE" in the corner of each envelope instead of a stamp…servicemen overseas didn't have to pay for stamps.

When my husband was shipped to Italy as a turret gunner in September 1944, his letters often were cut up by a censor. So much of what they did each day couldn't be talked about.

Before long, his letters stopped coming. Then came a telegram saying he was missing in action over Yugoslavia. That terrible day will be etched in my memory forever.

I never lost hope for his safe return, and kept sending him letters every day. Eventually my letters started coming back to me, marked "Missing in Action". Then the Christmas boxes I'd sent him came back, crushed and stamped the same way. I felt so empty, but I kept on writing as if nothing had happened.

Finally, in January 1945, the mailman delivered a letter from my husband. The Army Air Force had managed to secretly move him and many other boys back to their base in Italy! That letter is the greatest I've ever received, and I still have it to cherish after all these years. ✪

Prayers Brought All Five Sons Safely Back Home

By Ray Ruby, Farmington, Missouri

WITH FIVE SONS serving overseas during the war, my mom became a dedicated letter-writer. Her letters, and those from other loved ones, were our only contact with home, so mail call was always greeted with great hopes and expectations.

I was on a munitions ship in the merchant marine, and our mail never seemed to catch up with us. When we were bound for India by way of the South Pacific, we asked about our mail at every port. The answer was always the same: "No mail for your ship. Probably at your next port of call."

Nearly 7 months had passed without mail when we finally anchored in the Mariana Islands. When we learned the port held mail for our ship, what anticipation we all felt! We lowered a lifeboat, taking a number of sacks to carry back the great bundles of mail that must surely be waiting. Unfortunately, one small sack would have been enough.

As the mail was distributed, I waited and waited, but my name was not called. I felt a great heaviness in my chest. Finally, with only a few letters remaining, my name was called. It was a letter from Mom! Now I would know whether all my brothers were safe.

I took the letter to my bunk and sat down to read the news. My hands trembled as I slit open the envelope…and…I could hardly believe what I saw. There was *no letter* in the envelope. After 7 months!

I felt a hard lump in my throat and a great pain in my heart. I turned the envelope over and over, not wanting to accept the fact that it was empty. Never in all my time in the service had I felt so alone.

Several weeks later, most of our mail caught up with us, but I never learned what had happened to that first letter until I got back home. Mom had written letters to all five sons, but accidentally placed my letter in an envelope addressed to my brother Leonard. Then she sealed and mailed the five envelopes.

I'm certain it was Mom's prayers and those of loved ones that brought all five of us home safely. Even when that one

"KEEP 'EM FLYING"
IS OUR BATTLE CRY!
DO YOUR PART
FOR
DUTY - HONOR - COUNTRY

RECRUITMENT POSTER emphasized that everyone had a part to play in the war effort. Elwood Krzyske of New Boston, Michigan shared it.

envelope came without a letter, I knew that her prayer—"Son, I love you, come home safely"—was sealed within. ✪

CENSOR AT WORK. Capt. T.M. Britton (left) got a chuckle out of serviceman's lighthearted poem about the woes of censored mail.

He thought it was pretty clever and sent me a copy. Here it is:

*I've got a girl so far away
And she is sweet and frail.
But how can I send my love to her
When the censor reads my mail?*

*This girl is oh so very sweet,
I love her willy-nilly.
But how can I tell her of my love
When in print it looks so silly?*

*I hate the thought of those tender words
Being read by a stranger's eyes,
The soul-writ words for her alone,
The lies and alibis.*

*So, read my letters gently, Sir,
They are not meant for you.
But for a girl so far away
I scrawl this silly goo.*

*But when you read my letter, Sir,
And chuckle with delight,
Remember, Sir, that another censor
May laugh at the letters you write.*

Poem Explained Frustration With Mail Censoring System

By Patsy Britton, Houston, Texas

FOUR MONTHS after we were married, my husband was sent to England to help organize the European Division of the Air Transport Command. One of his many duties was censoring the mail.

"I do get some masterpieces sometimes," he wrote to me, "but it's all in a day's work. The average censor never pays much attention to the content of a letter unless it contains something detrimental to our security."

One of the boys wrote him a poem.

Sailors' Codes Didn't Always Get Past Censors

AS A NAVAL boat captain, censoring mail was part of my job. Boat captains censored all outgoing mail for our own crews and some of the base personnel. Whenever possible, we passed on this onerous chore to the lowest-ranking officer in sight.

One fellow officer on Guadalcanal said his favorite memory of John F. Kennedy, then boat captain of the PT-109, was seeing that skinny, tanned young man frowning intently while attacking a pile of letters with shears, ink pad and official Naval Censor stamp.

Security officers sold us on the importance of responsible censoring, because "Leaks lost lives". Knowing who and where we were was important to the enemy. So we read and clipped with righteous confidence, hating every minute of this very un-American invasion of privacy.

Censoring letters for my crew was easy—they were young and rather innocent. (At 24, I was "the old man".) In their letters they griped about food and seemingly silly restrictions, told tales about their buddies' antics, and made plans for the great day when they would arrive home. I could have stamped "censored" on most of those letters without reading a word.

Base personnel were another matter. These sailors were usually older, wiser and married. These letters were a real problem to the conscientious censor, because married sailors often developed codes with their wives before setting sail. By placing a rough map of their hometown over an ordinary atlas chart of the South Pacific, it was simple to relay squadron movements.

I once read a letter a sailor wrote to his wife in Madison, Wisconsin, my hometown. He recalled the happy day when they saw a movie at the Eastwood Theater and then dined on Park Street. I'm sure his wife quickly figured out we had moved from Oahu to Majuro and that he was still working in the commissary.

By numbering and cross-referencing their letters, there was no limit to the information the men could transmit. We did our best to thwart this minor espionage with sharp scissors.

Just a few years ago, at a gathering of old wartime buddies and their wives, I was approached by an attractive grandmother. Waving a yellowed letter full of square-cut holes in my face, she said, "I've waited a long time to find the guy who did this to me!" —*L. Franklin Anderson
Woodland, California*

LETTERS HOME often were jotted down whenever a soldier had a few minutes to spare. This soldier used his pack as a writing desk.

but the rest made it past the military censors, and my anxious parents finally learned where I was stationed.

—William Smith
Federal Way, Washington

Delayed Letters Brought News of Son's Birth

MAIL CALL was probably the most important part of my tour of duty in the infantry, second only to staying alive. It was like a shot of adrenaline to get a letter from home.

My wife, who was 2-1/2 months pregnant when I shipped out, wrote me every day. She didn't know then, and maybe not even now, what a morale booster she was.

Suddenly the letters stopped coming when I was hospitalized. I was moved from one place to another so fast that my forwarded mail never seemed to catch up with me.

When I got out of the hospital and was stationed in one spot for a while, I finally got all my mail—70 letters, most of them from my wife. Excited? You bet! I didn't know whether I was a father yet! I sat down and sorted all the letters by the date on the postmark and began to read.

After several letters, there it was: Richard Allen Fluck, born June 21, 1945! Eleven months after that, my son and I met for the first time.

—Clifford Fluck, New Ulm, Minnesota

Seabees' Mail Censor Took It on the Nose

WHEN MY WIFE complained that my letters were often cut up, I explained, "The censor has a job to do, and if he thinks something is wrong, he cuts it out." All the mates in my Seabees company thought the censor was having a lot of fun cutting up our mail. So I added a P.S. to my letter.

"Honey," I wrote, "if he cuts up *this* letter, you tell me to punch him in the nose, and I'll do it just for you."

Two days later, I got a special delivery letter from the lieutenant who was our censor. It said: "Meet me down at the ring Thursday night at 7 p.m."

I did, and the battalion commander made a lot of money. He had bet on me to win that match! —Peter Le Blanc
Dunstable, Massachusetts

Soldier's Code Helped Calm Worried Parents

BEFORE SHIPPING out of New York City, I worked out a code so I could let my folks know where I was. If there was a word scratched out in the first paragraph, they knew the first letter of each

ensuing paragraph would spell out my location. It worked like a charm. They knew where I was at all times.

—Clark Cowburn
Ulysses, Pennsylvania

Folks Found Out There Was Plenty in a Name

CENSORSHIP was very tight to prevent the enemy from learning of any troop movements or placements. So, of course, no one could write home and say exactly where he was stationed. But I was determined to break the censorship code!

I wrote to my father, M.O. Smith, that I wanted him to save all my letters so I could reminisce when the war was over. I also asked him to save the envelopes, especially the next five.

The next five letters were addressed:
Mr. and Mrs. M.M. Smith
Mr. and Mrs. M.A. Smith
Mr. and Mrs. M.N. Smith
Mr. and Mrs. M.U. Smith
Mr. and Mrs. M.S. Smith

The five middle initials spelled "MANUS", the largest island in the Admiralty Islands, just north of New Guinea. One of the five letters was lost,

PROUD PAPA. Richard Fluck met Dad at the age of 11 months. Papa Clifford learned of his son's birth in much-anticipated letter from home.

POW POSTCARD of Harry Bumgarner (above) let family know he was okay.

Card from Missing Brother Was Perfect Christmas Gift

IN OCTOBER 1943, we had a letter from the War Department. My brother, a gunner in the Air Force, had been shot down over German territory and was missing in action.

Weeks passed, and we still didn't know anything. Was he alive, hurt, taken prisoner, hiding out somewhere? We didn't know.

Christmas was coming, but not much could be done in the way of preparations. The wartime economy, with rationing, shortages and stepped-up defense production, didn't leave much for gift-buying and holiday cooking. Not many people were in the mood anyway.

Christmas morning dawned cold and clear, but we definitely weren't filled with Christmas joy. The war was dragging on. There was so much uncertainty, so many casualties, so much sadness in so many households. There really wasn't much to be happy about.

That afternoon, we decided to drive to the post office and pick up the mail. (In those days, you could do that every day except Sunday.) I was glancing carelessly through my mail when an address caught my eye—"Guffey, Colorado, USA". Who would put "USA" on a card to me? I turned it over.

"Stalag 17—Somewhere in Germany. I am a prisoner of war but am OK. Do not worry." Suddenly everything was all right, and it was truly Christmas. I had just received the best present of my life. —*Ardath Bumgarner Canon City, Colorado*

Prayer Sustained Family With Three Sons at War

AS A CHILD, I couldn't understand fully what the war was all about, but I did understand my parents' prayers and tears. I had three brothers serving in the war, and I was scared. I'd never known the loss of a loved one.

I saw Mom and Dad eagerly waiting for letters from Leonard, Dan and Doyle. I saw them listening to the war news on our radio. The looks they exchanged when battles were described and casualties listed soon told me more than words ever could. Their hearts ached with fear for their sons, and for the sons of all their friends and neighbors.

Our occasional visits to the Palace Theater in Spur, Texas now always included newsreels about the war. As I saw bombs and shells exploding, planes being shot from the sky, ships being sunk, soldiers falling, I really grew up. Suddenly I, too, realized the loss we could face—I might never see my brothers again. The fear of losing any of them was almost too much.

Then the first feared news came! On July 23, 1944, I was in the front yard when a man from town drove up with a telegram. He asked if my folks were home, and I went to the door and called Mom. When she saw the telegram in his hand, I thought she would faint.

As the man handed her the message, he said, "I'm sorry to have to bring this."

MISSING IN ACTION. Flier Leonard Pritchett was shot down after 28 missions. Telegram told family the news, but they never gave up hope.

It was word that my brother Leonard, a combat engineer stationed in Italy, had been missing over Yugoslavia since July 9.

Words cannot describe the grief this message brought our family. But our faith in God saw us through. Mom and Dad simply said, "He's alive and in God's hands. We have to have faith and pray for him, and for Dan and Doyle."

That's just what we did. And God protected all three of them and eventually brought them back home.
—*Nancy Pritchett, Lubbock, Texas*

SILVER DOLLAR that Harold Gerbers tried to mail from Ohio to Indiana returned to him in France, 3 months and 4,000 miles later, postage due!

Mail Followed Him For 4,000 Miles!

WE GOT ONE DAY'S notice that we were shipping out of Camp Millard, Ohio. We would leave for Europe the following day, July 15, 1944. I had a silver dollar and several other items I didn't want to take overseas, so I put them in an envelope and sent them home to Fort Wayne, Indiana, only 2-1/2 hours from camp.

On Aug. 1, we were working in train shops in Wales. By mid-August we were stationed in France. At mail call Sept. 24, my name was called. Much to my surprise, it was the envelope that contained my silver dollar. It had been returned to me for 10¢ postage due!

That envelope had traveled 3 months and close to 4,000 miles, when it had started out only 120 miles from its destination!
—*Harold Gerbers Fort Wayne, Indiana*

GOOD NEWS FROM HOME always lifted a soldier's spirits. Military authorities did their best to deliver precious letters quickly, but had trouble trying to catch up to troops that were constantly on the move.

Sister's Home-Canned Food Went All the Way to China

WHEN I SENT food to my brother Tom in China, I knew it would arrive safe and sound—I packed it in tin cans! I'd started canning meat in cans rather than jars some time before, and used that method to send fried chicken to Tom.

One time Tom wrote and said he was hungry for strawberry jam. I packed it in a quart can and put it in a box with several other goodies.

When it arrived, Tom opened and shared everything in the box—*except* the can of jam. He pretended that was more chicken, and said he'd save it for the next day. That night, he and three buddies took four loaves of bread to their tent, waited for quiet and then devoured every bit of that homemade jam!
—*Olivia Wiese*
Davenport, Iowa

She Sent Son Secret Stash In 'Goodie Box'

MY BROTHER loved cookies and candy, and when he joined the Air Force our mom sent him a big box of goodies. He wrote and thanked her, but said his buddies ate everything the minute he opened the box! When the next box arrived, the same thing happened.

But as soon as my brother was alone, he removed the box's false bottom—just as Mom had told him in a separate letter—and he thoroughly enjoyed the rest of the goodies. —*Joan Griffith*
Smicksburg, Pennsylvania

It Was 'Bombs Away' For Unwelcome Gift!

I WAS a pilot in the 98th Bomb Group, flying B-24 Liberators out of southern Italy.

While overseas, it became a custom for all 10 members of our bomber crew to gather 'round when one of us opened a package from home. It was share and share alike whenever one of those precious boxes arrived, and no one minded if the baked goods were dried out from lengthy periods in transit.

One day a Christmas package arrived from my mother, and the crew watched as I ripped off the layers of paper and opened the cover. When we saw what was inside, 10 pairs of eyes bugged out and we screamed in agony.

Neatly wrapped in tissue were four cans of Vienna sausage—the ex-act same "delicacy" our mess hall served as a main course *twice a day*! My bomber crew buddies bolted from my tent to avoid the sight of it!

It just so happened that one of our most dreaded targets was the heavily defended city of Vienna. On our next mission there, we released a payload of 500-lb. bombs, including all four cans of that dreadful sausage!
—*Russell Dexter*
Glastonbury, Connecticut

Package from Home Had Him Cackling with Joy

MOM SENT ME many packages during my stint in the Army, but they weren't the usual boxes of cookies and tidbits. Mom's packages always contained things like whole salamis, pepperoni, jars of artichoke hearts, cans of special homemade cookies, bottles of anisette and other delectable items.

The topper came when I wrote home from Fort Knox, Kentucky and complained about the tough Army chicken (we called it "armored chicken"). The next package from home included a well-sealed quart of cooked chicken!

Mom had seasoned and broiled the chicken, then put the jar in the center of a block of dry ice to keep it from spoiling on the 4- to 5-day trip from New Jersey. When I received it, the ice had just about evaporated.

I ate the chicken for dinner that night and shared some with a couple of buddies. They couldn't believe it—eating home-cooked New Jersey chicken in the middle of Kentucky! My mom... God bless her. —*Joseph Petti*
Bayonne, New Jersey

UNWELCOME GIFT of Vienna sausage, a "delicacy" that was all too familiar to one bomber crew, became part of the payload on their B-24 Liberator.

'Our Christmas Gifts Survived a Sniper Attack!'

By Albert McGraw
Anderson, Alabama

IN 1944 I was one of two mail clerks for our company in the Philippines. By December 1, the men were already harassing us, anxious to get the Christmas packages their relatives had sent in October. Most of the harassment was in jest, but sometimes it got intense—especially as Christmas neared, with no packages in sight.

A couple of days before Christmas, the other clerk and I drove to the central post office, about 10 miles away. There we heard a rumor that the ship bearing gifts destined for our outfit had been sunk by the Japanese. We returned to camp with only a handful of letters, dreading the thought of telling our comrades the news. But rumors flew so fast that they'd already heard about it by the time we got back.

Many rumors had no basis in truth, but it was close to Christmas and no packages had arrived, so this one was easy to believe. Our morale was as low as our combat boots. Our area was usually bustling; now it felt like a funeral parlor.

The supervisor at the post office said he'd call us if our packages arrived Christmas Eve, or even Christmas Day. No call came on the night before Christmas, and the following morning, things looked bleaker than ever.

Late in the afternoon on Christmas Day, a call finally came through. Our packages had arrived! The other clerk and I bounded to an old 2-1/2-ton truck and sped away for the post office.

Before we were halfway there, I thought I saw three or four enemy soldiers run across the road and into a dense bamboo thicket. The other clerk concurred, but nothing happened. We got to the post office without incident.

Such was not the case on the return trip. As we approached the area where we'd seen Japanese soldiers, bedlam broke loose. Our truck, with its mountain of packages, was being fired on by snipers!

At least 100 rounds of ammunition were fired at us. One rear tire was shot to shreds, and the windshield was shattered. Bullets swarmed around us like bees, but somehow we got through unscathed.

When we limped

MAIL CLERKS had a few surprising stories to relate after the war. One clerk and his buddy had to navigate through sniper fire in the Philippines to deliver Christmas packages to their company!

into camp, the men were so thrilled about receiving their packages that our close call didn't register—until they found bullet holes in some of the boxes. At least three fruitcakes were hit by gunfire and torn to pieces.

It was a terrifying experience, but it had its blessings. My buddy and I were almost in a state of shock, but seeing the radiant happiness on 240 faces calmed us down. We had helped make Christmas 12,000 miles from home a little more bearable.○

HOLIDAY GREETINGS. Gerri Lucia of Woodbury, New Jersey says her dad sent this card to her mom at Christmas. "It's not my idea of a Christmas card, but it's all we can get," he wrote. The card is from a huge scrapbook Gerri's mom kept during the war.

Kids Took Turns Waiting for Mail

EACH OF THE six children in our family took turns waiting for the mailman after our father was sent to the South Pacific. I still remember standing on the front porch, praying for a letter from Dad.

The first mail came just before Christmas. There was a separate card for each child, and a letter for Mom. We felt *so special*; Dad had taken the time to send *each* of us a card! It was like receiving a Christmas gift from far away.

It was a difficult time for us. But as the war progressed, those cards and brief letters were like a hug and a kiss from a far-off place.
—*Florence Leephart*
Newhall, California

Artwork Envelopes Stamped with Love

By Cecile Cowdery
Long Prairie, Minnesota

MY LATE HUSBAND, Ray, was considered an extrovert by most people. He dearly loved to be noticed, even if he had to do ridiculous things to accomplish it. For instance, he once rode up to my door on a goat!

But early on in our relationship I realized he was really a shy young man whose behavior was a cover-up for the fact that, deep inside, he simply felt insecure.

With the onset of World War II, Ray was inducted into the Army. He was just a number in the military, and lost in the crowd. Whenever he tried to become "noticed" it usually backfired, resulting in KP or latrine duty.

Ray coped as best he could, but his letters to me were anything but joyful tidings. That disturbed me and I tried to think of a way to cheer him up. Since I'd always enjoyed doing artwork, I decided to illustrate the envelopes I sent him.

When Ray's first illustrated envelope arrived, he let me know it had drawn a lot of attention from the other soldiers. From the day I learned that it made a difference, I dared not let up!

I drew these scenes to help Ray feel special. While other soldiers got "Dear John" letters, my man was assured daily by my sharing of remembered things. But decorating those letters was therapy for me, too!

When the war wasn't going well and I couldn't sleep, I'd stay up producing envelope after envelope. Some designs only Ray would understand, others were for the benefit of "the boys".

I guess the real proof that my personal war effort was worthwhile came when Ray was sent into combat in the Pacific. Before he left, he sent *all* my envelopes home for safekeeping.

When the war finally ended, Ray, too, came home for safekeeping.

Editor's Note: *Cecile's envelopes have been published in a book entitled World War II Envelope Art. The book is available from USM, P.O. Box 810, Lakeville MN 55044 for $19.95 post-paid (Minnesota residents add $1.30 sales tax).*

ENVELOPE ART enlivened Cecile Cowdery's letters to husband Ray as a way of cheering him up and boosting his morale after he'd been inducted into the Army. "From the day I learned that it made a difference," she says, "I dared not let up!" Her artwork included sketches of herself (right and below), caricatures of Hitler (left) and humorous depictions of Army life (above and below left).

SPECIAL CARDS noted efforts of servicemen. This one was sent by Nancy Allan of Greenfield, Wis.

All Were Not Called During Mail Call

BECAUSE OF OUR Navy carrier's schedule of invasion support, it was sometimes 2 to 3 months before our mail caught up with us. When it did, the men in my division would gather in our sleeping compartment for mail call. Hearing my name called over and over gave me a great feeling—the people back home cared about me!

But mail call was never a completely happy time for me. There were about four men in my division who never received a letter. Each time mail call was sounded, they were there, waiting, *hoping* that maybe this time their names would be called. They never were.

I can still see the disappointment in their eyes as they turned away empty-handed. They always tried to pretend it made no difference, but the look in their eyes told a far different story. That's why I always shared as much as I could with these men. —*Ron Vaughn Eastland, Texas*

Speedy Letter Broke Records—and GI's Heart

WITHOUT MAIL from home, the members of the Allied forces overseas never could have survived. It was our umbilical cord. Of everything shipped to us overseas, mail was the No. 1 priority.

I served in North Africa and Italy, and the men in my company held a monthly lottery for recipients of letters that arrived fastest, counting the days between postmark and delivery dates.

The man who received the quickest "regular" letter would split the pot with the man who got the fastest V-Mail letter (written on a small form, photographed and reduced in size by the postal authorities to conserve space). The record was 5 days for a regular letter, 4 days for V-Mail.

When a letter came from my betrothed in the States, it broke *both* records, arriving in only 3 days! Everyone felt electrified by that letter. Imagine, a letter all the way from home, mailed only 3 days ago!

According to the rules of the lottery, any record-breaking letter had to be read aloud. That didn't bother me—it wasn't my sweetheart's style to write anything suggestive. So, as the proud new "champion", I started to read.

About halfway through the letter, the message began to sink in, and I felt as though I was reading to myself. She wanted to end our engagement! It was another Dear John letter, hitting a vulnerable target 6,000 miles from home.

I'm happy to report that none of the guys laughed. Instead, they sympathized and shared my regret. GIs were never more compassionate than when they consoled a buddy who'd received a Dear John letter! —*Joseph DeCurtis Commerce Township, Michigan*

Packages from Home Were Worth the Wait

IT SEEMED TO take an eternity for letters from the States to reach us in the Philippines. Packages seemed to take

even longer. One day I got a package from Mom and eagerly opened it, but found that the cake inside had spoiled a little bit from the long trip in muggy weather. But once I realized that other GIs had no mail at all, that cake tasted pretty good after all! —*John Bedner Colonia, New Jersey*

Mangled Message Nearly Got Soldier in Hot Water

HARRY AND I had been married almost 6 years when he was sent overseas with the 1144th Engineers. I went back to our hometown, found a job, became a volunteer nurse's aide at the hospital, and wrote and mailed daily letters to an APO address. Harry wrote as often as possible, at least once or twice a week.

Letters never came to either of us except in bunches. Perhaps on the day I received 10 from Harry, he got none from me. His letters had sections snipped out by the censors, and sometimes said little more than "I love you and miss you". Mine tended to be longer. Did he really have time to read them?

After V-E Day, Harry got a furlough and sent a cablegram from southern France. The message was telephoned to me and came through as: "On furlough with Vera wish you were here". Vera? You can bet *I* wished I was there, too!

When the actual cablegram was mailed to me a few days later, I was delighted to read: "On furlough Riviera wish you were here". We've had many a laugh about that over the years!
—*Leone Weber, Wild Rose, Wisconsin*

WISH YOU WERE HERE. Leone Weber and husband Harry wrote to each other often. When Harry was furloughed after V-E Day, his cablegram from France arrived promptly. Unfortunately, the garbled message gave Leone the impression that he was celebrating with another woman!

The Fun We Found

The Fun We Found

Mostly, wars are fought by youngsters. World War II was no exception. What we had back then was a military force largely made up of feisty, undisciplined, easily bored—and homesick—young people. Fortunately, Americans of all sorts decided to adopt and entertain them whether they were in Memphis or Manila, Louisville or London. Many of us can look back and truthfully say we were never among strangers, no matter how far away from home we were.

USO clubs sprang up everywhere in the U.S., providing everything from snacks to Saturday night dances complete with scores of smiling young ladies who danced and danced...and then danced some more. Bless them all.

And when you got overseas, there were the USO clubs. And the young ladies who cheerfully danced far into the night, and hardly ever winced when you stepped on their toes.

Home Away from Home

I particularly remember a Servicemen's Club in Houston that became my home away from home for many months. It had one indispensable feature: a tiny, sparkling, 60-something lady we all called "Mom".

She mended broken hearts, listened to our "someday-when-I'm-out" dreams, and had sage advice on proper birthday presents for the girl back home.

She also had a gentle way of asking about the last time you wrote your mom and dad. "Here's paper and an envelope, so why don't you just sit down at that desk right now and drop them a line," she'd urge.

Entertainers gave unstintingly of their time, putting on shows wherever there was a stage and an audience, be it a bomber base hangar in Great Britain or within sound of shellfire in New Guinea.

Comedy Brought Hope

I particularly remember catching one young comic's act on Leyte as a tropical moon filtered through the palms. We all agreed that this guy Bob Hope had a great future.

Then there were the tireless Red Cross and Salvation Army volunteers. They were there with coffee and doughnuts when you boarded the ship—and still there when you came home. They set up canteens in bombed-out buildings almost before the fires were extinguished.

Largely unsung were the hometown Red Cross workers, who helped frightened young wives cope with their new duties of motherhood, and even helped out with money until the next allotment check arrived. They comforted the grieving and served in hundreds of small ways that often went unnoticed.

Local groups were on hand in towns where troop trains paused, passing out sandwiches and cookies. I still wonder if those folks in Laramie (or was it Cheyenne?) really knew how delicious a homemade sandwich tasted after 2 days of troop train fare.

Yes, bighearted America adopted us all. It showered us with friendship, time, talent, love and countless kindnesses. Being on the receiving end of it was a lasting lesson in how good people can be.
—*Clancy Strock*

CUTTIN' THE RUG! USO dances—complete with young ladies who somehow managed to smile and dance ceaselessly—lifted the morale of servicemen, no matter how far from home they might be stationed.

Don Condon

Weary Fliers Found Safe Haven in Red Cross Club

By Betty John, Albuquerque, New Mexico

I HELPED ESTABLISH the Red Cross Officers' Club in Essex, England in the midst of the Marauder (B-26) bases.

One night, two helpers and I were preparing to lock up when the phone rang. At first I wasn't going to answer. Midnight was too late for further business, especially since I'd been there since 10 a.m.! But, realizing it might be an emergency, I answered.

It was my friend Lyle Forsythe, director of the GI Club.

"Betty, can you feed 36 men?"

"At this hour?" I asked. "Why?"

He explained that his club's larder was locked up for the night and he didn't have the keys. And these boys *needed* food. They'd been picked up all over the southern coast after parachuting out of their wrecked "Fortresses", and none of them had eaten in 36 hours.

"Send them right along," I said.

Back to Work

My helpers dragged tables back onto the dance floor while I hurriedly made coffee and scrambled eggs. Three officers came down from the dorm to help slice and butter bread.

When the Fortress boys arrived, they were haggard, silent and pale, wearing 2 days' growth of beard. And they *were* ravenous, shoveling down eggs as fast as I could make them. None of them spoke.

Soon the men began to thaw out a little. Bit by bit, their story came out. They had been returning from a bombing run in three crippled "Forts", trying to stay together for protection. Over the south coast, they realized the planes were in such bad shape they couldn't even be crash-landed. So all the men had jumped. Most of them landed safely, although two had sprained ankles and one man with a flak-riddled arm thought he'd hurt his back.

The first man to get to his feet had run to the closest house and called the base for transportation. It had taken most of the day to round everyone up.

The men tried to get back to their base without stopping to eat. But when they saw the warm welcome of the Red Cross emblem at the GI Club, hunger overcame them and they stopped. They still had a long way to go, and nowhere they could get food at that hour.

I asked one boy, all clumsily bandaged, why they hadn't taken him to a hospital.

"Because I won't let them," he said. "I want our base doc to take care of me. If I go to the hospital I may lose my outfit."

One thing these boys hated most was separation from their unit by long hospitalization. I could see the suffering in his face, but I knew he'd stick it out.

One of the men looked like someone I'd met before, at another Red Cross club. "Weren't you at Andrews Field?" I asked.

He nodded. "When I walked through that door downstairs, it was just like coming home," he said. "I didn't think there'd be any doors open for us tonight—and here you are, just like old times. Nothing has changed." ✪

Dance Halls' Popularity Paid Off for Teen Musician

AFTER I STARTED high school, I had the opportunity to join a small dance band as an accordion player. We played almost every night of the week, and sometimes had only 2 or 3 nights off in a month! The dance halls were always full, no matter what night it was. The servicemen got in free, and for every serviceman who came, there were about five girls!

I was still going to school every day, too. Whenever our homeroom had a war bond drive, I always won—I bought a war bond every week.

Once my teacher asked me how I got the money to buy all those bonds. I explained that I made an average of $75 a week with the band. "Girl," he said, "do you realize you make more money than the teachers?"

—*Rosemary Gast, Davenport, Iowa*

Artie Shaw Gave GIs a Memorable Show at Sea

By Andrew Balog
Dearborn Heights, Michigan

IN MAY of 1943, my ship, the destroyer *USS Pringle*, had just completed an emergency overhaul in the Pearl Harbor navy yard. We were bound for combat areas in the South Pacific.

Before we left, my shipmates and I had some time to relax, enjoying liberty in Honolulu. We lingered long at a daytime club called "The Breakers", to

---

"Artie gave the downbeat, and the band swung into his theme..."

⭐

---

hear the swinging sounds of Artie Shaw and his Navy Band. It was great, but we knew the good times wouldn't last.

On May 8 we sailed past Diamond Head, leaving the shores of Hawaii far behind. Our destroyer was escorting the battleship *USS North Carolina* to New Caledonia.

After 5 days at sea, we crossed the equator and received orders to fuel up alongside the *North Carolina*. For some reason, there seemed to be a holiday spirit in the air.

Ice cream was passed to us from the battleship, and then a band began to form on the *North Carolina's* deck. Word spread quickly. It was Artie Shaw and his Navy Band! They'd been sent to the South Pacific to entertain the servicemen! As the band set up, we lined the port rail of our ship, waiting for Artie to give the downbeat.

Soon, that Big Band swung into Artie's theme, *Nightmare*. Then followed all the latest tunes, like *Begin the Beguine* and *Stardust*.

I glanced along the rail of the ship and saw reflected in my shipmates' faces the same thought I was having: How I wish the people back home were here to see this! The only other sounds were the sloshing of the waves between the ships and the shouts of the hose and line handlers.

It was by far the most unique and spine-tingling band session I've ever had the pleasure to hear. There we were, in the middle of the Pacific—in the middle of *nowhere*—listening to the music

ARTIE SHAW was an early volunteer in WWII, leaving his 32-piece Big Band to put on a uniform. He fronted a Navy band that toured throughout the Pacific.

of Artie Shaw! Was there a war on? Not that day!

I like to remember that musical interlude as a highlight of our ship's career. We may have had a "Nightmare" in the Pacific, but it was a pleasant one! ✪

AP/Wide World Photos

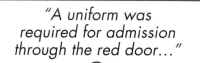

'We Left Our Hearts at The Stage Door Canteen'

By Edythe Freeman, Brooklyn, New York

THE STAGE DOOR CANTEEN.

During the war, civilian radio listeners, movie watchers and newspaper readers across the country grew to know that name well—and most folks could only dream about it.

A uniform was required for admission through the famous red door on West 44th Street in New York. Civilians peeked in with awe at the place that had become synonymous with the "glamour" of the war.

As a junior hostess, I spent at least 1 night a week at the canteen, dancing with lonely servicemen. I quickly learned how little glamour was involved. A single pair of shoes wore through in 2 months, and a pair of hose would run to ribbons after only 1 night.

We danced the rumba with Mexican fliers; Brazilian soldiers taught us the samba; and we learned the polka from Norwegian sailors.

The small dance floor was so crowded we couldn't help but get kicked in the shins and ankles. We'd silently count to 10 and then tell ourselves wryly, "I'm due for my Purple Heart any day now— black and blue in the line of duty."

Rewarding Work

But none of that really mattered. The grateful look from an RAF flier or the gruff "Thanks, you're a swell bunch of girls" from a tough master sergeant were more than enough reward.

One night, after hours of dancing, I was just about to throw in the towel when a French soldier asked for the next waltz. He told me about his hometown, which he hadn't seen in over 4 years. He told me of the family he could contact only once a year through the Red Cross.

Then he expressed wonder over our hospitality, our welcome, our "untiring efforts" on the servicemen's behalf. I lowered my eyes, ashamed of accepting his appreciation. *I* should have been thanking *him*.

Work at the canteen was never boring. Show me the gal who honestly gets bored among a couple of thousand men in uniform! Sure, we did have to quiet the howls of a few uniformed wolves. But the bother of that was nothing compared to the feeling of pulling some shy, lonely lad out of a corner for

---

"A uniform was required for admission through the red door..."

---

a dance. Invariably, these homesick boys were alone and in New York City for the first time.

Some of those boys were just youngsters of 17 or 18. They might have been wearing campaign ribbons, their hats at a cocky angle as they talked of "shakedown cruises" and "dames". But speak with one of them alone for a minute and he'd pull out his wallet and show you snapshots of his mother and dad, his sister, his dog.

When we saw, through their eyes, the suffering of war, the lack of silk and nylons on the home front didn't seem so important anymore. I no longer missed long automobile rides, extra pats of butter or thick steaks.

From them we heard the war's amusing incidents, the tragedies, the human and inhuman stories. There was no glamour attached to any part of their job, or ours. As we said good-bye to those leaving for the infested waters of the Atlantic, the jungles of New Guinea or the windswept landscape of the Aleutians, we did it with a prayer in our hearts and unspoken thanks on our lips.

We appreciated their courage, their sacrifice and their determination. And we appreciated having the opportunity to meet such a grand group of men.

Irving Berlin wrote the hit song *I Left My Heart at the Stage Door Canteen*...and many of us who worked there really did.✪

Kiss from Film Star a 'Hedy' Experience

By Hal Winter, Schenevus, New York

NO SERVICEMAN who ever visited the Stage Door Canteen could forget it—certainly not me!

It opened in March 1942 in the basement of a former New York City nightclub as an entertaining refuge for anyone in uniform. It proved so popular that critic Brooks Atkinson called it "the biggest hit Broadway has had for weeks".

Stage and screen celebrities rolled up their sleeves to take turns serving behind a food-laden counter. No alcohol was served, but who needed it? Having Tallulah Bankhead or Ethel Merman offer you pie and coffee was intoxicating enough!

Tables and chairs hugged the walls and bordered a dance floor, with a small stage at one end. Big-time bands and top stars appeared on alternate Saturday nights. There were plenty of swell-looking girls eager to dance with you, but dating them was taboo.

One night was especially memorable. It was a Saturday in September 1942—my 20th birthday. I had no special plans, so I sauntered into the Stage Door Canteen.

The place was jammed, and every table was taken. When I elbowed my way to the dance floor, I found it filled with servicemen sitting cross-legged on the floor.

Suddenly the lights dimmed. Silence spread over the packed house. On stage,

HEDY LAMARR was one entertainer who served coffee, sandwiches and soft drinks—all free—to soldiers at the Stage Door and Hollywood Canteens. She greeted this man from behind the snack bar in 1942.

a pale pink spotlight hit an empty chair. Then, out of the darkness walked...

Hedy Lamarr. The greeting she received could have cracked the plaster on the walls!

As the noise trailed off, she beckoned the men in front to come up and gather around her. I expected a stampede, but the guys were timid.

"Come on, boys," she said, waving them onstage. "I won't bite."

When they settled in, Miss Lamarr began telling us stories about her film career, then took questions from the audience until closing time approached.

But before she left, she did one thing that endeared her to us for life. She came down among us, and gave every man who was celebrating a birthday a kiss!

As she drew near me, all I could think was: Be still, my heart! I don't remember when I came down to earth, but it was a long time before I washed the spot where Hedy Lamarr kissed me.

Kate Smith Treated SPARs To Concert of Their Own

WHEN I SIGNED up with the SPARs, the Coast Guard division for women in the service, our training station wasn't ready yet. We took our boot training with the WAVEs at Hunter College in New York.

In May 1943, Kate Smith gave a concert there for the WAVEs—but the SPARs weren't invited. When Miss Smith found this out, she insisted on giving a second concert just for us!

We were already in bed, but we got up, threw coats over our pajamas and marched to the auditorium. This wonderful lady sang for us for about 2 hours! The next day, she invited all the girls named Smith to have lunch with her.

It's been 50 years, but I'm sure none of the women who were there ever forgot that concert. —*Gwen Nekrewich, Milford, Connecticut*

AP/Wide World Photos

SMILING THRONG of servicemen crowded the Hollywood Canteen as stage star Shirley Temple dished up the snacks in August 1944.

Film Industry Workers Made Hollywood Canteen a Reality

By Jeannette Lindner, Escondido, California

WHEN A HUGE number of servicemen began coming through Hollywood at the start of the war, actress Bette Davis knew just what to do. The film community would build them a canteen!

With the help of her boss, Jack Warner, head of the Warner Brothers Studio, and actor John Garfield, a vast piece of property was leased on Vine Street. Carpenters, electricians, set decorators and others from film industry trade unions donated their time to build a kitchen, dance floor, stage and other necessities.

Other studios were contacted to provide stars, services and staffing. Studio musicians provided the music. Food came from various sources, and studio commissaries donated supplies.

I was a motion picture editor in those days, and I drove to the canteen every Monday night with my friend Alexis Smith to dance and talk with the enlisted men. Sometimes they were lined up around the block when the doors opened at 7 p.m.

The canteen was open every evening and all day Sunday. Servicemen could sit at tables, dance, watch the entertainment or ask stars for autographs. Where else could you hear Betty Grable sing or watch Ann Miller dance while eating a sandwich served by Rita Hayworth?

It was a wonderful, exciting time, and the canteen remained open until the war ended. Hollywood did have a heart, and the canteen proved it. I'm glad I was a part of it.✪

Secret Singer Found Himself Crooning to Packed Canteen

AS A SAILOR stationed near Long Beach, California, I often visited the USO's Hollywood Canteen. Famous bands, movie stars and everyday people mingled freely, and it wasn't unusual to see a star take the stage or sit down to chat with a stranger.

One evening, I wandered backstage behind the curtain. The band was playing *Paper Doll*, a particular favorite of mine. When I saw what I thought was a "dead" mike, I walked up to it and, pretending to be a popular crooner, started singing with the band.

With a start, I realized the curtain was opening, with me alone at center stage. I practically tore holes in the floor getting off that stage!
—*William Amey*
Southern Pines, North Carolina

Friendly Dinner Companion's Identity Stunned Soldier

By Donald Lang
Kane, Pennsylvania

THE OFFICERS' CLUB was bulging with people when I arrived at Fort Meade, Maryland. The Glenn Miller Orchestra was performing, and military activity had come to a virtual halt. No one wanted to miss the show.

I didn't want to miss it, either, but I did want to eat first, so I went to the dining hall early. I went through the line and came away with a plate full of goodies, only to find every chair occupied.

After a few frustrating minutes of standing in the middle of the hall with a full plate in my hands, I spotted an Army Air Corps captain sitting alone at a small table with one empty chair. He motioned for me to join him. We introduced ourselves briefly. There were no name tags then, and I'm sure he forgot my name as quickly as I forgot his.

Dining with the captain was a pleasant experience. We casually discussed military matters, swapping opinions on how we should go about winning the war, but I never got around to asking about his job.

Finally the captain glanced at his watch and announced, "Well, it's time for me to go to work now." Only after he got up and left did I recognize that face and voice. I'd just had dinner with Glenn Miller!

Glenn Miller Show 'Lifted Our Spirits as Nothing Else Could'

EARLY IN 1944, our B-17 squadron was assigned to an 8th Air Force base in England. Those were dark days of the war, filled with anxiety about the next mission and, too often, grieving for friends who were killed or missing in action.

Sometime late in the year, a poster appeared in the enlisted men's club announcing the arrival of Glenn Miller and his Air Force Band at our base. I couldn't believe it. My favorite band!

Most of the B-17s were moved out of the largest hangar and a makeshift stage was set up. That hangar was jammed the night of the show. Hundreds of officers and enlisted men and women occupied every available space.

The famous Glenn Miller sound and the unforgettable renditions of Johnny Desmond and the Crew Chiefs filled the cold night air. Those classic arrangements propelled us above the homesickness and frustrations of wartime, and for a few brief hours, lifted our spirits as nothing else could!

None of us could have guessed during this euphoric experience that this would be Glenn Miller's final performance. A few days later, he took off in a small plane to prepare for an Armed Forces Radio broadcast in Paris. It was foggy and a light rain was falling as the plane headed across the English Channel, never to be seen again.

Thanks for the memories, Glenn. That's one night I'll never forget!
—*Dick Keller, West Covina, California*

At the concert, I stood as close as I could get for the opening theme, *Moonlight Serenade*, and was thrilled by the band's rendition of *String of Pearls*. Never had I heard such beautiful music, or seen people do their jobs so well.✪

GLENN MILLER, second from right, formed the war era's most popular service band. Yvonne Kent of Middleburg Heights, Ohio shared this photo. Her husband, Al, is at Glenn's right. Al played for a base band that Glenn guest-conducted.

FUN AT THE FORT. NBC Blue Network announcer Gil Newsome introduces singer Betty Bradley at Fort Hayes, Ohio in 1943.

Clever Pals Made Sure Music Filled the Air at Rec Hall

By John Moore
Westfield Center, Ohio

WHEN I ENTERED the service at Fort Hayes, a reception center in Colum-bus, Ohio, I was pulled out of the pro-cessing lines because I could type. I ended up staying there 4 months.

Shortly after I arrived, I met Sgt. Dusty Rhodes, who ran the post's recre-ation hall. We discovered we both were fans of Big Band music. We also dis-covered that an Army regulation per-mitted us to hold musicians for 6 weeks before shipping them off for basic train-ing. What great news! Some of the men coming in for processing had been top-flight sidemen, playing 7 days a week in the hottest bands in the country!

After these musicians were processed, I'd notify Dusty, and he'd put through the 6-week order. We ended up having eight to 10 musicians at any one time, and they performed for dances at the rec hall two or three times a week. It didn't take long for word to get around that Fort Hayes had excellent dance bands! Many Big Bands performed at the rec hall, too.

Those performances meant so much to the kids coming in. Going into the Army was no picnic, but at least they had some fun before shipping out of Fort Hayes.✪

Popular Songs Reflected Concerns of War Years

WHEN I STARTED high school in 1942, I never realized how big a role the war would play in my education. It influenced every facet of our days.

Nearly all our teachers were women. The few male teachers were older men who had been classified as 4-F. During history class, we spent most of the hour studying maps and discussing the latest news from the front. Even ancient history was discussed in relation to current events.

Noontime sock hops were our favorite part of the day. We danced in our stocking feet until the bell rang, then scrambled for our shoes and raced to class. Glenn Miller records were the most popular, but the other songs on the Hit Parade reflected the times. *White Cliffs of Dover, That Russian Winter, Don't Sit Under the Apple Tree, On a Wing and a Prayer* and *Say a Prayer for the Boys Over There* reminded us of our involvement in the war.

—*Margaret Anderson, Irwin, Iowa*

Puppeteer 'Pulled Strings' For Paul Muni

By Robert Vern Longfield, Morro Bay, California

BEFORE I JOINED the Army, I spent several years puppeteering in vaudeville. After spending a year in North Africa, I was sent to Fort Sam Houston, Texas, where I produced GI shows, managed a large theater and served as an escort for visiting actors and movie stars. With a GI buddy, I also did puppet shows several times a week.

One day I found a note on my desk that read, "Paul Muni will be in tomorrow. Show him every courtesy." I'd escorted several stars by then, including Gary Cooper, Red Skelton and Mickey Rooney. But I was still star-struck at the thought of meeting the leading movie star of the day!

The next morning, I drove to Mr. Muni's hotel to pick him up. Aside from his beautifully tailored clothes, there was nothing to indicate he was a great movie star—no sign of ego or conceit. I'd called him "Mr. Muni" about three times when he said, "We're going to be together all day, so if you don't mind, let's make it Bob and Paul."

During the drive to the post, I asked him why a famous actor would spend his time visiting GIs across the country.

"I'm not going to tell you the old story about it being my patriotic duty, that it's the least I can do or that it's for publicity," he said. "The fact is that I really do enjoy every minute of it. It's great to talk to these fellows. I'd rather talk to one GI than a hundred fans or autograph seekers."

He Was Sincere

As the day progressed, I learned that was true. At one point I dropped him off at headquarters for a visit with the brass, and dozens of them were waiting, all decked out in their spit and polish and salad. When I picked Paul up later, he said, "Well, now that *that's* over, let's go talk to the fellows."

Paul also asked about my interest in show business. I told him I'd been a professional puppeteer before the war, and that I had my puppets at the company theater. He said he'd like to see them. I took his remark as a simple courtesy and forgot it.

Later in the afternoon, Paul asked, "When do I see the puppets?" I told him there was so much to do that I didn't think it was all that important. "I want to see them," he replied. "I used to have puppets back in Austria when I was a kid. Let's take a few minutes right now."

With dozens of GIs tagging along, we went to the theater and I did four of my acts for him. Paul was so enthusi-

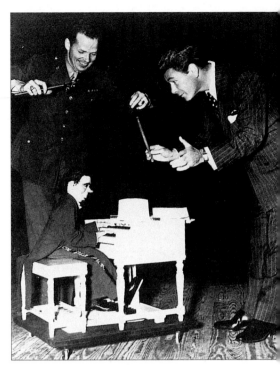

PICTURE THAT! Proud moment for puppeteer Robert Longfield was captured by cameraman at fort in Texas.

astic I couldn't believe it! He even came up onstage and asked if he could operate the puppets himself!

He particularly liked "Professor Keyzanpedals", who played the Hammond organ. Suddenly he said, "I think we need a picture of this. Where's that cameraman?"

The picture above shows Paul Muni directing, Professor Keyzanpedals playing, and me pulling strings. It was one of my proudest moments.✪

Movie Star Brought Message of Comfort to Worried Mom

DURING THE DARK years of World War II, I worked for a branch of Douglas Aircraft in Chicago. My husband was in the Navy, and my colleague, Helen Cragg, had a son on a submarine in the Pacific. Helen and I became closer than sisters, exchanging news from our loved ones so far from home.

Word came that a war bond drive would be launched, and Cesar Romero, the handsome and dashing movie star, would visit Douglas Aircraft to get it started! At this point Helen had received no mail from her son, Duffy, for several months. Her nerves were raw and she wept easily. We all suffered and worried with her.

One day a company executive gently approached Helen and whispered in her ear. She jumped up from her desk,

her eyes streaming tears of surprise and joy, and cried out that Cesar Romero wanted to meet her. He had a message from Duffy! We all watched Helen as she stumbled on trembling legs after that executive toward his office.

Half an hour later, Helen returned, her face beaming. As we gathered around her, she told us Cesar Romero had visited a submarine and become acquainted with the bugler—Duffy Cragg!

Duffy had begged the actor to let his mom know he was okay, but homesick. "I love you, Mom, and miss you and my sis," he had said. "And I'm proud of your efforts to build airplanes to help us win."

Women like Helen Cragg were some of the unsung heroines of the war. —*Glenna Manig, Laramie, Wyoming*

A REAL ROAD SHOW it was, as Effie Hazlett (left) and Eileen O'Leary Stein played music and sang for troops from the back of a Red Cross truck.

Red Cross Entertainers Grew Accustomed to 'Close Calls'

SERVING WITH the American Red Cross in Europe, I helped operate a mobile entertainment truck called a "Cinemobile". It had a piano, movie projector and screens, records, loudspeakers and built-in bunks. A stage folded down from one side of the truck, allowing us to do live shows.

My partner, Effie, and I often drove through pouring rain and darkness to entertain isolated GI units in France, Belgium and Germany. We'd sit on our helmets in the mud with a tarp over the projector while the movies ran. Later, we'd drive in complete blackout back to headquarters.

One cold November day in Metz, France, we were sent to entertain the artillery corps, just 3 kilometers from the front. We drove through the mountains to a small village, where we were billeted in a charming white cottage.

We set up in an old town hall, showing films, playing piano and singing for 2 days. It was nerve-racking trying to drown out the sound of artillery fire!

On the third day, we learned Mickey Rooney was arriving with his USO show, so we returned to Metz. Since the road we'd taken had been bombed out, we followed a bulldozer and minesweeper all the way back through the densely wooded mountains.

The next day, an artillery officer came to Metz for supplies. Chuckling, he asked me if I carried a lucky shamrock. When I asked why, he told us an 88 shell had landed in our bedroom right after we left our little cottage! Close calls were so much a part of our lives that we just said a quick prayer and went on our way.

My 3 years with the Red Cross were a mix of laughter and tears, camaraderie and loneliness, terror and joy. But I had the wonderful feeling of being part of a close-knit family of Americans doing all we could to win the war.
—*Eileen O'Leary Stein*
Oak Creek, Wisconsin

Red Cross Clubmobiles Were Hospitality on Wheels!

IN 1942, the first American Red Cross Clubmobiles began operating in England. The idea behind them was to bring a touch of home to GIs not able to enjoy Red Cross clubs in cities and camps.

Early Clubmobiles were often English vans equipped to carry hot coffee and doughnuts to fliers returning from sorties over Europe and to GIs disembarking at all hours of the day and night from the United States.

After the invasion of France in June of 1944, Clubmobile operations changed drastically. By that time, there were about 1,000 young American women in Red Cross uniforms in the service, and my wife, Milly, was one of them.

Each Clubmobile was assigned three women who were responsible for its operation under all kinds of weather and battle conditions. The vehicles used on the Continent were rugged GM 2-1/2-ton trucks capable of keeping up with rapidly moving troops.

Clubmobile crews worked in groups of 10 vehicles under a group captain. Red Cross women were assigned areas of operation by the Army as combat conditions permitted. It was routine for them to make, transport and serve 2,000 doughnuts and 90 gal. of coffee a day while playing popular music over their speakers for battle-weary GIs.

They also carried cigarettes, candy and gum, which were much appreciated by the soldiers. These Clubmobile girls never received much publicity and their work has remained largely unknown. But the grateful GIs they served will never forget the invaluable contribution these women made to the war effort.
—*Robert Cox, Vicksburg, Mississippi*

Visit from 'Red Cross Girl' Made Injured Soldier's Day

INJURED SOLDIERS greatly appreciated the efforts of Red Cross volunteers. The following account, submitted by Emeline Malpas of Littleriver, California, was written by veteran Richard Peil.

"She usually comes in the mornings,

CLUBMOBILE CREW. This trio trucked comfort and hospitality to GIs in Europe. From left are Bunny Clapp of Connecticut, Milly Cox of Mississippi and Petey Goff of Rhode Island. Photo was shared by Milly's husband, Robert.

sometimes in the afternoons. After you're here a while, you start to watch for her. You just want to see her. It's not for the cigarettes she passes out, but the regular things she does—the letters she helps you write, the card games, the conversations that are like volleys in a good Ping-Pong game. She'll swap you story for story and jibe for jibe.

"But there's another reason you look forward to her daily visits. For a few minutes, the gal from the 'Red X' becomes your gal back home, your wife—anyone you want her to be. She helps you relive the scenes that have become foggy with time. With her help, you find yourself replaying all your favorite memories.

"When she moves on to the next bed, leaving you with your thoughts, you're happy and content. You may have just taken her on a tour of Central Park, but now she's somewhere else, maybe a farm in Kansas. The girl in the Red Cross uniform is just doing her job—and doing American womanhood a great honor."

Young Woman Offered Food, Conversation at Canteen

MY CONTRIBUTION to the war effort was serving servicemen coffee and doughnuts from midnight to 8 a.m. Fridays at a Salvation Army canteen in Philadelphia, Pennsylvania.

I was just out of high school, and traveled an hour each way to get to the canteen, but my parents never had to worry for my safety. I felt blessed to be able to provide food and friendly conversation to the fellows who were serving our country.   —Florence Clay
St. James City, Florida

Brigadier General Never Forgot Volunteer's Courage

LITTLE HAS BEEN written about the hard work of Red Cross workers during World War II. Many of their courageous efforts were overshadowed by the more dramatic moments of the war.

But there are those who never forgot. Julia Davignon of Lancaster, California received the following letter after her sister, Jessie "Jean" Brake Weldon, died in 1987. The writer was Harold W. Bowman, a retired brigadier general with the U.S. Air Force.

"Even though I haven't seen Jean Brake since World War II, she has lived

TIRELESS VOLUNTEER Jean Brake (top photo, left) lives on in the memory of grateful servicemen. This Red Cross worker dispensed coffee and doughnuts to pilots and crews after bombing runs.

in my heart, and I speak for some 7,000 members of the 401st Bombardment Group stationed at Deenethorpe, England.

"In 1944, prior to an early-morning mission, I had stopped at a remote blackout area of the base to check on airplane maintenance about 2 a.m. There was a windy, dreary, icy drizzle. Ground crews were struggling to perform their difficult tasks, with no time off to rest next to the heater in the hangar.

"Then I saw a small figure, bundled beyond recognition in heavy, fur-lined leather clothing, dispensing coffee and doughnuts to the men. As I stopped to participate, I expressed my appreciation. I was startled to learn that the Good Samaritan was a Red Cross lady, alone in her Jeep. Why wasn't she in the comfort and safety of the Red Cross Club?

"She replied, 'I joined the Red Cross to help win the war, where I could be most needed. I think this is it.' I asked her name, and I assigned a driver to assist her thereafter and to make sure she was safe.

"I was never able to forget that scene, or that young patriot."

Town Treated Each GI on Furlough to His Own Party!

OUR MAIL CARRIER in Garden Valley, Idaho thought every boy home on furlough should be treated to a big party. So that's just what we did!

The mail carrier was usually the first to hear when a serviceman was coming home, and he'd spread the word. When the young man arrived, we'd have a big dance, and everyone in the valley came. No one even thought of hiring baby-sitters back then—the kids came with us!

The women prepared lots of food, and at midnight, tables were set up and loaded with goodies. After everyone had eaten, the food and tables disappeared, and the visiting and dancing resumed until dawn. The children were put down to sleep on the big stage, where I played the piano for dancing.

What fun it was! Best of all, every boy who came home on leave knew he'd get a chance to see everyone, because they'd all show up for his "serviceman's dance".   —Goldie Charters
Boise, Idaho

FIRST DANCE. Sailors in Waukegan, Illinois jammed this new USO hall for its first formal dance. Norma Connell worked as hostess at the Valentine's Day affair, as did her sister, Lawana, at left in print dress, holding a paper heart.

'I Was a Hostess at Nation's First USO'

WITHIN A WEEK after Pearl Harbor was bombed, the government began building a USO in my hometown of Waukegan, Illinois. It was the first in the country, and it was finished in time for a Valentine's Day dance in 1942.

The girls at the YWCA were asked to serve as hostesses and formed the GSO, or Girls' Service Organization. My sister and I became members, and my mother recruited women to act as chaperons.

A Navy band played for dances every Wednesday night. The third Wednesday of each month was "formal night", and the girls wore full-length dresses. There'd be about 400 men and only 50 girls for every dance, so there was lots of cutting in. The girls would dance for 3 hours straight!

The USO offered more than just dances. Sailors could play Ping-Pong, cards and marbles, or just read and visit. For 50¢, a boy could spend the night and get breakfast in the morning. Sunday afternoon talent shows featured local singers, dancers and musicians, and any sailor who wanted to join in was welcome.

Sailors also could take dance lessons, go on picnics or attend roller-skating and ice-skating parties. There were

By Norma Connell Cerand
Vestal, New York

hayrides in fall, and sleigh rides and wiener roasts in the winter.

Our family became close to many sailors over the years. Some were like brothers. We took several home with us for coffee, snacks and conversation after every dance, and shared many a holiday or Sunday dinner with them. By the time the war ended, we had addresses for almost 600 boys. I myself corresponded with 37 sailors at once between 1943 and 1945!

The USO days were a wonderful time in my life, and I'm proud of the 10 years I served as a GSO hostess.⊙

'Honeymoon' Was Yet To Come for His Co-Star

DURING 1944 and '45, I was proud to perform with the "USO Camp Shows" that toured military bases.

We presented a popular play at many bases in this country, then took a 9-month swing through the South Pacific, covering the region from Australia to the Philippines.

Our show was Mike Todd's *Mexican Hayride*. I played the role of leading man David Winthrop. Our leading lady, "Montana", was played by a young woman named Audrey Cotter.

WHO'S future celebrity sitting beside Robert Tavis? See above!

Some years later, this same Audrey Cotter changed her stage name to Audrey Meadows. When television came along, she would become famous as "Alice" on *The Honeymooners*!
—*Robert Tavis*
Highland Village, Texas

Magician Traveled by Sub To Entertain the Troops

By Ralph Pierce, Urbana, Illinois

WHEN I WAS drafted in 1944, I was a professional magician. After boot training, I started performing with the Ray Anthony Band, which was entertaining servicemen in Hawaii. Before long, I was working as a solo act.

The Navy sent me all over the South Pacific via submarine to entertain the troops. Because of my act, I was even given special permission to wear a goatee!

Many of my audiences were in hospital wards. Sometimes I appeared between reels at outdoor movies, working from a flatbed truck in front of the screen. The most appreciative audience I ever had, though, was a group of five guys who were guarding some ammunition in a remote area of Saipan.

Being attached to the submarine division, I traveled from island to island, working on Wake, Johnston, Okinawa, Guam, Midway and Tinian, to name a few.

Later on, I performed as the warmup act for entertainers such as Jack Benny, Betty Hutton and Spencer Tracy.

Over the years, I received many letters of commendation from generals and admirals. But the best compliment I got was on Guam, when a Jeep rolled up to the platform and a hand shot out.

"You're the best magician I've ever seen!" barked Gen. "Vinegar Joe" Stillwell. It was a great feeling to know I was doing something to boost morale.

GIs Hand-Delivered Gift to Bogart

AFTER MORE THAN 60 days on the front lines in Italy during 1943, our division was sent for some well-deserved rest and recreation. Everyone in the outfit got a pass to visit Naples.

When my turn came, it was Christmastime, and I was lucky enough to attend a USO show featuring Humphrey Bogart and Red Skelton.

During the performance, Mr. Bogart displayed a German machine pistol an American GI had given him, and said he'd like to shoot it, but had no ammunition. After the show, a friend told me he had a bagful of ammunition for that German gun. Why not deliver it to "Bogie" at his hotel?

We walked miles to the hotel, but had a bit of an argument when we asked the desk clerk to see Mr. Bogart. The actor heard the racket, appeared on the second-floor balcony and asked what was going on.

When my friend explained why we were there, we were immediately invited up to his room. Bogie was very pleased with the gift. His wife, Mayo Methot, offered us a piece of cake and a glass of wine, and introduced us to Red Skelton when he came in from an adjoining room.

We spent about an hour chatting with the Bogarts. He told us of his early days in the Navy during World War I, and was very interested to learn our division had captured Casablanca. He'd made his famous movie by the same name in 1942.

I'll always be grateful to the USO. It not only did a fine job of entertaining the troops, but made it possible for a couple of lonely soldiers to meet two of the most famous people in Hollywood. —*Joseph Watters Friesland, Wisconsin*

Boy Learned of War's Toll Through 'Hillbilly Songs'

By Wayne Daniel, Chamblee, Georgia

I WAS 11 years old in 1940, and the radio became my link with the world outside my rural Georgia home.

Big Band music was sweeping the nation then, as were the voices of Bing Crosby, Frank Sinatra and Kate Smith. But with my rural roots, I preferred to listen to radio programs like the "Grand Ole Opry", the "National Barn Dance" and the "Wheeling Jamboree".

We called country music "hillbilly music" back then. Sung to the accompaniment of fiddles, banjos, mandolins and guitars, those 1940s songs held my interest, and when they dealt with the war, they stirred my emotions.

The first war-inspired country song I remember was Red Foley's *I'll Be Back in a Year, Little Darling,* recorded in spring of 1941. Many battle-related songs followed.

Bob Wills and his band, the Texas Playboys, played a type of music known as Western swing. Their song *Stars and Stripes on Iwo Jima* painted a word picture of the historic flag raising on that island. And *White Cross on Okinawa* surely brought tears to many a listener's eyes, telling of a mother's prayers silently crossing the ocean, and of how each white cross on Okinawa brought a gold star to some mother's home.

Cowboy singer Tex Ritter lamented the gold star mothers with *Gold Star in the Window*. Meanwhile, Roy Acuff, the "King of Country Music", expressed the feelings of most Americans with his song *Cowards Over Pearl Harbor.*

Many songs were written about wives, girlfriends and mothers back home. In Floyd Tillman's *Each Night at 9,* a soldier asked his wife to pray for him every evening. Gene Autry sang about Dear John letters in *At Mail Call Today.* Ernest Tubb's *The Soldier's Last Letter* told the story of a GI who wrote to his mom just before dying in battle.

The most popular and inspiring song was *There's a Star-Spangled Banner Waving Somewhere* by Elton Britt. It was about a mountain boy who longed to fight for his country, but was denied the chance because of a handicap.

Those songs taught me there was more to war than just the battles. The war was also about real people and their sacrifice, loneliness, heartbreak and heroism.✪

COUNTRY SINGERS who recorded patriotic songs were: Tex Ritter (1) *Gold Star in the Window;* Red Foley (2) *I'll Be Back in a Year, Little Darling;* Elton Britt (3) *There's a Star-Spangled Banner Waving Somewhere;* Gene Autry (4) *At Mail Call Today;* and Ernest Tubb (5) *The Soldier's Last Letter.*

CHAPTER NINE

Victory!

"THE WAR IS OVER!" News of the war's end spread like wildfire, and celebrations erupted everywhere. The agonizing wait for news of loved ones far away would soon be over. The brave men and women who had served their country so long and so well were finally coming home.

CONFETTI AND STREAMERS filled the air on Lower Broadway in New York City on V-E Day. Euphoric workers streamed out of their office buildings to share in the heady moment of spontaneous celebration.

I have one shining, indelible memory of World War II.

I was aboard a Navy troop transport ship that had started its voyage in Calcutta, paused in Manila to pick up me and several hundred others and then headed east for the United States.

Around sunset one evening, the word spread—San Francisco was near! The railings and decks were packed as we strained for our first glimpse of the country that some of us had not seen for as much as 4 long years.

Excitement mounted among the entire throng on deck. Slowly the ship came around a headland and there, tall and proud, stood the Golden Gate Bridge. Beyond, glowing red in the setting sun, were the hills and buildings of San Francisco.

At precisely that moment, the ship's loudspeakers blared out a rousing version of *California, Here I Come*.

It was the purest moment of high drama I've ever known. Hollywood could never stage anything to top it.

Put Tears in Our Eyes

We stood there in silence soaking up the glorious sight, unable to speak and unable to hide our tears. Finally, as the ship passed under the bridge, a great cheer went up. We were home!

The ship dropped anchor in the bay and we spent the night on board. But few went to bed. We watched as the lights came on in office buildings and homes. We marveled at the enchantment of it all. Yes, we were home.

That was my homecoming. There were millions of other homecomings after V-E and V-J Days, each unforgettable in its own way.

Some servicemen and women came home to ticker tape parades and hometown celebrations. Many returned home much later, when the excitement had palled and a serviceman with a shirtful of ribbons was no big deal. No matter. We were home!

Hugs and Kisses Waiting

When we docked the next morning, crowds of impatient people waited below, anxious for their first hugs and kisses in years. There was a lot of getting reacquainted that lay ahead.

Some came home to children they had seen in snapshots but never held in their arms. Some came home to wives whose voices and faces were just hazy memories.

The bad dream was over. War had been scary, but now something even scarier faced us. What were we going to do with the rest of our lives?

Hopes ran high. Thanks to the G.I. Bill, nearly 6 million of us had a chance to go to college. Millions of others used the G.I. Bill to get training in everything from welding to flying an airplane. Some had jobs waiting for them—but others found that somehow their old job didn't exist anymore.

It made no difference. The war experience had seasoned and toughened us. We had reason to be confident about the future.

The world had changed while we were gone. It had gotten along just fine without us, but now it was time to find our new place in it. —*Clancy Strock*

Ewing Galloway

Three Little Words: We're Goin' Home!

HEADED FOR HOME. William Draves stood in front of a "welcome" sign on the dock at Le Havre, France (left) before boarding the *Colby Victory* (above) with more than 1,500 other GIs to return to the States in December 1945.

By William Draves
Fond du Lac, Wisconsin

"GOIN' HOME! We're goin' home!"

Those magical words were on every man's lips and beat in every chest as 1,568 World War II GIs lined up on the battered, rock-strewn quay in the French harbor of Le Havre on December 6, 1945. The little ship tied up there, the *Colby Victory*, would carry us back to America.

After 18 to 22 months in Europe, we were goin' home. Maybe we'd even see our loved ones by Christmas!

The long line of tired, anxious returnees moved slowly along the dock. We inched toward the gangplank, each of us lugging our gear—GI stuff, personal effects, war souvenirs…and millions of memories.

Since I was near the front of the line, I was among the first to board and was directed down into the *Colby*'s deepest hold, below the water line.

Room for a Writer

I'd always observed the soldier's credo—"Don't volunteer for nothin' "—but when an announcement came that staffers were needed for the ship's newspaper, I leapt at the chance to do something. I would have done anything to escape the heat, dim light, boredom and noise of the ship's hold!

Since I had some newswriting experience, I was named the editor of the paper, called *Ship-Shape*. I was told to haul my belongings to what had been a stateroom for nurses, behind the captain's quarters on the top deck. I even had a bed with clean sheets!

For 7 days, two writers, a cartoonist and I prepared a two-page mimeographed publication for everyone on board. To obtain world news, I climbed to the radio room, put on wireless headphones and jotted down brief reports.

My lead story for the paper of December 10 began: "At separation camps, all GIs will be allowed to make their first telephone calls home." The final banner headline read: "*Colby* Due in New York Sometime Saturday; 3,230-mile Transatlantic Voyage Took 9 Days".

"A Great Day!" was the heading for my diary entry on December 15. I pushed my way to the forward deck at 1 p.m. and sighted land 2-1/2 hours later. Those of us on deck saw a huge sign reading "Welcome Home, Well Done" on the Brooklyn shoreline. In the distance, an Army band played a musical greeting.

We didn't think we could see the Great Lady with the torch through the heavy fog, but there she was—welcoming home the boys in khaki who'd been away from America so long. Some just smiled, others thanked God. Many, like me, had lumps in their throats and tears in their eyes.

When we docked at 4:40 p.m., the Red Cross was there to serve us milk and doughnuts. "The first *real* milk in 19 months," I noted in my diary.

We were home at last…*home at last!*

NEW YORK CITY SKYLINE, photographed from the deck of the *Colby Victory*, moved returning soldiers to tears. Most hadn't been on U.S. soil in many months.

War's End Stunned Soldiers into Silence

By Edward Laliberte
Provincetown, Massachusetts

I WAS ON a huge troop ship on August 14, 1945. There were thousands of men aboard, packed in like sardines. Every inch of the deck was filled. We'd been at sea for several days, and now were sailing into the Pacific.

I'll always remember that night. The sky was full of stars, the air was warm and we were sailing along smoothly. I was thinking about what was to come. After all, I'd already earned two battle stars in Europe. Could

I possibly be lucky enough to survive battle in the Pacific theater, too?

All of a sudden there was an announcement over the public-address system. "Attention! Attention! This is the ship's captain. Japan has surrendered. The war is over!"

Despite the thousands of soldiers on board, you could have heard a pin drop at that moment. The silence was deafening…I guess we must have been in shock for a few moments. Then it came—the shouting, the crying, the laughter. Chills shot up and down my spine. It was a dream come true.

Several minutes later, the captain made another announcement. His words may have been the most beautiful I have ever heard. "Watch the bow of the ship," he said, "as it turns around and heads for New York Harbor." You can imagine the happiness aboard that ship as it made a giant U-turn and headed for home!

Several days later, as we passed by the Statue of Liberty, I came to realize just how much that symbol meant. I fell to my knees on the deck of that ship and thanked God…and I was not alone. ✪

At Long Last, Lady Liberty Welcomed Weary Troops Home

DAWN WAS BREAKING as our ship entered the world's largest harbor. After 2 years of combat, 3,000 battle weary boys were on deck, eager to catch the first glimpse of home.

As the huge ship glided softly over the water, a husky voice broke the quiet. "There she is!"

Everyone stampeded to starboard. And there it stood —the Statue of Liberty, standing proudly on its pedestal like a sentry. It reminded me of an Olympic champion with its bare, muscular arm lifting the torch of liberty to the heavens.

I wondered why the statue was called "The Lady in the Harbor". To me, it had the face

By Elwood Krzyske
New Boston, Michigan

"THERE SHE IS!" Mel Peters, Tomahawk, Wisconsin, snapped photo at the moment these GIs spotted the Statue of Liberty.

of a clean-cut warrior, with deep, penetrating eyes that seemed to speak its message in every language. Those warm, friendly eyes seemed to say, "Welcome home. We missed you."

Two years before, we had sailed out of this same harbor. There was no joy then— only curiosity about what lay ahead. Many of those faces were missing now. They would never share the joy and happiness of watching this symbol of liberty come into view.

As I stood silently amid thousands of khaki-clad men, I whispered a quiet prayer. For the first time in 2 years, I began to feel real peace and serenity returning within me. ✪

"WE MADE IT!" Jubilant soldiers from the 1st and 9th Armies crowded the deck of the Navy transport *Monticello* as it sailed into New York Harbor from Europe. The ship brought home 6,893 servicemen and women, as well as civilian passengers.

Ships' Horns and Whistles Created Symphony of Joy

By Francis Mahoney
Casselberry, Florida

MY UNIT WAS involved in air and sea rescue in the Pacific. When the Japanese surrender was announced, some of the pilots buzzed the ships in our harbor, flying so close that we could feel the downdraft. Even a few gigantic B-29s joined in these "flybys". After a while I wondered if, having survived the war, I would survive the peace!

Meanwhile, every horn and whistle in the harbor was blowing at once, creating a symphony that expressed the joy we all felt. Our patrol crew's reaction was nothing less than delirious. We danced like fools, alternately hugging, punching and pounding each other.

As the news sank in, we all began to think of home. Finally, it was really over. The nightly prayer, said for months on end, had been answered; the victory was won. The joy of that realization is difficult to explain to anyone except those who endured those times.✪

GIs Training for Invasion Were Relieved by Surrender

WHERE WAS I on V-J Day? Trying to sleep!

Our ship was anchored off the coast of an island in the Philippines. We had been storming the island's rice paddies every day, practicing for the invasion of Japan. At night, we were under total blackout conditions. Sleep did not come easily lying on the steel deck of an LST.

About midnight, the ship's loudspeaker blared: "Japan has surrendered!" The shouting of hundreds of infantrymen on that steel deck must have been heard for miles! There could have been no greater joy than ours regarding V-J Day.

—*Maurice Heath*
North Chili, New York

MPs Expected Riot Duty, But Had Peaceful Night

I WAS A SERGEANT in the military police near Salisbury, England when the news came that the war was over. Our entire MP contingent was ordered to remain in the barracks, ready for riot duty. The brass feared there would be a rowdy celebration by GIs. We didn't know what to expect—especially at night, when the GIs and civilians got together.

It turned out to be one of the quietest nights of my entire tour of duty overseas. We didn't have a single call about trouble!

The GIs and civilians gathered together at pubs, churches, public halls and in the streets. They sang songs, danced, and expressed their thanks to each other and wished each other well. Then they quietly returned to their homes and barracks and went to bed.

—*Henry Troutman*
Bernville, Pennsylvania

A Soldier's Plea: Remember Those Who Gave Their Lives

THE DAY THE war ended, Sgt. Ralph Lewis Jr. wrote this letter to his parents. He was stationed at Brooke Field, Texas and now lives in Erlanger, Kentucky.

V-J Day

August 14, 1945

"Well, the day for which the world has been waiting these many dreary years is now here with startling suddenness. I could not let it go by without at least a few lines to express the joy and thankfulness that overflow my heart at this moment.

"At precisely 6 p.m. this evening, two air raid sirens on the field began wailing long and loud to proclaim that Japan had accepted the surrender terms. Almost at once, soldiers began streaming from their barracks, shouting, smiling, laughing, dancing and slapping each other on the back.

"There were cries of 'Hey, guys—the war's over!' 'We'll be goin' home now—tell Mom to dust off my civilian clothes'. 'My soldier days are over!' 'The next day we're waitin' on is V-H Day—*home*!'

"Yet despite the atmosphere of joy and gaiety, I couldn't help but notice the grim, unsmiling faces of many overseas veterans. I, too, felt rather sad.

"While this day means personal happiness for us all, in that we'll be going back to our homes and loved ones, we couldn't help but think of the guys 'over there'—our buddies, the ones who will never know the joys of this day or realize how much they gave to make it all possible.

"These boys who sleep now in many foreign lands are the ones to whom the world should turn and be eternally grateful. They, too, dreamed of their homes, wives and sweethearts and longed for the day when they could go back. Today, the world must remember them—and tomorrow, the next day and forever! The day the world forgets, they will truly have died in vain.

"I, for one, will never forget them. In my heart, I will always see the rows and rows of little white crosses I saw so many times in Africa and Italy.

" 'They died that others might live.' How very fitting and true!

"So, folks, it's up to you and me and the rest of us to remember how much was given to bring peace to the world. We must never betray these boys that wanted life so very much and who had so much to live for, but died so that future generations might be entitled the right to freedom and happiness."✪

WAC Was There When Germans Studied the Surrender Terms

WHEN OFFICERS from the German army arrived at Reims, France to sign the surrender agreement, I was there, serving them coffee while they read over the terms.

I felt very uneasy, especially when one officer made a wise-crack about my serving coffee to the Germans while my husband was still shooting at them. He thought that was funny. I didn't.

When we served them, one officer, an admiral, thanked us. But General Jodl—the highest-ranking German officer still alive—didn't even look up. They were so arrogant! I never saw anything like it.

But General Eisenhower had the last laugh. When we told him that the Germans had asked for schnapps, he said, 'No schnapps. Just coffee.' " —*Agnes Pernazza Lansdale, Pennsylvania*

SUPREME COMMANDER. General Dwight Eisenhower led the Allied troops in Europe during the war and orchestrated the campaign that led to the German surrender at Reims, France in 1945. When German officers arrived to sign the terms of surrender, they asked for schnapps. Ike said no.

PACKED SHIP. More than 14,000 service personnel crammed the decks of the *Queen Elizabeth* as they sailed into New York City. Used as a transport throughout the war, the huge ship could outrun anything at sea and was able to travel without escort ships.

Ship Passing in the Night Carried Cheering GIs Home

By Patricia Coole
South Weymouth, Massachusetts

I WAS CROSSING the Hudson River on the Jersey Central ferry after working late at the office one night in 1945. The war wasn't over, but it was winding down. It was a pleasant evening, so I was standing outside on the bow. I couldn't see anything—New York and New Jersey were still blacked out—but I was enjoying the cool evening breeze.

Without warning, the ferry stopped dead in the water. I heard a faint roar in the distance. There were only a few people on the boat, and they all came to the bow. "What's happening?" several asked. No one knew, but the roar was getting louder.

Suddenly we dimly saw a huge hull looming up in the darkness right in front of us. The roar became deafening. It was the *Queen Mary*, her decks jammed with cheering, whistling, shouting GIs joyfully returning to the American shore.

It was a strange and wonderful experience to hear them, although we couldn't see them. There were so few of us on that dark ferry to welcome our soldiers home, and they didn't even know we were there.✪

IT'S ALL OVER NOW. Mrs. J.W. Blackman of Loudonville, New York had her photograph taken with historic front page on V-E Day.

Connecting GIs' Calls Was Labor of Love

AT THE START of World War II, I worked for the New York Telephone Company. Although I donated blood and knitted many a sweater for servicemen, my work as an information operator contributed nothing to the war effort. I truly wanted to do more.

In 1943, the phone company started recruiting operators to work in California, and I was transferred to the long-distance office in San Francisco. At last, I felt I was doing something real for the war effort! How rewarding to be the one who connected a lonely serviceman to his family, or to place that last call before he was shipped overseas.

And what an exciting time it was in 1945, when our servicemen began returning from those distant South Pacific islands. It was not at all unusual to have a young man tell me he'd just gotten back from a 2-, 3- or 4-year tour of duty. I was as happy to connect his call as he was to place it.

The most special calls were those placed from the local veterans hospital by returning wounded men. They usually had to reverse the charges, so the operator was on the line for the first few seconds of the call.

When family members heard a loved one's voice after so many anxious years of separation, they weren't the only ones with tears in their eyes.
—*Mary Rath, Mahopac, New York*

Andrews Sisters Serenaded Returning Hospital Staff

ON A COLD February day in 1946, I sailed into New York Harbor with the rest of the 108th Evacuation Hospital after 21 months overseas. The war had been over for months, and we had waited a long time to come home.

When the ship entered the harbor, it was met by a boat—with the Andrews Sisters on deck! They sang all their popular wartime songs for us. We may not have been war heroes, but we felt as if we were after getting such a great welcome.
—*Robert Warrner*
Muncie, Indiana

BON VOYAGE. When Don Condon of Janesville, Wisconsin boarded ship at Le Havre, France for the voyage home, he and other GIs were greeted by a sign reading: "Go west, young man...here's to the lady with the lamp in her hand."

VICTORY KISSES. Many a rejoicing serviceman swept up a young woman or two for a celebratory kiss. This particular lady submitted to one such kiss—but she also made sure she had a tight grip on a girlfriend's hand the whole time!

Night Turned to Day as Coney Island Rejoiced

By Carole Burg, Dallas, Texas

I WAS 10 years old in 1945, living with my family in New York City's Coney Island. We spent idle summer days on the beach, but stayed close to home at night. We were all waiting breathlessly for news of the war's end, which we knew was coming soon.

It came during the evening of August 14, a night I remember as clearly as though it were yesterday. It was Tuesday, and we were listening to our favorites on the radio, George Burns and Gracie Allen, when suddenly the announcer broke in excitedly, saying, "Japan has surrendered!" The guns of war were at long last silent.

We shared a strange mix of intense emotions. We cheered and danced, then fell meditatively silent. My father offered a prayer, and my mother wept as my sister and I held hands.

The news spread like a grass fire. Shouting and laughing drifted up to our second-floor apartment from the street below. We caught the excitement, grabbed our sweaters and raced downstairs. The crowd kept swelling, and the joyful noises got louder and louder. Carried along by the crowd, we headed in the direction of the boardwalk.

The scene there was unlike any other I've ever witnessed. The boardwalk was teeming with people who were laughing, crying, shouting, dancing and jumping. The boards were strewn with

---

"Carried along by the crowd, we headed for the boardwalk..."

⭐

---

confetti. One group of people carried a soldier aloft. Music blared from a hundred jukeboxes and radios. Thousands of lights, darkened throughout the war, turned the night to day.

Suddenly, I was grabbed from behind and hoisted onto the shoulders of a triumphant sailor. He twirled around and around, plopped his hat on my head, gave me a kiss and put me down. "It's over!" he shouted. "I'm going home."

Soldiers and sailors started celebrating in restaurants lining the boardwalk. The crush of bodies formed virtual blockades, and after a while, no others could jam into these establishments. The rejoicing lasted through the night and into the next day.

As we walked home, my parents talked about the block party we would have the following Sunday. Our block would be just one of the thousands across America to commemorate the end of World War II with a party. When I finally fell asleep, I was enveloped in the warmth and security of the peace we had dreamed of for so many years.

August 14, 1945 was a day I will remember forever. I have but one regret about that night of celebration, and it concerns the sailor who kissed me. I wish I had told him, for all Americans who cherish freedom: "Thank you."✪

V-J Day Marked End of an Era

By Gay Sorensen, Lacey, Washington

AT THE FIRST sound of sirens, we knew something momentous was happening. The shrieking soon was joined by the peals of church bells and the blaring of hundreds of horns—all sounding to proclaim the end of World War II.

Thousands of happy, shouting people poured out of office buildings and into the streets of downtown Seattle, Washington. Many of those who heard the news at home jumped into their cars and careened downtown to join the throng.

To say we were happy is an understatement. We were jubilant, and the scene was one of joyous pandemonium. The misery of war was over for our young men and women in the armed forces. Our country was the victor, and we were at peace again!

I was working at the Federal Reserve Bank that day. My friend Merrilyn and I were sorting mail when we heard the first sirens. We looked at each other, wide-eyed, then threw the mail into the air and ran to the window. Wherever we looked, people were cheering and throwing streamers out of windows or swarming to the streets below. We clattered down the stairs to join them.

Another friend, Kathy, was at a downtown dentist's office that day, being fitted for some new bridgework. The dentist was checking the fit when they heard the sirens. Kathy snatched the bridge right out of his hand and dashed outside!

We knew from news reports that victory was close at hand, so Kathy, Merrilyn and I had made plans with two

---

> ## "The crowd was massive and the din was thunderous..."

---

other friends to meet downtown the minute the war ended. By the time we all bumped into each other, the crowd was massive and the din was thunderous.

A sailor leapt onto a lamppost, circled it with one arm and waved with another. Another sailor grabbed me, bent me over in his arms—just like a scene from a movie—and planted a kiss. Two Marines wreathed in smiles passed us, one carrying the other on his shoulders. But the one on top couldn't wave. He had no arms. It was a sudden, sobering reminder of what the war had been all about.

We finally decided to start for home and somehow managed to squeeze onto a bus that would take us within a few blocks of Kathy's house. Even after getting off the bus, we couldn't stop celebrating. We danced, skipped and sang all the way there.

We had a celebration at her house that night, joined by many friends, neighbors and relatives. Kathy's Uncle Bruce, just released from the Army, was there with a buddy. They'd been in the thick of the fighting throughout Europe and North Africa. Kathy's cousin Dwight also was there. He'd been in Hawaii's Schofield Barracks the day Pearl Harbor was bombed. These men were only a few years older than us—just boys when they went off to war.

Our friends from high school were there, too. We celebrated well into the night, feeling happy, safe and secure. The war was finally over, and our boys were "home free".

It was the end of an era—for the world, and for us, too. Soon after V-J Day, our close-knit group of friends went off in various directions—college, marriage, moves to other parts of the country. But for that day, we were all together, blissfully united in the new state of worldwide peace.✪

CHEERING CROWDS thronged into Times Square on V-J Day. As elsewhere all across the country, this New York City celebration lasted through the day and deep into the night.

HEROES' WELCOME. Citizens lined the streets of Brooklyn, New York to welcome veterans home. Sal Catrini of Lindenhurst, New York shared this parade photo.

Neighborhood Youngsters Staged Impromptu Parade

WHEN CHURCH BELLS began ringing and the Great Northern Railroad yard's whistle blew, we knew something momentous had happened and ran for the radio. The war was over! When we heard the news, everyone in my family danced, hugged each other and cried.

We neighborhood kids got together immediately and planned a parade. In about an hour, 25 of us were lined up in red, white and blue crepe-paper outfits.

We started in formation down the street on bicycles, tricycles, scooters and roller skates, pulling flag-decorated wagons carrying little brothers and sisters. We blew whistles, harmonicas and an old trumpet, playing *God Bless America*.

As our little procession slowly moved down the street, we were delighted and amazed to see all the adults standing in their yards, laughing, shouting and waving at us. We were euphoric.

We glowed with the giddiness of that memory for weeks afterward. I'd never before witnessed so much joy and solidarity. As young as I was, I truly felt the emotional impact of that great moment in our country's history.

—*Pat Lassonde, Lakeville, Minnesota*

Noise, Confetti—and Song— Filled Air at Celebration

I WAS AT A friend's house, and her mother was listening to the radio in the kitchen. Suddenly she ran into the room jumping and laughing, yelling, "The war is over! The war is over!"

My four brothers and sisters would be home soon—after all those years! I was only 7, but I'll never forget that day. At last, those dark years of war were gone.

My friend's mom grabbed some pots, lids, forks and spoons, and the three of us ran into the front yard and made as much noise as we could. It was wonderful to do this without an adult telling us to be quiet. In fact, an adult was joining us! Soon, others joined in the noisemaking, honking horns, ringing bells and doing whatever they could to make a racket.

That night, my parents took me downtown for the most wonderful celebration I've ever witnessed. The streets and sidewalks were crammed with people. The air was filled with confetti, streamers, balloons, firecrackers, horns and so much noise we couldn't hear each other talk!

A man from a radio station was interviewing people, mostly adults, about the war's end. Someone had lifted me to the steps of a fire escape, and the man held up his microphone and asked if I could sing a song.

The only one that came to mind was *Don't Fence Me In*, but I sang it in the loudest voice I could muster. When I finished, the crowd cheered and applauded. It was one of the biggest thrills of my life.

—*Mary Lou Sprowle Pagosa Springs, Colorado*

Horns, Whistles Alerted Theatergoers War Was Over

ONE HOT AUGUST day, my mother and I went to the theater to see a well-known war story, *Mrs. Miniver*. At some point during the movie, we heard car horns blowing and factory whistles screaming.

My mom told me to go ask Mr. Cooke, the theater manager, if he knew the reason for all the commotion. He told me the war was over and my daddy would be coming home!

After telling Mom the news, I don't think my feet touched the floor at all! We flew out of the theater to join the celebration in town. And what a celebration it was! Soldiers rode on the hood of our old Plymouth, and others lined the running board. We got hugs and kisses from strangers, and there were smiles and tears everywhere. The memory of it is still strong even today.

—*Marilyn Byerley Nevada City, California*

Victory Was Sweet for Mom Who Gave Birth on V-J Day

MY HUSBAND WAS a staff sergeant with the 2nd Marines, attacking one island after another in the South Pacific. This was Harry's second stint of overseas duty, and he left fearing he might not come back alive.

On August 13, 1945, I entered the hospital to give birth. The delivery was difficult, lasting well into the next day.

At long last, however, the doctor announced, "Mrs. Mohn, you have a healthy baby boy. The war is over. Are you going to name him Victor?"

The whole country was celebrating. Bells were ringing, horns were blowing and flags were flying. The air was charged with excitement and joy. My husband would be coming home, and I had our bouncing baby boy (we named him Frederick!) in my arms.

Every year on August 14, the flag flies at our house—for our son, and for our country, in memory of V-J Day.

—*Gladys Mohn Eau Claire, Wisconsin*

TOGETHER AT LAST. Harry Mohn met his son, Frederick, after the war. Frederick was born just as the Allies clinched victory over Japan.

Trip to See Fiance Landed Her in Midst of Celebration

SEVERAL WEEKS before V-J Day, my fiance wrote to say he was being sent home for reassignment. He would arrive in California, then take a train to Virginia. Along the way, the train would stop in Chicago, where I could see him for a few minutes if I wanted to make the trip. Of course, I agreed—I hadn't seen him in almost 2 years!

I lived about 40 miles from Chicago and would have to take a bus into the city, so I asked my future mother-in-law to go along. I was young and a little afraid to be alone in the big city at night. All I can say is, thank God she went with me!

About halfway to Chicago, a man ran out into the highway, waving his arms wildly. When the driver stopped and opened the door, the man hollered into the bus, "The war is over! The war is over!" Everyone started screaming, crying and hugging.

By the time we got to Chicago, the entire city was going crazy! People were hanging out windows, dancing in the streets, honking their horns, doing whatever they could think of to celebrate. When we got off the bus, we were ankle-deep in confetti!

Somehow we managed to get to the train station. I only saw Harold for a few minutes, but at least I knew the war was over!
  —*Bernice Maske*
  Joliet, Illinois

Canteen Workers Swept Along For Train Trip to Chicago

I WAS WORKING at the soda fountain at the Great Lakes Naval Station's canteen in Illinois on August 14, 1945. It was a hot day, and we'd been busy making sodas, sundaes and milk shakes.

Suddenly a Marine came running through the building, shouting, "The Japanese have surrendered! The war is over!" He tore open bags of potato chips and popcorn and threw them into the air as everyone ran out into the street.

My three co-workers and I closed the canteen and joined the celebration. We were shoved toward the North Shore line, where the trains ran to downtown Chicago. The conductors were letting all service personnel ride free to Chicago's Loop. We girls were still wearing our canteen uniforms, and we'd forgotten our purses in all the excitement, so we were allowed to ride free, too.

It was nearly dark when we got off at the Loop. All the big nightclubs had their bands playing in the street, and people were dancing and jitterbugging their hearts out. Balloons and confetti filled the night air, and champagne bottles were popped and passed around. It was V-J Day! We were free! The war was over! What excitement!

I leaned against a wall to rest and look around. An elderly couple sat on a bench, crying and holding hands. A Marine with one leg leaned on crutches as a young girl gave him a kiss. They were crying, too. A group of sailors sat on a curb, telling war stories.

So many sights, so many sounds, so much laughter—and, yes, so many tears. I remember it well. I was 18 then, and I sometimes wonder where all the people I met that night are now. I know they remember, too.   —*Shirley Peters*
  Rhinelander, Wisconsin

Girl Atop Tower Serenaded Town with Patriotic Music

THE DAY the war ended, a girl from the high school in Lamar, Missouri climbed the local water tower carrying her trumpet. I don't know how tall the tower was, but to my 6-year-old eyes, it seemed to reach the clouds.

When the girl reached the top of the tower, she lifted her trumpet and began to play *The Star-Spangled Banner*. People stopped whatever they were doing and came out of their houses to listen. Some couples stood in their yards, holding hands, as tears rolled down their cheeks. Others, including my sister and

ALL WET. Jesse Thompson of Bonita, California (at left, holding towel) watched fountain scene on V-J Day.

THE BEST OF TIMES. R. Hannan of Kings Park, New York shared this photo of celebrants in New York City's Times Square on V-J Day.

me, walked to the tower to listen.

We all gathered at the base of the tower and sang along as the girl played *America, the Beautiful* and other patriotic songs. Many tears were shed, and many prayers lifted to Heaven as we stood there. I never knew that girl's name, but I'll never forget her as long as I live.
  —*Faye McDonald*
  Fresno, California

Blowing Horns, 'V' Signs Marked Drive to Work

I WAS LISTENING to the radio in the bathroom as I got ready for work on August 14. When I heard the news, I started crying into my bath towel and could hardly move. My mom came running in and we cried together. My brother was in the Navy and my husband was in the Army.

When I finally pulled myself together to go to work, I drove past the little church where my husband and I were married. It was open, so I stopped in and said a prayer of thanks, then prayed for the safety of all the young men who would be coming home in a few weeks.

The rest of the drive was punctuated with horns blowing at intersections and people waving from their car windows and displaying the "V" sign for victory. It was really hard to get any work done that day. Everyone was in a party mood!
  —*Margaret Olesen*
  Gardnerville, Nevada

FAMILY REUNITED. Staff Sgt. George Deal greeted his 7-month-old son, Adrian, with a hug and kiss as his wife, Yvonne, looked on. George met Yvonne while stationed in England.

He May Have Been First To Buy Non-Rationed Gas

AFTER SERVING with a bomber squadron in Italy, I was back in the States, stationed at Chanute Field in Illinois. It was August 1945.

One day I was driving to nearby Champaign to see my girl and noticed the gas tank was almost empty. I checked the glove compartment—no ration stamps. Black market gas was available, but most of us wouldn't touch it. It was expensive, illegal and, worst of all, unpatriotic.

At that moment, the program on the car radio was interrupted by a news bulletin. The president had just announced the end of gasoline rationing!

Within seconds, I pulled in at a service station and told the attendant to "fill 'er up"—an expression not heard very often during the war. Before he started pumping, he said, "I guess you've got enough ration stamps, soldier?"

"I don't need them anymore," I told him. He frowned darkly and started to hang up the hose. Fortunately, I had left my radio on and the bulletin was repeated. The attendant happily filled my tank.

I believe I may have been the first person in the U.S. to buy gas without ration stamps—legally, at least.

—*James Mund, Bedford, Texas*

While Others Celebrated, Gold Star Mother Mourned

AFTER HEARING the war was over, I made my way up our street to join everyone who was outside, celebrating. Everyone was stopping to shake hands or wish each other well on this wonderful day.

Then I noticed Mrs. Dorman, one of our neighbors, standing alone on her front porch. She cried uncontrollably, tears streaming down her face, as she watched the happy scene before her. To those of us who knew the Dorman family, no explanation was necessary. Mrs. Dorman had just learned she was a gold star mother.

Imagine the feelings she must have been experiencing. The war was finally over, but her son would not be coming home. He was killed while trying to land his crippled bomber, but only after having his crew bail out first. It was a hero's death.

My feelings of jubilation were immediately replaced by guilt and remorse. I pushed through the crowd and up onto the porch. Mrs. Dorman met me on the top step, put her arms around me and wept in convulsive sobs that seemed to last an eternity.

She finally pushed herself back from me, hands on my shoulders, and said, "Thank you for coming up, Bob. I feel better now."

With that, she turned, opened the door with the gold star on it, and disappeared inside.

I stood there for a long time, reflecting on what had just taken place. When I reached up to wipe the tears from my face, I realized they weren't Mrs. Dorman's. They were my own.

—*Robert Gaskill Lansdale, Pennsylvania*

Kids Lined Up at Curb To Wait for Dad's Return

WHEN I HEARD on the radio that the war was over, I wanted my daughter-in-law to know right away. Her husband had been writing her every day from the war zone, but she was worried—she hadn't heard from him in a month.

I arrived at her house and saw my five grandchildren sitting on the curb, lined up and looking very pleased. "What are you kids doing out here?" I asked. It was the first time I'd seen them quiet and sitting still in months!

They all chorused, "The war is over! Daddy's coming home and we're waiting for him!" They'd just heard the news on the radio a few minutes before. And their daddy did come home several weeks later.

—*Opal Ethell Sublimity, Oregon*

Bells and Whistles Announced Soldier's Return

By R. Shelton Croom, Norfolk, Virginia

AFTER MY DISCHARGE from the Army Air Force, I boarded a train for the trip home to Norfolk, Virginia. As I chatted with another serviceman on the train, I learned he was heading to what was then known as South Norfolk, just across the river from my own hometown.

"My family doesn't even know I'm on my way home," he said. "They'll surely be surprised to see me. I can hardly wait to see my folks again."

The conductor was a friendly, talkative fellow, and he quickly found out about the soldier's plans. He was familiar with South Norfolk, and even knew the street where the soldier's family lived.

As the train sped on through the night, the soldier peppered the conductor with questions. When he asked if the train stopped at South Norfolk, the conductor replied, "I'm sorry, but this train never stops there. We go right on through and across the river to the end of the line, in Norfolk. That's the way it is, son—and at this late hour you'll have a hard time getting back to South Norfolk tonight."

The soldier was surprised and somewhat saddened by this news, but he took it in stride. At least he was getting close to home. As the train sped onward, the clock edging toward midnight, the engineer sounded the whistle in loud, continuous blasts.

"We must be close to South Norfolk right now," the soldier said excitedly.

Then the old conductor entered our coach. His face beamed as he yelled, "Next stop, South Norfolk! All out for South Norfolk!" Turning to the surprised soldier, he said kindly, "Come on, son, I'll help you with your bags."

As the train rolled to a stop, the engineer was blowing his whistle and clanging the bell loud enough to wake up the whole community. The conductor had undoubtedly alerted him long before to make an unscheduled stop at a certain street in South Norfolk, with whistle sounding and bell ringing.

And why not? A soldier was home from the war! And not just any soldier—a soldier from South Norfolk! ✪

Archive Photos

TRAIN WHISTLE announced soldier's homecoming at a small Virginia town. A kind conductor secretly arranged with the engineer to make an unscheduled stop so the soldier could step off the train almost at his parents' front door!

Surprise Homecoming Surprised Everyone—Including Soldier!

I WAS DISCHARGED shortly after the war ended, and wanted my homecoming to be a surprise. My train from Fort Dix arrived in Pittsburgh, Pennsylvania about 1 a.m., and it took $25 to convince a sleepy cab driver to drive me the last 17 miles to our home in the country.

The driver dropped me off at the end of our lane about 2:30 a.m. It was dark and quiet. Our dog wagged his tail in welcome. (I'd been hoping he wouldn't bark and ruin things!) My plan was to slip inside and surprise everyone at breakfast. But the front and back doors were locked, as were all the ground-floor windows.

Then I saw a dim light coming from the second-floor bathroom. I quietly got the extension ladder from the garage, leaned it against the house and slowly climbed up. I was about halfway through the window when someone grabbed me, pulled me through the window and knocked me to the floor. I had forgotten Dad was a light sleeper. Talk about a surprise homecoming!

Soon everyone in the family was awake, and we all watched a beautiful homecoming sunrise together.

—*William Veitch*
Knoxville, Tennessee

Letters Tell Story of Young Wife's Vigil

By Virginia Lytle
Saxonburg, Pennsylvania

FIFTY-ONE LETTERS. My husband brought them all home, marked "Special", in his duffel bag after the war. They turned up again in 1970, during an attic-cleaning spree. Bill and I decided to read them again, together, one letter a day.

Our oldest son, the one who waited it out with me in 1944 and '45, knew how special those letters were, and suggested I decide which child would get them when I'm gone. No way, I said—they're too personal!

But as Bill and I read the letters again, we decided to copy parts of them so our sons and daughters would know what life was like for a young mother waiting for her soldier husband to come home. These are some of the excerpts:

May 4, 1945—Bobby came over from next door to play with Tommy today. They went to the living room and Tommy pointed to your picture. "See, that's my daddy. He's a soldier." I got the picture down where they could look at it closely. Tommy was very proud and Bobby was much impressed.

August 4, 1945—I took Tommy to town this morning, and I chased him everywhere. He would rush up to people and say "Hello!" as if they were very dear long-lost pals. He upset a wastebasket in the post office, and he called a soldier "Daddy"!

August 8, 1945—You asked me to send you some of Tommy's hand-me-downs. I don't know what I'd have to

send. Tommy doesn't have much at a time—he wears them clean out, too. And things like his blue corduroy three-piece suit that I've taken especially good care of, I'm saving for the baby

A SALUTE FOR DADDY. Bill Lytle's 3-year-old son, Tommy, gave him a proud salute when Bill returned after 18 long months overseas.

brother he'll have someday. I like it that you think about the little kids you see over there and notice their needs. I'll talk it over with the other mothers and see what we can come up with.

August 11, 1945—Tonight I was

telling Tommy stories. Most of them started with, "Once upon a time". But one was different, and he liked it best. It started with "someday". It was about Daddy coming home and taking Mommy and Tommy to live with him in a little house that was all their own. "Daddy bought a little puppy for Tommy. Daddy, Mommy, Tommy and the puppy went for walks every evening and had lots of fun every day."

August 15, 1945—On the radio this morning, the announcer said today is the day to throw something at all the people who for the past 3-1/2 years have been saying, "Don't you know there's a war on?!"

And a special bulletin came over the wire. Gen. Wainwright is on his way to rejoin the American forces and will be telephoning his wife at any time. The way that bulletin affected me, you'd have thought I was Mrs. Wainwright. I feel so happy for all the families of men who have been prisoners in Japan. I hope they are all receiving cables from their soldiers.

August 18, 1945—I have such a good time telling everybody that my husband is eligible for discharge. I've taught Tommy to say "eligible for discharge"! We both like to say it.

September 9, 1945—In church this morning, there were two fellows in civvies. Last time they were in church, they were in uniform. Their wives were with them, and it made me feel so happy to think of someday being there with you.

September 12, 1945—The mailman grins so big when he brings letters from you. He likes the husbands to write real often. He must know of a few who don't. Keep making me and the mailman happy!

September 22, 1945—Tommy was telling me this morning, "When my daddy comes home, we're going to go for a walk. Daddy will have this hand and Mommy have this hand, and Tommy in the middle."

September 28, 1945—Ever write a diary when you were a kid? I did. I can't help comparing it with all these letters. I don't want you to be "Dear Diary". I want to tell you something and have you talk back, or say, "Yes, dear" —*right then.*

October 8, 1945—I'm going to sleep good tonight! Four letters came through this morning, dated the 10th, 12th, 18th and 24th of September. It's like being thirsty and drinking cold mountain water when I read those letters.

A month later, it was homecoming time—finally! Tommy and I watched through the living room window, looking down the road into the deepening November twilight. The magic moment would soon be there. After 18 months in

"The duffel bag went flying as Tommy jumped into Daddy's arms..."

Africa, Corsica and France, our soldier was coming home. Eighteen months... half a lifetime for our 3-year-old.

We had looked at snapshots taken at Fort Bragg before our captain went overseas. We reread the letters that had come to Tommy from faraway places. We talked about the fun we'd had together—rides in the Jeep, picnics, parades. Tommy nodded, as if he remembered.

At last, Tommy shouted, "Here he comes!" Yes, it was Bill—half running, half trudging up the hill, duffel bag on his shoulder. Tommy and I opened the door together. The duffel bag went flying as Tommy jumped into his father's arms.

Bill shot me a glance that said, as clearly as words could have, "You don't mind waiting, do you?" I shot Bill a grin that said, "This kind of waiting I like!" ✪

TEARS OF JOY were shed in thousands of long-awaited reunions as service personnel began returning home, ending months or even years of separation.

Archive Photos/Lambert

Train Trip Unexpectedly Reunited Soldier Brothers

WHEN THE WAR ended, my brother John T. had been in Europe for 4 years. I was at my parents' on leave, praying he would make it home before I shipped out for the Far East.

A small local "milk train" with a passenger car ran past my parents' house. One morning, my wife and I flagged it down for the 2-1/2-mile trip to her mother's house. When we returned in the afternoon, the train was crowded with servicemen. Pollie found a seat near the door, and I took the only seat left, next to a soldier.

He was staring out the window, as if searching for something. I couldn't see his face, but sensed something vaguely familiar about him. I looked at his unit shoulder patch and a thrill began to well up inside me. It was the same unit as my brother's!

I gently touched his arm and asked, "John T.?"

The soldier turned to face me, and there he was—my 22-year-old brother! He looked 35 now, his hair streaked with gray and his face lean and deeply lined, but it was my brother.

We stood, embraced and began to cry. All the other passengers stood, too, and began to applaud. The applause didn't stop until we reached our parents' house.

Mama was in the yard when Pollie and I stepped down from the train. When she saw a soldier get off behind us, she began walking slowly toward us, peering to see who it was. When she recognized her son, her knees gave way. She knelt in the grass and shouted for all the world to hear, "Praise God! That's my baby!"

Without a doubt, that was one of the greatest days of our lives.

—O.D. Withem, Ashdown, Arkansas

Dad's Arrival Caught Daughter Off-Guard

I KNEW THE war was over and that Daddy was coming home, but I didn't know when.

Very early one morning, the doorbell rang. When I went to answer it, I saw my dad through the glass. "Daddy! Daddy!" I screamed and ran to Mama's bedroom to wake her. I was so excited I didn't even let him in the apartment!

As Mama and I ran back to unlock the front door, Daddy was standing there laughing and crying at the same time. He picked me up and hugged Mama and me so hard that *all* of us were laughing and crying!

After Mama made us a big breakfast, I asked Daddy to pick me up from school later—in his uniform. When I got out of school, there he stood. I was so proud! I can still see how handsome he looked. *—Janet Stufflebeam Middlebury, Indiana*

One Special Christmas: a Family Reunited

COUNTING THEIR BLESSINGS. As families reunited, they bowed their heads in prayers of gratitude. At long last, their loved ones were safely home.

By Marlyce Peterson
Willow Lake, South Dakota

MY OLDEST brother, Lyle, was the first in our large family to join the service. I was only 8 when he left in 1941, but I got to know him very well through the loving, longing letters he wrote to each of us. I missed him, especially at Christmas.

The following Christmas, my sister Avis was in Washington, D.C. with the WAVEs, and one more chair was empty at our table. The prayer before our Christmas Eve supper was the same one we prayed at every meal, ending with "bring our boys and girls safely home".

Although my brother Harvey was badly needed on our farm, he enlisted in the Marines the following summer. He wanted to be the toughest and best in his outfit. Maybe he was, but that didn't stop tears from glistening in his eyes as he stopped by our country school to tell us good-bye.

That winter we skated on the pond near the house, singing *God Bless America*, *The Marine Hymn* and *Anchors Aweigh* at the top of our voices. Perhaps I didn't fully realize the dangers of war, but I was filled with a stirring of pride for my sister and brothers.

One day we received a telegram that read: "LYLE WOUNDED IN ACTION". The neighbors came to show their concern. My youngest sister and I went to our playhouse behind the lilac bushes, where we hugged each other and cried.

When the church bells rang all over the world to tell that the war had ended, our family knelt at our own church and said a thankful prayer. Lyle, Avis and Harvey all came home separately. Each

> *"We knelt at our church and said a thankful prayer..."*

homecoming was a wonderful, joyous reunion.

All through the war years, I had dreamed that someday we would celebrate Christmas together again, and my dream finally came true. The memories of laughter and happiness from that holiday are like family heartbeats sounding through the years.

But the strongest memory of all is of the Christmas Eve service in our little church, with the whole family together...hearing again the story of a baby boy born years ago who would bring peace to all mankind...Pop, his head bowed in humble prayer...Mom, her hands folded, with a tear spilling down her cheek when the blessing was given...and me, sitting next to Lyle.

As the church bell rang, Lyle reached across and took my hand, squeezed it, and held it between his two big hands. It's a memory that will always live in my heart, waiting to whisper back to me.✪

Dad's Return Made Her Christmas the Best Ever

THE LAST WORDS Daddy said to my mother, sister and me before shipping out were, "I love you all, and I'll be home soon." Daddy had never lied to me, so I knew he'd come home. Meanwhile, we went to live on my grandfather's farm. We had no car, and our mailbox was 2 miles away.

A few weeks before Christmas, Mother walked to the mailbox through heavy snow. She came back about half-frozen, but she had a big smile on her face. She held up a letter and said, "Guess what I have?" I knew right away.

"It's a letter from Daddy," I said. "He's coming home!"

"Yes," Mother said. "Real soon."

On Christmas Day, we were walking through the snow to church when a car pulled up alongside us. Almost before it stopped, Daddy jumped out, picked me up and hugged me *so* tight! Then he grabbed Mother, who was carrying my little sister, and hugged and kissed them. We got in the car and drove on to our little country church.

Everyone wanted to know what I got for Christmas that year. I told my friends, "I got my daddy home for Christmas, and that's all I wanted." It was the best Christmas I ever had. —*Jearl Dean Burgess, Decatur, Tennessee*